# PUPIL STRATEGIES

# Pupil Strategies

## EXPLORATIONS IN
## THE SOCIOLOGY OF THE SCHOOL

**EDITED BY PETER WOODS**

CROOM HELM LONDON

© 1980 Introduction, selection, editorial matter, Ch. 1 Peter Woods.
© Martyn Hammersley and Glenn Turner, Ch. 2. © Martyn Denscombe,
Ch. 3. © Margaret MacLure and Peter French, Ch. 4. © Cathy Bird, Ch.
5. © Robert J. Meyenn, Ch. 6. © Stephen J. Ball, Ch. 7. © Andy Hargreaves, Ch. 8. © Martyn Hammersley, Ch. 9.

Croom Helm Ltd, 2-10 St John's Road, London SW11
ISBN 0-7099-0116-X
ISBN 0-7099-0343-XPbk

British Library Cataloguing in Publication Data

Pupil strategies.
    1. Educational sociology
    2. Educational psychology
I. Woods, Peter, *b. 1934*
301.5'6          LC191

    ISBN 0-7099-0116-X
    ISBN 0-7099-0343-X Pbk

Printed in Great Britain by
Biddles Ltd, Guildford, Surrey

# CONTENTS

# ACKNOWLEDGEMENTS

The articles in this book, as in the companion volume on *Teacher Strategies*, derive from a conference held at St Hilda's College, Oxford, in September 1978. On behalf of the contributors, I would like to thank the SSRC, who funded the conference, the Open University, who provided administrative support, and all who attended and contributed to the discussions. I owe a special debt of gratitude to Gill Norman for unfailing secretarial assistance.

# INTRODUCTION

Sociological research on the school shows an imbalance to date of studies given over to, on the one hand teachers, and on the other pupils, and between manifest activities and 'hidden' activities in respect of them both. In short, we know something about formal teaching methods, pupil background and forms of achievement, school organisation and so on, but we know very little about what teachers, and especially what pupils actually *do* in school. It is clear however, that the official business of the school is only a proportion, and to many pupils only a very small proportion of their total school career, and that the remainder is not only of interest in its own right, but enormously relevant to teacher aims.[1]

For pupils have their own aims, which sometimes accord, sometimes conflict with teachers'. They are not empty vessels to be filled, nor pieces of clay to be pressed into shape. They are, rather, complex individuals in their own right, with developed characters and infused with rich cultural forms, within which they interact as full contributory participants. Some basic parent cultures, as is well known, conflict with those of teachers, and this has been particularly well demonstrated by studies of language and communication.[2] What is much less known, however, is how conflict is worked out on the spot, how new cultures specific to school arise and develop, and how these relate to wider concerns.[3]

In *Teacher Strategies* I argued that the concept of 'strategy' focuses attention on situated, intentional action, that is the active component of cultures, and that it offers clear opportunities for relating to 'macro' theory.[4] Herein lies one of its major attractions for sociologists. For teachers as well, not to mention pupils and parents, it forces us to look behind the public façade of the school to the real stage and players behind, but in a theoretically systematic way. Here, we might find some surprising things, such as that 'conformist' pupils are not so conformist after all, and that in fact it is not a very meaningful term;[5] or that anarchic pupils are hidebound by rules, or apparently dull ones possessed of great skills and intelligence.[6] We might gain a grasp, too, not only of the conflicts and disputes, but of the humanity that pervades the sinews of school life. We might find help also, with questions like why some of our institutions have such alienating tendencies, why teachers cannot teach as they would wish to, nor pupils learn; or how important to people such activity is within their total lives and careers.

There is, then, both sociological and educational promise in the concept of strategy, and these articles, together with those in *Teacher Strategies*, are an illustration of current work in the field and prognoses for the future. Their content and interrelationships I discuss in the first chapter, against the background of how pupil strategies develop.

## Notes

1. Several books now illustrate this. See, for example, P. Willis, *Learning to Labour* (Saxon House, Farnborough, 1977); P. Woods, *The Divided School* (Routledge and Kegan Paul, London, 1979); M. Hammersley and P. Woods (eds.), *The Process of Schooling* (Routledge and Kegan Paul, London, 1976).

2. See, for example, B. Bernstein, *Class, Codes and Control* (Routledge and Kegan Paul, London), vol. 1, 2nd ed. 1974; W. Labov, 'The Logic of Non-Standard English', in P. Gigliolo (ed.), *Language and Social Content* (Penguin, Harmondsworth, 1972).

3. We have, of course, the earlier works of Hargreaves and Lacey; of Wakeford, making an application of Goffman to a public school, and the later studies by Furlong, Gannaway and Birkstead, as well as those mentioned in note 1. The article by Hammersley and Turner in this volume takes this point further. See D.H. Hargreaves, *Social Relations in a Secondary School* (Routledge and Kegan Paul, London, 1967); C. Lacey, *Hightown Grammar* (Manchester University Press, Manchester, 1970); J. Wakeford, *The Cloistered Elite: A Sociological Analysis of the English Public Boarding School* (Macmillan, London, 1969); E. Goffman, *Asylums* (Doubleday, Garden City and Penguin, Harmondsworth, 1968); V. Furlong, 'Interaction Sets in the Classroom: Towards a Study of Pupil Knowledge' in M. Hammersley and P.E. Woods, *The Process of Schooling*; V. Furlong, 'Anancy Goes to School; A Case Study of Pupils' Knowledge of their Teachers', in P.E. Woods and M. Hammersley (eds.), *School Experience* (Croom Helm, 1977); H. Gannaway, 'Making Sense of School', in M. Stubbs and S. Delamont, *Explorations in Classroom Observation* (Wiley, London, 1976); I. Birksted, 'School Performance Viewed From the Boys', *Sociological Review* (1975).

4. P. Woods (ed.), *Teacher Strategies* (Croom Helm, London, 1979). This is a companion volume to *Pupil Strategies*, and for general educational and sociological background and discussion of the concept of strategy, readers are referred to the introduction and first chapter of that book.

5. See Hammersley and Turner, in this volume.

6. See, for example, E. Rosser and R. Harré, 'The Meaning of "Trouble"', in M. Hammersley and P. Woods (eds.), *The Process of Schooling*.

# 1 THE DEVELOPMENT OF PUPIL STRATEGIES

Peter Woods

In one of his books, Fred Davis adopts the view of person as

> A perplexed, somewhat anguished, yet essentially well-intentioned character groping his way among alternatives, most of which are given him by the world and some more nearly of his own making. He sees none of the alternatives as ideal, although he reasons that one *must* after all be better than all the rest. The object of his quest is to decide on that alternative. Since life can offer no certainty that he has indeed chosen best, what else to do but fashion with the help of others a small 'master plot' of language, thought and action which in its playing out convinces him, most of the time, that he has chosen wisely.[1]

This may be, as Davis says, only an image (he uses the term 'homunculus') of the real person, but images, according to Schutz, are all that the social scientist is able to construct of his subjects.[2] This particular image of person as coper, manager, dramatiser, rationalising his way through means to ends, adjusting behaviour according to situations and contingencies, continually monitoring the process of action, checking and re-casting his own thoughts and intentions in line with changing possibilities and expectations, in short, as a deviser of strategies, is basic to interactionist approaches, and particularly apt for the study of largely conflictual situations like schools.

Such an image of person carries obvious implications for pupil, and indeed all human development. The process of socialisation includes learning strategies to cope with the world. Highly appropriate to this concept is the notion of primary and secondary socialisation.[3] The situation of childhood is given, and one has no choice over the significant others through whom the world is mediated in the first years of life, when primary socialisation occurs. It consists of acquiring perspectives, becoming accustomed to certain cultural forms and learning some basic strategical techniques—how to behave as boy or girl, how to act at table, speak to strangers, play games, relate to parents, brothers and sisters. Some of these may be seen as given properties of personality, such as patience, persistence, tolerance, when they may well be attributes

11

learned socially, so deeply are they internalised. For the child, at this stage, before going to school, the family *is* the world, and what is mediated to him is the only reality that he knows. This reality is a basis for life, has an obdurate completeness; it is the root stock on which later secondary socialisation is grafted. Thus the child internalises these mediations, builds up his own identity, and also learns the valuable lesson of 'Taking the role of the other', that is of seeing things from others' points of view and not simply his own.[4]

Secondary socialisation, according to Berger and Luckmann, involves 'the internalisation of institutional or institution-based "sub-worlds" . . . the acquisition of role-specific knowledge . . . role-specific vocabularies . . . and tacit understandings.'[5] Some of these sub-worlds phase into each other. For example, the first lesson the child has to learn on going to school, is how to become a pupil, in general terms, as distinct from 'a certain mother's child'. In the early years of infant school, the boundaries between school and home are softened to ease this transition. Eventually, however, other sub-roles come into play as the pupils become categorised into good or poor academically, well or badly behaved, proficient at certain subjects rather than others, and so on. There are fairly well defined types, of which there are fairly clear expectations, and pupils, having signalled the appropriateness of their allocation to them, further learn to respond to these expectations. One's identity, thus, takes a further twist in sub-roles, but this is not so intractable as in primary socialisation.

This is mainly because, as a corollary of learning to take the role of the other, the child may also learn — though perhaps with varying degrees of success — to cultivate the art of 'role-distance'.[6] These roles, then, that are encountered in secondary socialisation, even with their various specific languages, semantic fields and legitimations, may not be internalised to the same degree as those of early childhood. They can be held at arm's length, as with the prisoners studied by Taylor and Cohen, when they steadfastly refused to allow their own sense of themselves to be changed or overcome by the dehumanising tasks they were forced to do;[7] or they can be used in the furtherance of the self, as with Goffman's surgeon, who used joking asides while doing surgery, to show personal command over the role.[8] That, perhaps, is not a bad recipe for education in modern industrial society, that is learning to accommodate to a variety of roles in a flexible way, with maximum command but personnally adjustable commitment. In his ability to change readily according to the situation, the perplexed coper, when he is winning, becomes protean man.[9]

The art of role-distancing is aided by the different character of the individual's relationships with the secondary sub-worlds. The affective ties with parents are very strong; with functionaries, they are formalised. The child

> does apprehend his school teacher as an institutional functionary in a way he never did his parents, and he understands the teacher's role as representing institutionally specific meanings—such as those of the nation as against the region, of the national middle-class world as against the lower-class ambience of his home, of the city as against the countryside. Hence the social interaction between teachers and learners can be formalised. The teachers need not be significant others in any sense of the word. They are institutional functionaries with the formal assignment of transmitting specific knowledge. The roles of secondary socialisation carry a high degree of anonymity; that is, they are readily detached from their individual performers . . . the consequence is to bestow on the contents of what is learned in secondary socialisation much less subjective inevitability than the contents of primary socialisation possess. Therefore, the reality accent of knowledge internalised in secondary socialisation is more easily bracketed . . .[10]

The child therefore moves from the confidence and certainty of primary socialisation, where the world is one and indivisible, and within which he is totally immersed, to a functionary world of many parts, which he quickly learns are of a different order—more distant, more utilitarian, more manipulable. The groundwork for the development of strategical thinking and behaviour is laid during this process.

The child learns this ability to change and to adapt according to circumstance mainly through negotiation, a key concept in interactionist thought, and basic to strategical action.[11] Indeed, for a view that lays stress on strategies, negotiation is life. Though the individual has learned to take the role of the other, he still likes to maximise his own interests. Being able to put himself in the other's position adds sophistication to his negotiative skills, a keener sense of when to press harder, when to give way, what gratifies the opponent, what displeases, how to make the best out of a situation, how to turn loss into gain, disadvantage to advantage. All school life is of this kind, for even the most conformist pupil will fall short of the teacher's ideal, and somewhere along the line there will be a truce, agreement or compromise, that will reflect the nearest both sides can approximate to their aims, given the opposition's alternative aims and resources. Negotiation is the activity that lays the basis for the truce, and it is composed of strategies.[12] Elsewhere, I have suggested a typology of pupil negotiations in respect of work, from at one extreme 'hard work' implying full commitment and near complete identification with teacher goals, to, at the other, 'work avoidance', implying total lack of commitment, and rejection of any negotiative base.[13] In between, there is 'open negotiation', where parties move some way to meet each other of their own volition, and 'closed negotiation' where the parties 'independently attempt to maximise their own reality in opposition to and conflict against the other, and each makes concessions begrudgingly, and only if forced'.

The concept of negotiation rests on certain assumptions. One is to do with power. Though generally recognised that teachers have more power than pupils in the sense that they create the demands, set the scene, and are imbued with authority, all against a background of compulsory education, the extent to which a teacher can influence pupils in accordance with his intentions in any given situation is highly problematic. This is what the art of teaching is all about—getting pupils to do what you wish—and for the teacher of course, this is just as much a matter of learning and devising strategies.[14] It cannot be achieved, as many new teachers find to their cost, by a straightforward appeal to authority or exercise of power—this latter can be quite ethereal, especially in secondary schools. It can be argued that the teacher's authority has considerably diminished in recent years, and the rights of the pupil improved, together with the rights of other underprivileged groups in society. The teacher's resources are slender in terms of the job he is expected to do, especially in the stark confines of the classroom, where he is vastly outnumbered, and, unless he is careful, stands to be outmanoeuvred. For many pupils do not have the same purpose, nor even the same basic reality as the teacher, and the order is ever a precarious one.

Another assumption is that relationships are variable, that is to say that teacher-pupil relationships are not all of a kind, except in the general functionary sense which defines the boundaries of them. Instead, the interactionist view is that teachers and pupils are continually creating relationships, changing them, shifting the bases of them, gaining a point here, conceding one there, devising new forms of them, new ways of getting round them, plugging holes in one's own version, detecting weaknesses in others. It is the greatest exercise of one's powers of ingenuity, for both teacher and pupil, and at its best can be attended by the subtlety of manoeuvre, respect for opponent, and joy in accomplishment, whether winner or loser, that accompany the best of games. At its worst, it can be humiliating in the extreme for either teacher or pupil, for here it will breach the strategical defences constructed during primary socialisation, and hence the basis of one's identity. Relationships will vary according to certain conditions, such as how pupils relate to a certain teacher, subject or activity, what the particular constellation of the group happens to be, how they are feeling at the time. Of course, some negotiations and strategies will be more routinised than others. Even with established relationships between teacher and pupils, however, the forms of negotiation are still acted out, and subject to revision. For individual relationships are also changeable, especially where they rest on broad categorisations rather than intimate detailed knowledge of each other.[15]

A third assumption is that the parties to the negotiation have different interests. I have discussed elsewhere the range of adaptations of pupils to secondary school in relation to their association with institutional goals and means as mediated through teachers.[16] The majority of pupils appeared to have conditional relationships with their teachers. But even with those that might be viewed as 'conformist' types, there are, as Hammersley and Turner suggest in the following chapter, great problems of definition. The concept can be seen, fundamentally, as oppositional to interactionist concerns. For these, conformity in the generally accepted sense does not exist. The most dutiful pupil will vary his or her behaviour to some degree in accordance with one or some of the factors discussed above. Intentions will be liable to change, both at a local everyday level, and on a longer term basis. At times they may well coincide with those of a teacher, or teachers, but there is no bland internalisation of institutional goals. Thus, conformity, if and when it occurs, is only one form of negotiation. For example, a teacher's demands might frequently be pitched well above what he expects a pupil will do, or what a pupil is even capable of, as a bargaining position. The sheer impossibility of such goals necessitates negotiative strategies.

As it is, most pupils' favoured mode of adaptation appears to be some form of 'colonisation', and this neatly fits our conceptual mould. For if we regard primary socialisation as the home base, then during secondary socialisation the individual colonises other areas of activity in the outer world, gets out of them what he can to further his own interests in true imperialistic fashion, though in some areas he might feel more at 'home' than in others, and on occasions shift the locus of his identity to one of these sub-areas. Here is the classic conflict between self and society. How can the individual both maximise his own interests, and avoid conflict with others all engaged in the same enterprise? Negotiation is the interactionist's answer.

An instructive example from a related sphere is Howard Becker and others' study of medical students, a group with strong commitment to a common aim – becoming doctors.[17] But his observations revealed that the students were less concerned, in the day-to-day action of their lives, with learning how to become doctors, than with learning how to become students. They had 'impossible' demands made on them in the form of extent of knowledge they were expected to absorb, and in work assignments set. The ultimate vocational call to medicine became more distant under the pressure of having to pass examinations. They were forced to devise short-term measures to cope, quite cynically, in order to qualify, but they preserved their long-term aim of becoming good practising doctors after qualification. Becker introduces the notion of 'time-perspectives' to explain this disjuncture, and argues that it is essential to see the short-term strategies as a temporary expedient to meet present contingencies against a much broader career backcloth. One might wonder, however, whether the ideal doctor *ever* emerges, any more than the ideal teacher, or barrister, or whatever. For constraints on action and variable resources, both personal and in the situation, follow one throughout life, and the moment is often a compromise between aspirations, possibilities and strategical knowledge. In this way, the short-term and the long-term are not as discrete as Becker suggests, but firmly related. In practice they remain inseparable. Our 'perplexed coper' is perplexed for life. Though he finds out more answers as he progresses through life, and though some areas of thought and activity may become routinised, he also discovers more questions, so that his bewilderment in some respects may appear to increase. The point is therefore that such strategies may appear temporary, but they become part of the individual's stock of experience, which provides a resource for meeting future contingencies which are bound to arise. The most striking example of this in recent literature is Willis's claims for the integral relevance of pupil counter-culture to shop-floor culture.[18] It would be an interesting exercise to investigate how far pupils' experience of strategies generally provided a basis for coping with the problems and vicissitudes of later life. A strong connection would support the view of secondary socialisation advanced in this chapter, and of the school's integral part in that sphere of experience.

Of considerable relevance to a developmental analysis of pupil strategies is another well-tried interactionist concept – that of 'career'.[19] In one sense, the 'pupil career' seems clearly and progressively constructed from infant to junior to senior, one passes examinations or goes through

grades toward the ultimate symbol of completion, a certificate or reference; even with respect to one's fellows there is often a clear route from
innocent freshman to seasoned veteran. There are appropriate strategies
at each point along these careers, influenced by such factors as status,
power and aspirations, and also different strategies between different
careers. For example, Hargreaves and Lacey identified pro- and anti-
school groups of pupils, Dale 'planners' and 'drifters', Willis 'lads' and
'ear'oles', Wakeford 'conformists', 'colonists', 'rebels', 'intransigents',
and 'retreatists'.[20] Though all of these might be better regarded as
modes of adaptation which pupils might shade in and out of, they might
also represent the major orientation of certain pupil careers, and clearly
the form of strategies deployed will differ considerably among such
types. But all, nonetheless, will progress, whatever their career.

The pupil's career is a series of steps or stages. Progression is through
a number of status changes occurring at significant points determined in
the first instance by the institution. One such career is: at 11 plus, as it
used to be, transfer from junior to secondary school, at 13 plus, translation from preliminary groundwork to examination-oriented schemes,
at 15 plus, movement into the new maturity of sixth forms, and at 17
plus, departure into occupations. At each such stage, there is a marked
change in the status and role of the pupil, the expectations required,
and treatment of him. Having 'mastered' the previous stage, new problems, new situations arise in the next, making new demands on coping
resources and ingenuities. The status change acts therefore as a stimulus
to increasing strategical sophistication. During the 11-13 period, the
new secondary school recruit learns to cope with the demands of the
new senior school; during the 13-15 stage, he learns new patterns, which
are superimposed upon the former, and so on. This socialisation into
ways of managing, solving problems, reducing perplexity, meeting
demands as efficiently and economically as possible is preparation for
later life, and arguably one of the most valuable lessons the pupil learns
at school. Of course, the progression is not arranged for this purpose,
nor should it necessarily take this form.

The properties of status passages have been considered at length by
Glaser and Strauss,[21] and discussed in relation to the career of the pupil
by Dale.[22] A glance at these properties reveals the perplexities that
might be initiated: the passage may be desirable or undesirable, voluntary
or involuntary; its features may not be clear, one's perceptions of them
inaccurate, and control over it negligible; one might go through the
passage alone, or with others, though awareness of this might be variable.
In negotiating the passage and learning to cope with new situations, one

might argue that behaviour might tend to take certain forms. For example, in a strange situation, the pupil might tend to be withdrawn, not active, a recipient rather than giver, consumer rather than creator. There is an initial reconnoitering phase, when those problematic elements of the passage are being worked out—what it constitutes, who else is involved, its duration, its relevance to one's own concerns, the space for manoeuvre, and so on; and when knowledge about how previous crossers of the passage coped, and similarities in one's own previous experience brought to bear. Perhaps the most obvious example is beginning at a new school. The comparative 'innocence' of first-year pupils is always endearing to teachers, and this 'innocence' appearance may be aided by another factor attending the onset of a status passage. While the reconnoitering is going on, there is a kind of 'playing safe'—meeting organisational requirements without fuss or contradiction, assuming, for the time being at least, that the passage is in one's own interests. To be sure, at later stages of the pupil career, this might be viewed with increasing scepticism. The pupil's increased stock of experiences will then provide him with more of a basis for a preliminary evaluation. But even then, on occasions, a status passage may offer a kind of redemption, an opportunity to round off one not entirely satisfactory episode in one's life, and to begin again. So that we may well see, in the early stages of such passages, a kind of ultra-conformity, a new and inspired investment of self.

The degree of conformity might vary according to the degree of consonance or personal fit felt by the pupil to these events. Pupils are not equal, either in their resources or in their aspirations, as they approach these passages. They differ in the degree to which they are already equipped to cope, and to which they are already familiar with certain indices of the passage, and to which the passage appears problematic to them. This may be connected to primary socialisation, to social class, to certain previous experiences and forms of secondary socialisation, to idiosyncratic differences, to different aspirations, or to different levels of mental or physical development. It might also vary according to the degree of role continuity or discontinuity.[23] For while a status change may imply a change of role also, some are more progressively continuous than others. Thus, if on change of school, a previously top stream child, for example, continues in this position in the new situation, the passage will be less problematic than if the new alignment involves a comparative demotion to mid- or bottom stream.

Following initial reconnoitring, there might be considerable experimentation in the sort of negotiative work discussed earlier, as one searches for ways in which to secure one's interests, perhaps also to identify what those interests are. In the last resort, the individual must work out his own passage, but he receives considerable help from his fellows, both those who have gone before, and current colleagues. Some strategies become routinised, almost folklore, and these are passed on tacitly and often unconsciously as ways of doing things that have been tried and tested over time, in many different ways, such as stories and legends, actual knowledge from, perhaps, siblings or parents, connivance from teachers who have learned the usefulness of such strategies for *their* purposes, or trial and error in discovering the norm. Much, however, is discovered in the company of contemporaries. On occasions, one individual might take the initiative in a certain lesson, perhaps with a piece of homework, with a new teacher, trying a new leisure pursuit, a new way of doing things, of answering questions perhaps, and getting things right, as well as exploring the boundaries of tolerance. Frequently, a group acts as a team, be it playing up teacher, or finding the best way to do the work, pooling knowledge, ringing the changes, taking cues from each other, changing tack as they take turns in experimenting.

Small wonder that a great deal of pupil activity has a brittle, transient quality about it. Some may never progress to the stage where negotiations are resolved, and where strategies settle into a well-laid plan of campaign, logically related to the individual's past and future, that is sensible within the individual's own conception of career. Such resolution takes the form, in the case of the group, of cultures, and there are several commentaries on how these come into existence in an academic environment.[24] Cultures provide a firmer platform for action. They prescribe the boundaries within and criteria by which strategies shall be devised and deployed, as well as their nature. Again, there will be a tendency for more experimentation earlier in a pupil's career rather than later, given that some of these matters, like identification of interests, together with knowledge of system, have proceeded apace. But radical changes are not unknown at sixth form level, and indeed it is becoming increasingly recognised that adults throughout life have much greater capacity for change than was formerly believed possible.[25]

Two other related factors complicate appearances. One is the manifest-latent discrepancy. Things are not always what they seem. Certain behaviours might be assumed for particular, transitory reasons, and might differ profoundly on different occasions. Dumont and Wax, for example, have shown how some Cherokee pupils appeared ideally conformist in their classroom behaviour; but this was because 'within their homes they have learned that restraint and caution is the proper mode of relating to others'—classroom and Cherokee culture coincided on appearances on this point, but differed in meaning—they apparently *learnt* very little.[26] The teacher did not detect the latent culture for what it was, interpreting it instead as conformity to her own. This could be a commentary on commitment and centrality. Pupils might become skilled at putting up appearances, reserving their best attentions, skills and efforts for other arenas and activities.

Similarly, Becker and Geer have discussed the importance of latent identities, that is that derive from cultures having 'their origin and social support in a group other than the one in which the members are now participating'.[27] This raises interesting questions about the relationship between primary and secondary socialisation, and between areas of secondary socialisation. The pupils' culture, like that of Becker and Geer's students, grows out of the problems of pupils as a group in the context of the school, and derives from their manifest identities as pupils—how to learn work, do problems, avoid failing examinations, or getting into trouble, relating to particular teachers, and so on. But just as it is possible to suggest ways in which pupil culture is strongly relevant to the future, so one can argue the potential significance of latent identities to such cultures, particularly when shared by a group. 'The girls from the Hurley estate' or 'the boys from Badcombe' may have such powerful, integrated and long-standing cultures developed that they display a collective identity that impinges powerfully on the school world. Complementary cultures, no less, blend in with those of school. Thus, latent cultures and identities may be very influential, providing a rich fund of resources for strategical action.[28]

Other significant features of the pupil's career affecting strategical development are 'transformational episodes', catalytic moments, periods or events when the pupil undergoes significant change. They may occur during status passages, but they may occur at other times also, for there are other catalytic agents. Strauss, in speaking of 'transformations of identity' has insisted that it is change, and not just development:

> As he 'advances', his earlier concepts are systematically superseded by increasingly complex ones. The earlier ones are necessary for the later; such advance depends upon the child's understanding a number of prerequisite notions. As the newer classifications are grasped, the old ones become revised or qualified, or even drop out entirely from memory.[29]

This is remarkably similar to our conception of strategical socialisation.

Strauss provides a list of 'critical incidents' or 'turning-points' that can lead to such transformations, such as the 'milestone', an event that brings home to one, or crystallises a progression or retrogression. As Berger and Luckmann point out, 'bring home to one' is a peculiarly apt expression for this experience, for it strikes into the world of primary socialisation.[30] Another 'critical incident' is playing a new role well, discovering perhaps hidden and unsuspected capacities. Two that we might insert that are particularly relevant to pupils, are the acquisition of new knowledge, and the influence of others, whether parents, teachers or peers.

The first is a factor which seems curiously absent from sociological literature. Perhaps this is because sociologists have been more interested in the social construction of knowledge, and in the 'hidden curriculum'. The impact of knowledge on self-identity is but little studied. But we know, from our own experiences at least, the power of knowledge to transform selves. Thus there may be revelations for pupils along the way – indeed this is what teachers are supposed to be providing – the discovery of an activity or area of knowledge that seizes the imagination, summons up new powers of application and ingenuity, that cuts through both the pupil's own possible undervalue of self and the labelling prescriptive of others.[31] This could lead to a re-routing of career, or a powerful impulsion to a new role level, from, for example, 'struggler' or 'drifter' to comparative 'expert'. We can speculate that, on occasions, the transformational agent is not unconnected with growing acceptance of future responsibilities. Yet others that occur later in life do so perhaps because they are elsewhere, that is to say generated not in the sphere of public, institutional life – the world of secondary socialisation – at all. Motor-cycling, stamp-collecting, hi-fi, photography, bird-watching, pigeon-fancying, fishing – these are all examples of interests that in a sense, for some, are oppositional to school, though it may have clubs and societies in some of those pursuits, because this deep, personal interest derives from the freedom of one's own initiative, which is more commonly experienced in the private sphere of life – the area more connected with primary socialisation. The 'progressive' movement in schools, which actually seems to recur quite regularly throughout history in some form or other, could be seen as an attempt to soften the school's own constraints and blockages to 'transformational episodes', and the public-private divide; while perhaps the greater success of the primary school in this respect, and in securing the pupils' motivation generally, is related to its proximity to the complete, real world of first childhood.

The second factor that might induce one of these 'transformational episodes' is an outstanding educational agent — perhaps a parent or other relative, a teacher or a friend. Most of what we learn, we learn from others, be it school learning, or learning about new situations, people and tasks, and events in life generally. An outstanding teacher can transform a pupil in an educationally beneficial sense. Some do the opposite, and cool out pupils who otherwise might have made progress educationally. Transformations are not always the result of beneficial incidents, but might arise from 'stressful situations'. Strauss suggests that these occur if 'motivations are inappropriate for further passages and when self-conceptions grate against arrangements for sequential movements'.[32] Dale adds two more factors — 'when no clear career-line is offered by the institution, and when an institutionally discouraged but competing value system is found'.[33]

If pupils' behaviour and attitudes often appear unaccountable, erratic and inconsequential, it may well be because of the extreme marginality of their position. It could be argued that the whole period of pupilhood is marginal. In Van Gennep's classic analysis of 'rites of passage', he distinguished three main phases — separation, transition and aggregation to a new condition or reincorporation.[34] The first phase is marked by behaviour symbolising separation from a particular point in the social structure or a set of cultural conditions. The second is distinguished by marginality or 'liminality', wherein the characteristics of the passenger are ambiguous, neither belonging to past or future status. In the third phase, the subject is reunited with the social order with the clearly defined rights and duties attaching to the state. Victor Turner says the attributes of liminality

> are necessarily ambiguous, since this condition and these persons elude or slip through the network of classifications that normally locate states and positions in cultural space. Liminal entities are neither here nor there; they are betwixt and between the positions assigned and arranged by law, custom, convention, and ceremonial. As such, their ambiguous and indeterminate attributes are expressed by a rich variety of symbols in the many societies that ritualise social and cultural transitions. Thus, liminality is frequently likened to death, to being in the womb, to invisibility, to darkness, to bisexuality, to the wilderness, and to an eclipse of the sun or moon.[35]

It might seem to be stretching a point to claim that pupilhood is marginal, since it is well established by law, custom, etc. However, the pupil leaves the primary world of early childhood at age five, and does not return to a 'primary' state until he leaves school. At school, he is under tutelage, subordinate, directed. He is 'growing' or 'becoming', without actually ever getting there. The whole period is transitional, from being a mother's child to being an independent citizen. Liminality, for the pupil, has been likened to 'prison', 'being in the army', 'Colditz', and 'Stalag camp 15'.[36] It is not surprising that strategies more associated with those institutions abound at school, from 'bunking off' to undermining the morale of one's captors and sustaining one's own.

'Stressful situations' and 'liminality' bring us back to our 'perplexed coper'. We are perplexed for life, but pupils have reasons for special perplexity. At school, they are initiated into secondary socialisation, and inducted into a functionary world of utilitarianism and manipulation among roles. They are especially subject to status passages and changes and transformational episodes, over which they have little control. They are exposed to a number of new experiences and phenomena, such as individual teachers, aspects of school organisation, problems of work and knowledge, class cultures, teacher and pupil cultures, peer groups, towards which they are required to make a response. Through this maze of activity and encounters the pupil negotiates his way, making the most of his power and abilities in furthering his interests, often in company with his fellows, discovering and inventing strategies of infinite number and complexity. It is, arguably, the pupil's most valuable lesson.

The remaining chapters in this volume suggest some of the forms, contours and influences on pupils' strategical experiences, and show that it is a wide and urgent field of enquiry, if we are to afford strategies the attention they deserve, and if our understanding of what pupil life means to the pupil is to advance. Hammersley and Turner examine previous approaches to the study of pupil perspectives and adaptations, and find them 'insufficient for explaining the rich complexity of pupil action'. The pro- and anti-school culture model most closely associated with Hargreaves's and Lacey's earlier work is too crude a measure, and arguably less relevant and indeed less evident than in the tight streaming situations in schools in the 1960s. The 'adaptation' model, deriving from Merton and Goffman, and most closely associated with Wakeford and Woods, is more flexible, but inevitably focuses attention on official goals and means, and possibly undervalues latent cultures and behaviour other than goal-directed. The authors propose an interactional alternative, which is based in the first instance in social interaction, rather than a theory of how the individual relates to society; and claim that this enables the detection of variability where the other models assume consistency, and that it provides a basis for work on subcultures and adaptations, and hence for viewing all three models as complementary, operating at different levels of generality.

One current debate concerns the relative influence of situation and social structure on action. Denscombe, following Becker's line on situational determinism,[37] argues that strategies are context specific, and examines how they are affected by different forms of organisation, namely 'open' as compared with 'closed' classrooms. He argues that much pupil activity is a reaction to events, thus supporting goal-directed models, and that therefore much of this activity is actually *counter*-strategic. For example, the use of 'noise', a key strategy in closed classrooms, was more tolerated in open classrooms, and the strategy thus negated. But more subtle forms of control engendered more subtle strategies. For example, 'friendliness' and 'indulgence' were used both as teacher strategy and pupil counter-strategy. 'Pupils could "get away with" doing little work or disturbing other pupils by exploiting a strategy which was more appropriate to the open classroom than the conventional situation.' Thus a new order, no less strategical, was negotiated.

Much teacher-pupil interaction is spent on 'chalk and talk' and 'question and answer' – it is the bread-and-butter teaching technique. Consequently considerable attention has come to be focused recently on the language employed by the teacher, and the strategies used by pupils in finding answers. Some of this has sought to show how this is basically teacher dominated, the whole discourse being governed by the social and pedagogic concerns of the teacher, but MacLure and French dispute this. They present data to show that the pupil employs various strategies, and that they derive from various sources. They include 'imitation', 'retrieving items previously introduced into the discourse', 'drawing on a stock of typical classifications', and 'cohort production'. It would appear that the child starts school already well equipped for demands such as these. Thus the teacher might establish the formal structure of the discourse, but her control over pupil meanings is by no means clear. The article is in part a commentary on the power of primary socialisation in a secondary arena.

'Labelling' has often been held to be a potent factor in the creation of its own content. Thus if pupils are persistently labelled deviant, this, according to labelling theory, will encourage them to adopt deviant careers. In any event, the definition depends on the label, and who affixes it. Labelling theory is not without its critics, however, and here Bird suggests more necessary qualifications. In her research she has found that few pupils see labelling as a cause of concern. In practice, it does not appear to have the imputed effect. Because of the variability of teacher-pupil interaction, the pupil may not be aware of it, and in any event may neutralise a hostile label. Like MacLure and French's chapter, this points to the powerful resources the pupil holds outside the school to bring to the 'negotiation' and to counter such a tendency. For many pupils, after all, school is but a small part of their everyday experience.

Pupil resources are sustained by the group. There has been much discussion lately on the form and nature of pupil groups and cultures, some disputing their importance as determinants of pupil action, as compared with more transient and variable arrangements.[38] Meyenn found, in the middle school of his research, that peer groups did indeed exist, and for the girls that he studied, were of critical importance. They were constant, they manoeuvred to keep the groups together, and developed their own cultures in relation to the school, all having a degree of commitment to 'teenage culture'. Thus the 'P.E. girls' like having a good time, playing practical jokes, getting round the school rules, helping each other with work; while the 'quiet girls', a group of low academic attainment, make light of this assessment of them, and create new meanings entirely within their own group, such that they can believe that it is more fun not to be clever. As a strategical base, the peer group, one suspects, will take a lot of beating.

A particular aspect of liminality in the status passage between schools is examined by Ball. This is the phase of 'initial encounters', when the marginality is at its peak. He is at pains to stress the developmental nature of teacher-pupil relationships. Much research gives us a snapshot of process frozen in time, and we rarely catch a glimpse of the dynamism involved, 'the ways in which strategies are tested or rules established'. Drawing upon his research in a comprehensive school, Ball goes on to discuss the 'process of establishment', during which negotiations are made and the terms of a 'truce' worked out. The monitoring of cues and information given off in the situation, strategies in the testing out of new teachers during a 'honeymoon' and a later reactionary period, and the teacher's response are explored, and analysed within the context of 'definition of the situation' theory. '. . . Definitions are tried out by participants and then accepted, rejected or modified in response to the reaction of others in the negotiation process.' The initial encounter, Ball concludes, is ultimately a 'pessimistic' environment, for it lacks the security and comfort of a sense of community, routine and trust, such as is embodied in Victor Turner's vision of 'communitas'.[39]

The last two chapters are of a different order, being concerned with the general sociological and methodological background to work on teacher and pupil strategies, and what the future requires. Not surprisingly perhaps, they come to different conclusions. Hargreaves, in giving an overview of the field, reminds us of C. Wright Mills's view that the ability and the desire to connect 'what we experience in various and specific milieux' to questions and conceptions of social structure is the core feature of the sociological imagination. One of the most fruitful ways of doing this, he thinks, is through the concept of 'strategy', though he is critical of some attempts that have been made in this respect. Such attempts include, for example, those of macro or micro theorists who take the other's concepts and translate them into their own paradigm, those who make inappropriate appeals to classical texts, and those who recognise the other area but give it inadequate exposition. He identifies three competing models of the relationship between school and society — direct reproduction (as represented by the work of Althusser, Bowles and Gintis), relative autonomy (Bourdieu), and split-level (Woods); and proposes that important areas of development are 1) definitions of boundaries of what can be embraced under the concept of strategy, and how strategies relate to factors such as biography, knowledge, rules and context; and 2) ethnographies of strategies.

Hargreaves's strong line on 'total' approach in the service of the sociological imagination is one not all would agree with, and a different view is put by Hammersley in the final chapter. Though he feels that there should be less insularity, he nonetheless argues for an explicit division of labour among sociologists, and sees interactionism as offering a good base for macro as well as micro analysis. He discounts the view that interactionism is inherently empiricist, though much current work in the field has empiricist tendencies, being ahistorical and ignoring institutional interrelationships. But it has fewer problems, he feels, than competing macro-structural approaches, which often have an inadequate data base or lack a comparative dimension, and are more 'closed' in conception than interactionism. Hammersley constructs a typology of approaches along macro/micro and formal/substantive lines, and while these might represent the basis for a division of labour, he feels there should be more cross-fertilisation. Interactionists, for example, have generally undervalued macro approaches, and are guilty themselves of not developing their own concepts. The way ahead, it is argued, lies in co-ordination, both between and within the four kinds of research through, for example, parallel studies, team research, and a historical perspective.

The research chapters in this volume are at least facing in this general direction in their attempts to fill out the detail of the data base and refine their concepts. But there is clearly a long way to go.

## Notes

1. F. Davis, *Illness, Interaction and the Self* (Wadsworth, Belmont, California, 1972), p. x.

2. A. Schutz, *Collected Papers* (Martinus Nijhoff, The Hague, 1967).

3. P. Berger and T. Luckmann, *The Social Construction of Reality* (Penguin, Harmondsworth, 1967). See also F. Musgrove, *Margins of the Mind* (Methuen, London, 1977).

4. G.H. Mead, *Mind, Self and Society* (University of Chicago, Chicago, 1934).

5. Berger and Luckmann, *The Social Construction of Reality*, p. 158.

6. E. Goffman, *Encounters* (Bobbs-Merrill, 1961).

7. S. Cohen and L. Taylor, *Psychological Survival* (Penguin, Harmondsworth, 1972).

8. E. Goffman, *Encounters*.

9. cf the concept of the 'protean family', as discussed in R. Rapoport and R.N. Rapoport (eds.), *Working Couples* (Routledge and Kegan Paul, London, 1978).

10. Berger and Luckmann, *The Social Construction of Reality*, p. 161.

11. A. Strauss *et al.*, *Psychiatric Ideologies and Institutions* (Collier-Macmillan, London, 1964). For examples of the application of the concept of negotiation to school life, see S. Delamont, *Interaction in the Classroom* (Methuen, London, 1976); D. Reynolds, 'When Teachers and Pupils Refuse a Truce', in G. Mungham and G. Pearson, *Working-Class Youth Culture* (Routledge and Kegan Paul, London, 1976); P. Woods, *The Divided School*; P. Woods, 'Negotiating the Demands of Schoolwork', *Journal of Curriculum Studies*, vol. 10, no. 4, 1978, pp. 309-27.

12. D. Reynolds, 'When Teachers and Pupils Refuse a Truce'.

13. P. Woods, 'Negotiating the Demands of Schoolwork'.

14. See A. Hargreaves, in this volume. Also A. Pollard, 'Teacher Interests and Changing Situations of Survival Threat in Primary School Classrooms', and M. Denscombe, '"Keeping 'Em Quiet": the Significance of Noise for the Practical Activity of Teaching', both in P. Woods (ed.), *Teacher Strategies*.

15. For teacher typifications of pupils, see N. Keddie 'Classroom Knowledge', in M.F.D. Young (ed.), *Knowledge and Control* (Collier-Macmillan, London, 1971); D.C. Lortie, *Schoolteacher* (University of Chicago Press, Chicago, 1975); D.H. Hargreaves, S.K. Hester and F.J. Mellor, *Deviance in Classrooms* (Routledge and Kegan Paul, London, 1976); P. Woods, *The Divided School*.

16. P. Woods, *The Divided School*. See also Hammersley and Turner in this volume.

17. H.S. Becker, *et al.*, *Boys in White: Student Culture in Medical School* (University of Chicago Press, Chicago, 1961).

18. P. Willis, *Learning to Labour* (Saxon House, Farnborough, 1977).

19. E.C. Hughes, 'Institutional Office and the Person', *American Journal of Sociology*, 43, November 1937.

20. D.H. Hargreaves, 'Social Relations in a Secondary School'; C. Lacey, *Hightown Grammar* (Manchester University Press, Manchester, 1970); I.R. Dale, *The Career of the Pupil* (Open University Press, Milton Keynes, 1972); P. Willis, *Learning to*

*Labour*; J. Wakeford, *The Cloistered Elite.*

21. B.G. Glaser and A.L. Strauss, *Status Passage* (Aldine, Chicago, 1971).

22. I.R. Dale, *The Career of the Pupil.*

23. R. Benedict, 'Continuities and Discontinuities in Cultural Conditioning', *Psychiatry*, 1, 1938.

24. For example, E.C. Hughes, H.S. Becker and B. Geer, 'Student Culture and Academic Effort', in B.R. Cosin, *et al.* (eds.), *School and Society* (Routledge and Kegan Paul, 2nd ed. 1977).

25. See F. Musgrove, *Margins of the Mind.*

26. R.V. Dumont and M.L. Wax, 'Cherokee School Society and the Inter-cultural Classroom', in B.R. Cosin, *et al.* (eds.), *School and Society.*

27. H.S. Becker and B. Geer, 'Latent Culture: a Note on the Theory of Latent Social Roles', in B.R. Cosin, *et al.* (eds.), *School and Society.*

28. See for example, P. Willis, *Learning to Labour.*

29. A.L. Strauss, *Mirrors and Masks* (Sociology Press, San Francisco, 1969), p. 92.

30. P. Berger and T. Luckmann, *The Social Construction of Reality.*

31. On labelling, see D.H. Hargreaves, S.K. Hester and F.J. Mellor, *Deviance in Classrooms*; also Bird in this volume.

32. A.L. Strauss, *Mirrors and Masks*, p. 106.

33. I.R. Dale, *The Career of the Pupil*, p. 82.

34. A. Van Gennep, *The Rites of Passage* (Routledge and Kegan Paul, London, 1960).

35. V.W. Turner, *The Ritual Process* (Penguin, Harmondsworth, 1974), p. 95.

36. P. Woods, *The Divided School.*

37. H.S. Becker, 'Personal Change in Adult Life', in B.R. Cosin, *et al.* (eds.), *School and Society.*

38. See, for example, V. Furlong, 'Interaction Sets in the Classroom: Towards a Study of Pupil Knowledge', in M. Hammersley and P. Woods, *The Process of Schooling*; and Hammersley and Turner in this volume.

39. V.W. Turner, *The Ritual Process.*

# 2 CONFORMIST PUPILS?*

## Martyn Hammersley and Glenn Turner

In recent years, the study of pupil perspectives and adaptations has been one of the growth points in the sociology of education. However, from Hargreaves to Willis, the focus has been predominantly on deviant or anti-school pupils. We can only speculate about the reasons for this, but two seem particularly plausible. The first is the overwhelming concern in the sociology of education since 1945 with the explanation of failure at school, and particularly the failure of working-class pupils. One of the consequences of this is that school success has not been treated as in need of explanation: 'successful' pupils simply have the personal characteristics, cultural backgrounds, material circumstances, etc., which 'failures' lack. Another possible explanation for the relative absence of studies of 'conformist' pupils is that researchers have taken over the pre-occupation of teachers with problem behaviour. Paradoxically reinforcing this, perhaps, is the influence of the sociology of deviance with its celebration of the deviant and exotic.[1]

This concentration on the deviant pupil has certainly advanced our knowledge of certain kinds of pupil and indeed of those pupils whose activities are most frequently dismissed as irrational. However, it has involved a neglect of the majority of pupils, or rather an assumption that their behaviour can be satisfactorily accounted for in terms of some combination of pro- and anti-school orientations. Thus, even where 'conformist pupils' have come into focus the pro-school/anti-school model has been retained, despite evidence of its shortcomings.[2]

In this chapter we examine the notion of conformity and evaluate the adequacy of currently available models of pupil activity. It is our view that these models are oversimplified and the purpose of the chapter is to demonstrate this, show some of the resources that are available for the construction of a better model, and indicate the direction this might take.

## Problems of the Deviant-Conformist Scheme

Once we begin to look at, or for, 'the conformists', a cluster of questions arise, and principal among them is: conformity to what? In the literature these pupils are usually portrayed as a pale mirror image of the deviants:

*We'd like to thank Peter Woods for his comments on an earlier draft of this paper.

they simply conform to middle-class or school values and norms. Where the deviants, on most accounts, develop novel values and strategies for dealing with their situation, the conformists simply conform to the school's definition of the pupil role.

However, only a little observation of 'conformist' pupil behaviour suggests that, at the very least, this is simplistic. Indeed, the inadequacy of the model is visible even in the data reported by the studies that have employed it. Consider, for example, Hargreaves's comments about 4A at Lumley School, the class with the highest 'commitment to school' and to 'middle-class values':

> The boys expressed their concern for academic achievement in their impatience with those subjects they did not intend to take in the CSE, RE and Music in particular were subject to criticism and ridicule. (Hargreaves, 1967, p. 13)

Furthermore,

> When they thought the lessons were inadequate in some way, the teachers were criticised. (Ibid., p. 14)

Clearly, the attitudes of 'pro-school pupils', or some of them anyway, are not identical with those of teachers. Furthermore, it seems most unlikely that there is a single set of values presented by the school and all the teachers. Nor, were there such consistency, could we assume that it represented a single coherent *'middle-class'* world view. Indeed, we can expect different segments of the middle class,[3] and teachers occupying different positions within the school, to promote rather different values and norms. We might also reasonably expect to find, on the part of particular teachers, 'official' and 'subterranean' values operating side by side.[4] Then again, values are often internally inconsistent and, even if they are not, drawing their implications for particular situations is always potentially problematic and open to decision and negotiation. Thus, even if we assume that 'conformist' pupils are totally committed to 'school values', there is much still to be explained concerning how they construct lines of action in conformity with these values.

But there is no reason to assume this. For one thing, we must recognise the ambivalence which underlies much social interaction,[5] and evidence for ambivalence on the part of pupils can again be found even in the existing literature. Thus, Lacey explicitly comments on the way in which pro-school pupils are committed to values other than those promoted by the school, and how they engage in a kind of balancing act which often relies for its success on the segregation of audiences.[6]

> Sherman was frequently top in 5B. He rarely misbehaved in class and was prominent in co-operating with teachers during lessons. On one occasion, however, I observed that after a lesson in which he was conspicuous for his enthusiastic participation, he waited until the master had left the room, then immediately grabbed an innocuous classmate's satchel and in a few moments had organised a sort of piggy-in-the-middle game. He passed the bag across the room, while the owner stood helplessly by, occasionally trying to intercept or picking up a fallen book. The initiation of this activity so soon after the lesson seemed to be a conscious demonstration of his status within the informal structure of the class. He was indicating that, although he was good at work, he was not a swot and would not be excluded from groups based on other than academic values. (Lacey, 1970, p. 87)

But secret deviance from school norms is unlikely to be the product simply of an attachment to alternative values and a concern with maintaining face in terms of those values. There are intrinsic long-term and short-term payoffs to be gained from 'unofficial' actions. Conversely, we can expect that much conformity to school demands is motivated as much by instrumental concerns, for example to get good exam results and thus a 'good' job, as by attachment to school values for their own sake. In other words, conformity may be a calculated strategy rather than *simply* the product of successful socialisation into school values and norms.

Once we recognise the multiplicity of orientations which even 'official' school values can produce, and also the existence of multiple alternative values and interests, it becomes clear that the pro/anti schema does not adequately capture the complex patterning of pupil perspectives.

## An Alternative: The Adaptation Model

The pro/anti model has its immediate origins in the work of Miller and Cohen on delinquent subcultures.[7] There is, however, an alternative scheme available based on the earlier work of Merton on anomie.[8] Merton was concerned to show that deviance is systematically generated by the mismatch between socialisation into common goals and the opportunities for individuals differentially placed within the society to achieve those goals by legitimate means.[9] He outlines five adaptations individuals could adopt towards the social order, each representing a unique combination of positive and negative orientations to the goals and means embodied in that order:

> We here consider five types of adaptation, as these are schematically set out in the following table, where (+) signifies 'acceptance,' (−) signifies 'rejection,' and (±) signifies 'rejection of prevailing values and substitution of new values.'

## A TYPOLOGY OF MODES OF INDIVIDUAL ADAPTATION

| *Modes of Adaptation* | *Culture Goals* | *Institutionalized Means* |
| --- | --- | --- |
| I.   Conformity | + | + |
| II.  Innovation | + | − |
| III. Ritualism | − | + |
| IV.  Retreatism | − | − |
| V.   Rebellion | ± | ± |

A number of people, most notably Harary (1966) and Wakeford (1969), have developed this model, and more recently Peter Woods has reworked it to relate to pupils in state secondary schools.[10] Woods's model provides for the following possible pupil orientations (Figure 2.1).

The adaptation model, especially the Woods' version, clearly allows for much more variation in pupil orientation than the pro/anti schema. It does this by distinguishing between goals and means and by recognising that a number of different attitudes can be taken to each. As a result it also marks a shift away from a rule-based model of action in which action is portrayed as the product of attachment to values and is produced by following institutionalised rules which derive from and are legitimated in terms of those values. Instead, a decision-making model is assumed in which pupils select adaptations to school according to their goals and the means available to achieve them. This seems a far more promising basis for the explanation of pupil activity; even if, as we want to argue in the remainder of the paper, further development of this model is required if we are to advance our understanding of the complexity and diversity of pupil behaviour.

## Problems of the Adaptation Model

### 1. *The problematic nature of 'official' goals and means*

With the adaptation model, as with the pro/anti scheme, the primary

Figure 2.1: Revised Typology of Modes of Adaptation in the State Secondary System

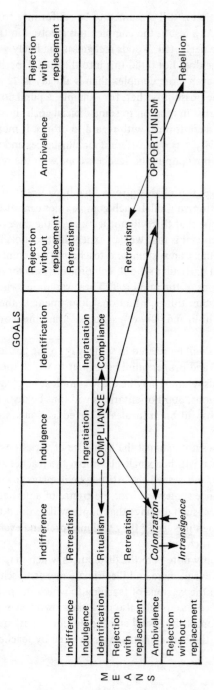

| | GOALS | | | | | |
|---|---|---|---|---|---|---|
| M E A N S | Indifference | Indulgence | Identification | Rejection without replacement | Ambivalence | Rejection with replacement |
| Indifference | Retreatism | | | Retreatism | | |
| Indulgence | | Ingratiation | Ingratiation | | | |
| Identification | Ritualism | COMPLIANCE | Compliance | | | |
| Rejection with replacement | Retreatism | | | Retreatism | | |
| Ambivalence | Colonization | | | | OPPORTUNISM | Rebellion |
| Rejection without replacement | Intransigence | | | | | |

KEY

Capitals  typical of earlier years
Italics    typical of later years
Arrows    some typical movements

axis of pupil orientation is still presumed to be conformity to or deviance from school values. As a result, the complexities involved in the notion of 'school values' are neglected. Woods recognises the likely variation in 'official' goals, but he does not build this into the model, perhaps because this would render it even more complex than it already is. It would involve theorising the possibility that, for example, a pupil could simultaneously be a retreatist in relation to some official goals, intransigent towards others, and a conformist with regard to others. It means examining how pupil activity varies in different circumstances and we would also need to explain how pupils and teachers cope with the resulting 'inconsistencies'.

In our view, though it probably gives a final blow to the elegance and force of the Mertonian model, such complexities cannot be ignored. One small sign of hope that this will not leave us in the mire but lead to a more satisfactory model is that we can expect that schools in different locales within the education system, and teachers at different points in the organisation of a particular school, will project *systematically* different values and conceptions of the pupil role. These variations will be the product of, among other things, situational adjustment,[11] the moral division of labour within and between schools,[12] and the work of missionary movements.[13]

Pupil orientations will be related in some way to the particular conceptions of 'success' and proper pupil behaviour to which the pupils are exposed. Though this relation may be quite complex, involving multiple and shifting adaptations, pupil orientations will thus be distributed in systematic ways across different locales of the education system and school.

However, this does not exhaust the influence of variations in 'official' values on pupils. Even within a single classroom the teacher acts towards pupils differentially, and indeed the attitude he displays toward the same pupil may change somewhat over the course of a particular lesson. It is, in the first place, such displays that pupils will respond to not abstract values; though it is likely they will interpret and evaluate these displays in terms of such values.

Finally, we can only note here the differences which may arise in views about what are legitimate and illegitimate means to school success. These will vary with the versions of teaching to which the pupils are exposed.[14] And, of course, pupils also have their own views about this. Indeed condemnation of the 'swot' and the 'teacher's pet' are not always restricted to pupils, they are sometimes also voiced by teachers.[15]

## 2. *The assumption that 'official' values/goals are the primary feature of the school environment for pupils*

This assumption seems rather implausible.[16] Pupils have various latent identities and cultures which they bring with them to school. Class cultures are the most obvious example, but equally there may be gender-specific and generational orientations,[17] and perhaps also child cultures.[18] Furthermore, these different latent cultures may be interrelated in various ways producing multiple subcultures. The use of traditional sociological concepts such as the local-cosmopolitan distinction can also be productive. Thus, in Willis's work there is a hint at one point of the contrast between national (cosmopolitan) and localised adolescent subcultures.[19]

Of course, because pupils are dealt with in batches, the potential for the generation and maintenance of alternative conceptions of status becomes much greater than it would be were each pupil taught in isolation from others (as in home tutoring).[20] For this reason, it is actually misleading to regard class, gender, generation, etc., simply as latent identities. To the extent that any such identity becomes a key orientation for some pupils, it is made manifest and has an important presence *within* the school. This can occur in another way too. It has been noted by Woods, in another context, how aspects of latent pupil cultures are incorporated and mobilised by teachers for the purposes of maintaining order.[21] A consequence of this is that part of a pupil's response to school may be a response to mediated forms of his own latent cultures. This opens up an intriguing area of research: the way in which pupil adaptations are accommodated to by schools and how, through these accommodations, these adaptations act back on themselves.

We can even playfully speculate, reversing the Merton and Cohen models, that conformity to 'official' goals might sometimes be the product of failure to succeed in other subcultures. This might, for example, explain the academic success of some working-class pupils.[22] It might also be that, as with deviance, 'success' can be amplified by the process of social interaction.[23]

The important point is that we must begin from concrete description of the orientations of pupils rather than by imposing prior assumptions about what the key features of their environment are and how they react to them.[24] If we do this we may well find a group of pupils strongly committed to 'academic success' for one reason or another, and perhaps also another group whose activities are centrally organised around opposition to school. But these two groups would probably only account for a small number of pupils in any school, the perspectives of the remainder not being explicable simply in terms of conformity to or deviance from school requirements.

### 3. *Adaptational Careers*

It is clear that Woods assumes that middle-class pupils are more able and more likely to conform than others, and there is some evidence for this. However, his model does not provide any basis for explaining why particular conformist and deviant adaptations are likely to be adopted by particular kinds of pupil.[25] In this sense it has less power than Merton's original, where different social locations are specified as conducive to different adaptations: notably, the working class to innovation and the middle class to ritualism. We have suggested earlier that systematic variation in exposure to 'official' values and norms may provide some basis for the explanation of differences in pupil adaptation. But this could only be the sole source of such differences if we assumed a direct, unmediated, relationship between 'official' goals/values and pupil adaptations. That would be to abandon one of the important advances made by the adaptation model: recognition of the role of pupil decision-making.[26] Even so, we can expect to find some kind of relationship between the official and unofficial cultures pupils are exposed to and their orientations.

The development of Merton's model has not been restricted to its application in the sociology of education. Thus, for example, in their work on delinquency Cloward and Ohlin (1960) have added an important new element which can be fruitfully applied and developed in the field of pupil adaptations. The central point they make is that Merton assumes that particular adaptations are freely available for actors to adopt. Thus for Merton the crucial factor determining which adaptation is adopted is the nature of the contradiction between goals and legitimate means experienced by the actors. Cloward and Ohlin argue that adaptations have to be learned, and thus that an equally important determinant is access to others who can socialise the actor into a particular mode of adaptation.

While we may not want to press the argument too far, since then it becomes difficult to account for the emergence and development of adaptations, this is clearly an important point. Indeed, we reached it earlier by another route in talking about the way in which batch treatment had the potential for turning latent into manifest cultures. Thus, for example, working-class culture is not simply something working-class pupils are able to draw on as a result of their out-of-school experience. To the extent that they act on it, and even celebrate it, within school, working-class culture has an intra-school presence to which middle-class pupils must adopt some attitude and through which they can gain access to it. However, the perspectives of other pupils may not only facilitate the adoption of a particular adaptation, as Cloward and Ohlin suggest, they may also prevent it, or at least make it very difficult. For example, a pupil may be faced with a choice between working for his exams or keeping his friends.[27]

This argument can be developed further. Thus, it seems likely that some adaptations to school would require negotiation with teachers to create the space for them; and this may be more or less possible at different places within the education system and within a particular school. Indeed, we should perhaps treat pupil adaptations as involving not only conceptions of how the pupil himself should behave, but conceptions of social order that, if successfully negotiated, become a working consensus or contract.[28] We can speculatively illustrate this by reanalysing some data provided by Willis (1977, pp. 11-12):

[In a group discussion on teachers]

**Joey** ( . . .) they're able to punish us. They're bigger than us, they stand for a bigger establishment than we do, like, we're just little and they stand for bigger things, and you try to get your own back. It's, uh, resenting authority I suppose.

**Eddie** The teachers think they're high and mighty 'cos they're teachers, but they're nobody really, they're just ordinary people ain't they?

**Bill** Teachers think they're everybody. They are more, they're higher than us, but they think they're a lot higher and they're not.

**Spanksy** Wish we could call them first names and that . . . think they're God.

**Pete** That would be a lot better.

**PW** I mean you say they're higher. Do you accept at all that they know better about things?

**Joey** Yes, but that doesn't rank them above us, just because they are slightly more intelligent.

**Bill** They ought to treat us how they'd like us to treat them.

( . . .)

**Joey** ( . . .) the way we're subject to their every whim like. They want something doing and we have to sort of do it, 'cos, er, er, we're just, we're under them like. We were with a woman teacher in here, and 'cos we all wear rings and one or two of them bangles, like he's got one on, and out of the blue, like, for no special reason, she says, 'take all that off'.

**PW** Really?

**Joey** Yeah, we says, 'One won't come off', she says, 'Take yours off as well'. I said, 'You'll have to chop my finger off first'.

**PW** Why did she want you to take your rings off?

**Joey** Just a sort of show like. Teachers do this, like, all of a sudden they'll make you do your ties up and things like this. You're subject to their every whim like. If they want something done, if you don't think it's right, and you object against it, you're down to Simmondsy [the head], or you get the cane, you get some extra work tonight.

**PW** You think of most staff as kind of enemies (. . .)?

— Yeah.

— Yeah.

— Most of them.

**Joey** It adds a bit of spice to yer life, if you're trying to get him for something he's done to you.

There are a number of different ways of interpreting this passage, none of which can be securely established, including Willis's claim that it displays 'entrenched, general and personalised opposition to "authority"'. One alternative interpretation is that what we have here is a conflict between two forms of authority; indeed we may even be able to formulate it as a conflict between charismatic and legal-rational authority. On the one hand, there is the teacher who demands obedience from pupils on the basis of his institutional identity. On the other, there are 'the lads', or some of them, for whom authority has to be earned and maintained in interpersonal interaction. On this reading 'getting him for something he's done to you' is not simply a reaction against what they regard as the teacher's illegitimate authority claim, but is simultaneously action on the basis of their own conception of legitimate authority, which involves competing for status in interpersonal interaction.[29]

Academically oriented pupils will also have certain ideas about what a teacher should and should not do, in what kinds of circumstances and for what reasons; slanted, no doubt by their own particular interests. Furthermore, built into such conceptions are notions of the limits within which particular attitudes operate: thus the compliance of 'academic' pupils may only operate so long as the teacher does not claim control over areas not regarded as within his legitimate domain; and so long as he is thought to be competent. If these limits are transgressed, compliance may be replaced by intransigence or rebellion.[30]

4. *The Exclusive Focus on Goal-directed Behaviour*

The adaptation model is a general sociological theory which has been applied to many specific fields. It is a rudimentary form of decision-making theory, but it is a version which is rather limited in scope, only providing for combinations of specific attitudes to a single set of goals and a single set of means. As a result, it is incapable of incorporating some of the other general sociological models which, while inadequate as complete accounts, may capture some aspects of pupil activity not amenable to the adaptation model. An example is mass society theory which, deriving from Durkheim, conceptualises modern societies as having a low level of social integration with individuals cut off from one another and lacking any sense of purpose and direction.[31] One is struck by the similarities between the comments of school refusers about the anonymity and loneliness of life at school and the tenets of this theory.[32] It also fits the general complaints about boredom at school which are often voiced by pupils. Taken at face value at least, this suggests that the mass society model may have some application to pupils. One possibility is where a pupil is committed to academic success but finds the work he is required to do isn't relevant to this goal. Where this is not a shared experience paving the way for collective alternatives, the pupil may well come to feel bored, isolated and restless.

Goffman's discussion of adaptation to total institutions, in which inmate behaviour is a reaction to the loss of civilian identity and status, represents another model which we may be able to draw on in explaining pupil perspectives.[33] Thus, for example, it does seem that with recent changes in attitudes to children and in the social organisation of the family,[34] there may be a mismatch between the way pupils are treated in school and outside: outside, certainly among some strata, they are increasingly treated as 'semi-adults', whereas the school's authority relies to a considerable extent on their being 'children'.[35] Goffman's work also has the advantage of focusing attention on organisational structure as well as 'organisational goals'. The significance of the organisational structure of schools has been rather lost in the shift from the deviant-conformist scheme to the adaptation model.

If it is indeed true that these alternatives to the pro/anti and adaptation models do offer distinctive contributions to the understanding of pupil activity, any new model in this area should be capable of incorporating the relevant aspects of them.

## An Interactionist Alternative

There is one other key approach to the explanation of pupil behaviour which should be mentioned here: the work of Furlong.[36] Unlike the previous two models, which are derived from normative functionalism, this is interactionist. As one would expect, therefore, instead of starting with a theory about possible orientations to society, Furlong begins at the level of social interaction and stresses the importance of pupils' definitions of the situation for their behaviour on different occasions. He emphasises the variability of pupil behaviour across different contexts, in particular according to pupil evaluations of the teacher as strict or soft, effective or ineffective.

If one monitors the behaviour of the same pupil in different circumstances, the existence of considerable contextual variability soon becomes obvious: the 'disruptive' pupil is not 'disruptive' all the time and 'conformist' pupils often deviate from school requirements.[37] Furlong sets out to explain this variability by pointing to the importance of mutual support among pupils, employing the concept of interaction set: 'those pupils who perceive what is happening in a similar way, communicate this to each other, and define appropriate action together'.[38] And he documents some of the considerations which underly a pupil's perception of 'what is happening' and thus provide the basis for the development of interaction sets.

The great advantage of this approach is that it begins at the level of action and sets out to describe the actions of pupils and the perspectives on which these are based. It is because of this focus that Furlong detects variability where the other two models assume consistency. However, the model hardly begins to provide a viable alternative to these other models. Even at the level of action, the approach is schematic, giving no account of why a pupil might on one occasion join in a 'disruptive' interaction set and on another occasion ignore it. Even more importantly, Furlong's model does not relate the perspectives of the pupils either to their goals and values or to the structure of the school, let alone the society in which they find themselves. Thus we have no idea why pupils are interested in 'effective learning' or how their position 'one from the bottom' in the streaming system shaped the kind of teaching they were exposed to and their own orientations to schooling.

In summary, then, while it points us in the right direction, Furlong's paper only takes us a few steps on the way.[39] In the next section we attempt to build on this work in such a way as to make possible the incorporation, albeit in modified form, of the deviant-conformist and adaptation models.

## Towards Another Model

We can only begin to sketch the outline of a more satisfactory model here. An essential starting point is to recognise the different levels of abstraction at which the model must operate. The first two approaches discussed in this chapter work at the level of general adaptations to school. It seems to us that working solely, or even primarily, at this level is unsatisfactory for both methodological and theoretical reasons.

Methodologically, it tends to result in a reliance on interview data since in interviews participants can themselves provide generalisations about their own and others' behaviour across different settings. But the dangers of an exclusive reliance on participant accounts are well known.[40] To take one example, Woods (1979) documents his concept of ingratiation with the following piece of data:

> **Karen** If Jane does something, she gets ignored. If she don't do anything she never gets told off, all the teachers favour her.
>
> **Susan** She's so *good* in lessons, behaviour and work. She does *more* than they give them, she does *extra* work. If we have a film, she'll watch it, whereas others might talk a bit. If we have a book to read, she'll do it in a couple of days, and pointedly go and ask teacher for another one.
>
> **Liza** She goes up the library every lunchtime. She used to creep round.
>
> **Karen** If we do anything wrong, we get shouted at. If Jane does it, it's 'Oh Jane, do stop please dear'.
>
> **Susan** She copies in maths to get ahead, and gets ratty if she falls behind. She's not so good in maths, so she has to copy to keep up. She says 'Come on, let's have a look'.
>
> **Liza** She *always* does homework, so never gets into trouble.
>
> **Susan** She had a cousin from France who came over, she was flouting her about.
>
> **Karen** One teacher said, 'This is a girl who's going to get on in life'. It makes you sick.
>
> **Liza** Reading a passage in French, she'd volunteer. Beefy would say 'I think you've done enough, Jane'. She'd say 'I want to do it, I want to'.
>
> **Karen** Mr England told her 'Oh Jane! You should have been in the top stream, you know!' — as if she didn't know.
>
> **Liza** Beefy asked her 'Will you look after the library for me?' 'Oh yes sir' she said, 'certainly sir, thank you very much sir'.

What we have here are pupils' typifications of another pupil and these are, of course, an interesting topic in themselves. But we cannot assume that these typifications represent an accurate analytic account of Jane's action in school or of a particular kind of adaptation some pupils adopt. The case would be stronger if, in addition, we had Jane's own account of her orientation to school. But even that would have to be supplemented by observer description of her behaviour in school if we were to establish that Jane's general adaptation to school is that of ingratiation. It may be that ingratiation like deviance is not something anyone does all the time and that to formulate it as a general adaptation is misleading.[41] Certainly Woods provides no data to allay such doubts.

Focusing solely or primarily at the level of general adaptations to school is also problematic from a theoretical point of view: it is a central and well-established finding of interactionist work that actors do not re-act directly to general situations or social structural locations. Rather, they build their actions to deal with the particular configuration of circumstances that they perceive to be facing them at any moment in time.[42] Thus the actions of pupils in relation to moment-to-moment changes in their situation must be a central element in any model of their activity. Indeed, this level has a certain priority. At this level, when we talk of, say, retreatism, intransigence, etc., we are describing the in-tentions of pupils or at least our analytical descriptions are not far removed from those concrete intentions. When, on the other hand, we talk of general orientations to school, we are generalising about pupils' typical actions across a wide range of circumstances. Such generalisations are necessary, but they *are* generalisations; they are dependent on prior analysis and documentation at the more concrete level. Furthermore, it may not always be possible to specify a particular general adaptation adopted by a pupil: he/she may not have a single dominant mode of adaptation, but rather display a collection of orientations to various aspects of, or situations in, school.[43]

We must begin, then, as does Furlong, with the analysis of pupil action, identifying the intentions, motives and perspectives which underlie it. Once we do this we can see that at any moment in time a pupil is faced with choice from a range of different possible courses of action. For example, with whether to attend to what the teacher is saying, talk to his neighbour, carve his name in his desk, or make some initiative in the lesson, perhaps in an attempt to sidetrack the teacher on to some-thing more interesting. Each of these lines of possible action will have certain actual and perceived consequences. These will be evaluated as payoffs or costs, in terms of both extrinsic and intrinsic gratifications, including identity implications.

Operating at this level it is possible to specify a much more unequivocal definition of conformity. We can conceive of the teacher as, in the course of his teaching, setting up frames, projected patterns of joint activity which specify the proper behaviour of pupils. Frames vary in scope and several may be operative at any one time. Thus some will be virtually all-pervasive, specifying the appropriate behaviour of pupils at any time; though there may be occasions, for example, school trips, visits to the games field, etc., where even these are relaxed. Other frames are much more specific, being relevant to particular lesson phases[44] or relating to just one segment of a phase. An example of a very specific frame is where the teacher asks a question. Doing this he demands pupil behaviour which at other times during the same phase is illegitimate: he requires pupils to talk publicly to him and the rest of the class, albeit in an 'appropriate' manner. Directives play a similar role in specifying a certain form of action pupils are to engage in.[45] It is in terms of such frames, and specifically in terms of the frames operative at any particular point in time, that we can define pupil conformity to school requirements.

However, while, in most versions of teaching, the teacher is the only classroom participant who has an automatic right to set up frames, in practice pupils also propose frames, and sometimes these 'come off'. Much classroom deviance amounts, whether intentionally or not, to the proposal of an alternative framework to that the teacher is operating. Such alternative frames may be public, classroom wide, or they may be more localised, being confined to those who are sitting close to one another.[46] Where this occurs the other pupils are faced with a choice between conforming to the 'deviant' frame, joining a 'disruptive' interaction set, or conforming to school requirements and being seen to conform by fellow pupils as well as the teacher. It is at such times that the issue of being a conformist or a deviant, a 'lad' or an 'ear'ole', becomes particularly salient.

However, it is unlikely that such decisions are made on the basis of criteria which are simply momentary. In his article on interaction sets Furlong points to some of the criteria which the pupils he studied seemed to employ. However, underlying such typifications of teachers must be some basic concerns which make these particular aspects of teachers relevant to the pupils. Of course, we cannot assume a single integrated set of such concerns nor can we assume that these concerns are derived from school values or even from an inversion of school values. We indicated earlier the complex nature of 'school values' and the diversity of other influences likely to impinge on pupils. Furthermore, it is also clear that the salience and implications of these concerns will vary across different contexts in the schools; for example according to the reputation of the teacher or the composition of the pupil audience.

The field of possible actions facing a pupil, and the costs and gratifications associated with different lines of action, will also change over time. Thus, we must take account of the way in which pupils re-evaluate their positions over time and adjust their orientations to changes in their situation. Some of these changes will occur independently of the actions of the pupil himself. Others may be consequences of his own previous actions: for example, adopting a particular line of action frequently involves building up commitments which change one's situation in such a way that it becomes more and more costly to act in any other way.[47]

One particularly important kind of consequence linked with lines of possible pupil action is identity implications. It is not just social scientists who make generalisations about the typical or general orientations of particular pupils. Both teachers and pupils do this too. In adopting a particular line of action a pupil must take into account the way others will interpret and react to his action, since this may have important consequences for what options are open to him in the future. Of course the relationship between actions, identity ascription, 'societal reaction' and the options available to an actor in the future is fairly loose. Performing a particular action does not automatically result in the acquisition of a particular reputation, and having a particular reputation does not absolutely determine how others will act towards you. But there is a tendency for each to follow from the other.

The pupil may also have to make sense of his action in terms of his conception of his own identity and biography. Even so, we should not assume a great deal of consistency over time and across contexts in the behaviour of pupils. Not only will a pupil's assessment of the feasibility of achieving particular goals vary across different situations but, more than likely, his assessment of the *desirability* of the different goals will also shift. And, of course, he may frequently be faced with dilemmas: as we noted earlier, the existence of a deviant interaction set forces choice between open 'conformity' and 'deviance'. Such crises may have important implications both for a pupil's sense of self and for how he is treated in future both by fellow pupils and by the teachers.

How the pupil evaluates the desirability and feasibility of different courses of action, how dilemmas are resolved and thus the general drift in his school career (if there is one) may well be influenced by the gatherings and groups in which he participates. The structure of the school— whether pupils are streamed, banded, setted or taught in mixed ability

groups and how they are allocated to classes – is obviously of considerable importance here, as are the informal groupings which develop within and across classes. However, we cannot assume an isomorphism
between the adaptations pupils adopt and the interaction sets or groups
in which they participate.[48] Pupils may interact with their fellows for
many reasons, not necessarily because they share values or even goals.

## Conclusion

In this chapter we have reviewed the currently available models for the
interpretation of pupil activity: the pro/anti subculture model, the
adaptation model, and Furlong's interactionist approach. The first two
models have considerable scope but fail to account for the complexity
and subtlety of pupil behaviour revealed even in the evidence of those
who have employed them. On the other hand, Furlong's model, while
it certainly begins to take account of the contextual variability of pupil
behaviour, is very limited in scope: it seems stuck at the level of description. In the final section of the chapter we have sketched a slightly
different approach which should provide a basis for the integration of
these various models. While it *begins* at the level of the intentions,
motives and activities of pupils, it nevertheless also allows for the
*explanation* of patterns of pupil behaviour in terms of the structural
features of the school and the wider society. A pupil's social class position and his position within the school will have consequences for the
lines of action available to him and the costs and benefits associated with
these. But the operation of these factors only works through, and can
only be identified and documented in, the more shifting moment-to-
moment features of school process.

## Notes

1. A curious feature of this influence, however, has been the dominating
influence of subcultural and adaptational models deriving from normative functionalism rather than interactionism. For exceptions, see Furlong (1976) and D.H.
Hargreaves (1976). Also, Cathy Bird's chapter in this volume.
2. For example, Lacey (1970), Marsh, Rosser and Harré (1978) and Woods
(1978a) and (1978b). Delamont (1973) and (1976) are exceptions to this, taking
the form of straightforward applications of interactionist theory.
3. See Bernstein (1977).
4. Matza (1964). Also, we can expect differences between the values and
norms teachers project and those they live by.
5. Merton and Barber (1963); Lang (1977).
6. Goffman (1971).
7. For Miller (1958) delinquency, like crime, is the product of conformity to

working-class culture. Cohen (1955) treats it as the product of a youth subculture centred around the inversion of middle-class values. This is produced by status frustration on the part of working-class boys who do not have the resources to succeed in middle-class terms. However, despite their differences, both Miller and Cohen employ the contrast between two sets of values to explain contrasting behaviour: conformity and deviance. Paradoxically, therefore, both 'straight' and delinquent youth are treated as conformists, albeit to different sets of values and norms.

8. Merton (1957).

9. In this respect his version of functional analysis is an advance over that of Parsons which fails to provide any systematic basis for the social production of deviance. See Parsons (1951), ch. 7. For a critique of Parsons along these lines which, curiously, doesn't mention Merton's work see Lockwood (1956).

10. Woods (1977); Woods (1979), ch. 3.

11. See Becker (1977).

12. For an application of Hughes's concept which has particular potential in this context see Emerson (1969).

13. See Bucher and Strauss (1961).

14. For an attempt to differentiate versions of teaching see Hammersley (1977).

15. The issue of the perceived legitimacy of different routes to school success is an important area for investigation.

16. For a similar argument see Cathy Bird's chapter in this volume.

17. See Mannheim (1952).

18. Speier (1976); Silvers (1977).

19. Willis (1977), p. 38.

20. See Wheeler (1966).

21. See Woods (1977) on fraternisation.

22. For other, but not necessarily incompatible, explanations of this see Jackson and Marsden (1962), and Lacey (1970).

23. This is one possible explanation for Rosenthal and Jacobson's (1968) findings.

24. This is, of course, a central tenet of interactionism. Bob Meyenn's chapter in this volume represents a move in this direction.

25. He does, however, make the important suggestion, following Wakeford, that some of the adaptations tend to occur at characteristic points in pupils' school careers.

26. Though it should be said that the model stops well short of any analysis of the *process* of decision-making.

27. See Turner (1979).

28. See Geer (1977) and Werthman (1977). The classic discussion of negotiation is of course Strauss, *et al.* (1964). Also see Strauss (1978).

29. Another plausible reading is that some of 'the lads', including Joey, don't object to teacher authority as such, only to the degree or particular range of authority the teachers claim, for example, their attempts to control aspects of personal appearance.

30. See Bob Meyenn's (this volume) discussion of the 'science lab girls' reaction to restrictions on make-up and clothes. He suggests that their reaction was more extreme than that of the less 'conformist' girls. Incidentally, one curious feature of recent reworkings of Merton is that 'rebellion' is no longer taken to mean an attempt to reorganise society or school but the use of what space is available to follow alternative goals. Clearly the possibility of rebellion in its original meaning must be preserved, even if it is relatively rare.

31. See Bramson (1961), Kornhauser (1959) and Shils (1975).

32. See Lang (1977) on school refusers.

33. Goffman (1968). Later proponents of the adaptation model have incorporated some of the adaptations pinpointed by Goffman but not his basic model.

34. Shils's (1975) notion of the displacement of charisma in modern societies seems particularly promising as an explanation for these changes.

35. See Hammersley (1976) for the manipulation of the notion of 'child' in bolstering teacher authority.

36. Furlong (1976).

37. Turner (1979).

38. Furlong (1976), p. 27.

39. The same judgement applies to Delamont's (1976) application of this approach.

40. See Deutscher (1973).

41. Matza (1964) points out that deviants are never deviant all the time, they spend most of their lives conforming. He argues that this misconception has led to the incorrect presumption that deviants are a different type of person from conformists, for example having a different physical make-up, or personality.

42. See McDermott (1976) for documentation of this at a very detailed level.

43. Of course, some of those working with the adaptation model have recognised this, notably Peter Woods. But the adaptation model cannot deal with this problem because it focuses exclusively at the level of general adaptations to school values. While Woods recognises the complexity of pupil activity and of the situation they are responding to, he does not develop the model to cope with this complexity. In this sense his account amounts to a normative functionalist model dressed up in loosely fitting interactionist clothing.

44. For the concept of lesson phase see Hargreaves, Hester and Mellor (1975).

45. This concept of frame is an interactionist reformulation of the more structuralist notions of frame used by Sinclair and Coulthard (1975) and Goffman (1975). Also, see Hammersley forthcoming.

46. Though even the latter may encourage other localised side involvements elsewhere in the classroom.

47. See Becker (1977) for this concept of commitment.

48. This is an inevitable result of adopting a decision-making rather than a rule-based model of action.

# References

Becker, H.S. (1977) 'Personal Change in Adult Life', in B.R. Cosin, *et al.*, *School and Society*, Routledge and Kegan Paul, London, 2nd ed

Bernstein, B. (1977) 'Class Pedagogies: Visible and Invisible', in B. Bernstein, *Class Codes and Control*, vol. 3, Routledge and Kegan Paul, London, 2nd ed

Bramson, L. (1961) *The Political Context of Sociology*, Princeton UP, Princeton

Bucher, R. and Strauss, A. (1961) 'Professions in Process', *American Journal of Sociology*, 66, January 1961, pp. 325-43, reprinted in M. Hammersley and P. Woods, *The Process of Schooling*, Routledge and Kegan Paul, London

Cloward, R. and Ohlin, L. (1960) *Delinquency and Opportunity*, Free Press, New York

Cohen, A.K. (1955) *Delinquent Boys*, Free Press, New York

Delamont, S. (1973) 'Academic Conformity Observed', unpublished Ph.D thesis

Delamont, S. (1976) *Interaction in the Classroom*, Methuen, London

Deutscher, I. (1973) *What we say/What we do*, Scott Foresman, Illinois

Emerson, R.M. (1969) *Judging Delinquents*, Aldine, London

Furlong, V. (1976) 'Interaction Sets in the Classroom', in M. Stubbs and S. Delamont,

*Explorations in Classroom Observation*, Wiley, New York

Geer, B. (1977) 'Teaching', in B.R. Cosin, *et al.*, *School and Society*, Routledge and Kegan Paul, London, 2nd ed

Goffman, E. (1968) *Asylums*, Penguin, Harmondsworth

Goffman, E. (1971) *The Presentation of Self in Everyday Life*, Penguin, Harmondsworth

Goffman, E. (1975) *Frame Analysis*, Penguin, Harmondsworth

Hammersley, M. (1976) 'The Mobilisation of Pupil Attention', in M. Hammersley and P. Woods, *The Process of Schooling*

Hammersley, M. (1977) 'Teacher Perspectives', E202 Schooling and Society, Units 9-10, Open University

Hammersley, M. (1979) 'Towards a Model of Teacher Activity', in J. Eggleston, *Teacher Decision Making in the Classroom*, Routledge and Kegan Paul, London

Hammersley, M. (forthcoming) 'Putting Competence into Action', in M. MacLure and P. French, *The Sociolinguistics of Children's Conversation*, Croom Helm, London

Harary, F. (1966) 'Merton Revisited: a New Classification for Deviant Behaviour', *American Sociological Review*, vol. 31, no. 5.

Hargreaves, D.H. (1967) *Social Relations in a Secondary School*, Routledge and Kegan Paul, London

Hargreaves, D.H., Hester, S. and Mellor, F. (1975) *Deviance Classrooms*, Routledge and Kegan Paul, London

Hargreaves, D.H. (1976) 'Reaction to Labelling', in M. Hammersley and P. Woods, *The Process of Schooling*

Jackson, B. and Marsden, D. (1962) *Education and the Working Class*, Routledge and Kegan Paul, London

Kornhauser, W. (1959) *The Politics of Mass Society*, Free Press, New York

Lacey, C. (1970) *Hightown Grammar*, Manchester University Press

Lang, T. (1977) 'School Experience – More Sociological Ambiguities', in P. Woods and M. Hammersley, *School Experience*, Croom Helm, London

Lockwood, D. (1956) 'Some Remarks on "The Social System"', *British Journal of Sociology*, vol. VII, no. 2

McDermott, R.P. (1976) 'Kids Make Sense: An Ethnographic Account of the Interactional Management of Success and Failure in One First Grade Classroom', (unpublished Ph.D. thesis, Stanford)

Mannheim, K. (1952) 'The Problem of Generations', in K. Mannheim, *Essays on the Sociology of Knowledge*, Routledge and Kegan Paul, London

Matza, D. (1964) *Delinquency and Drift*, Wiley, London

Marsh, P., Rosser, E. and Harré, R. (1978) *The Rules of Disorder*, Routledge and Kegan Paul, London

Merton, R.K. and Barber, E. (1963) 'Sociological Ambivalence', in E. Tiryakian, *Sociological Theory, Values and Sociocultural Change*, Free Press, New York

Merton, R.K. (1957) 'Social Structure and Anomie', in R.K. Merton, *Social Theory and Social Structure*, Free Press, New York

Miller, W. (1958) 'Lower Class Culture as a Generating Milieu of Gang Delinquency', *Journal of Social Issues*, 15, pp. 5-19

Parsons, T. (1951) *The Social System*, Routledge and Kegan Paul, London

Rosenthal, R. and Jacobson, L. (1968) *Pygmalion in the Classroom*, Holt, Rinehart and Winston, New York

Shils, E. (1975) *Centre and Periphery*, University of Chicago Press

Silvers, R. (1977) 'Appearances: a Videographic Study of Children's Culture', in P. Woods and M. Hammersley, *School Experience*, Croom Helm, London

Sinclair, J. and Coulthard, M. (1975) *Towards an Analysis of Discourse*, Oxford University Press, Oxford

Speier, M. (1976) 'The Child as a Conversationalist: Some Culture-Contact Features of Conversational Interactions between Adults and Children', in M. Hammersley and P. Woods, *The Process of Schooling*, Routledge and Kegan Paul, London

Strauss, A. *et al.* (1964) *Psychiatric Ideologies and Institutions*, Free Press, New York

Strauss, A. (1978) *Negotiations*, Jossey Bass, California

Turner, G. (1979) 'Contrasting Conformist Action', paper given at the Conference on 'Pupils In and Out of School', Hertford College, Oxford

Wakeford, J. (1969) *The Cloistered Elite*, Macmillan, London

Werthman, C. (1977) 'Delinquents in School', in B.R. Cosin, *et al.*, *School and Society*, Routledge and Kegan Paul, London, 2nd ed

Wheeler, S. (1966) 'The Study of Formally Organised Socialisation Settings', in O.G. Brim and S. Wheeler, *Socialisation after Childhood*, Wiley, New York

Willis, P. (1977) *Learning to Labour*, Saxon House, Farnborough

Woods, P. (1977) 'Teaching for Survival', in P. Woods and M. Hammersley, *School Experience*, Croom Helm, London

Woods, P. (1977) 'Pupil Experience', Unit 11, OU Course E202 Schooling and Society, Bletchley

Woods, P. (1978a) 'Relating to Schoolwork', *Educational Review*, vol. 30, no. 2

Woods, P. (1978b) 'Negotiating the Demands of Schoolwork', *Journal of Curriculum Studies*, vol. 3

Woods, P. (1979) *The Divided School*, Routledge and Kegan Paul, London

# 3 PUPIL STRATEGIES AND THE OPEN CLASSROOM

Martyn Denscombe

The strategies adopted by pupils and teachers owe a great deal to the physical and institutional setting in which they occur. Pupils and teachers identify possibilities and constraints offered by the context in which they operate and adopt strategies which they regard as appropriate under the particular circumstances.

It is surprising, therefore, that relatively little attention has been given to classroom strategies as 'context specific' phenomena. Instead, there has been an apparent willingness to treat the context as a 'given'—as an obvious and unremarkable setting whose implications are self-evident and warrant little examination in the account of classroom strategies.

It seems reasonable to speculate that this situation results from the predominance of one type of classroom context in secondary education— the 'closed classroom'. It is, after all, the context with which most people are familiar and one whose implications might not be regarded as worthy of detailed comment. There are, however, alternatives to the closed classroom in secondary education. Quite apart from the games lessons, PE, art and other examples of situations which differ from the normal classroom context, there are occasional instances of innovation which also offer marked contrast. These innovations warrant some attention and, although emphasis on the closed classroom is certainly necessary in view of its prevalence in secondary education, as Hamilton[1] warns, the study of schooling needs to break from a myopic focus on the conventional and commonplace if it is to offer analyses pertinent to educational development.

For this reason, the study of classroom strategies in the open classroom is apposite. Open classrooms provide contexts which contrast with the conventional situation and thus promote comparisons which not only demonstrate the necessity for treating classroom strategies as part of the wider physical and institutional context in which they occur but also draw attention to practical possibilities and limitations affecting proposed innovations in the realm of education.

## Open School—Open Classrooms

The open classroom contrasts with more 'traditional' modes of schooling in terms of four factors: i) it integrates subject boundaries; ii) it integrates social groupings (sex, intelligence, social class, etc.); iii) the teacher role becomes that of a non-authoritarian 'catalyst' to learning; and iv) the pupil role becomes more active in terms of the content and pacing of work, with an emphasis on self-motivation and self-discipline at school. Attempts to implement open schooling, of course, will vary in scope and degree according to the wishes of those involved and the practical problems they confront, and it is unlikely that open schooling exists anywhere in its pure form. Realistically, attempts to implement open schooling should be viewed as a move along a continuum away from conventional schooling rather than a 'successful' or 'unsuccessful' break from traditional principles.

The point was well illustrated by the case of a Leicestershire community college[2] in which there existed a definite shift toward open schooling, but a shift which was neither total nor without its own contradictions. Opened in 1969, it was a co-educational school taking 14-18 year old pupils and had established for itself a reputation for being particularly progressive and innovative.[3] In many respects it aspired to open schooling. It was part of the official school policy, for instance, to move toward a more integrated curriculum and to provide the basis for integrating the social groups, a fact which found expression in a policy statement by the principal:

Subject boundaries are only one expression of man's preoccupation with fencing himself in. We have hoped in our social organization to break down barriers caused by class, money, neighbourhood, intelligence, sex—and to point the need—and provide the means—for a caring community. (Rogers, 1971)

Hannam (1975), in previous research at the college, has argued that the official policy largely reflected the principles of open schooling outlined by Bernstein (1967) in his well-known article 'Open Schools: Open Society?'. With its avowed aims of social and curricular integration, the school appeared to aspire to an organic solidarity which reflected, and was conducive to, authority relationships which differed from traditional schooling. There was a conscious attempt to promote self-motivation and self-discipline amongst the pupils so that reliance on punitive measures to achieve order became redundant. The school, indeed, aspired to a collaborative relationship between pupils and teachers (rather than authoritarian) and thus encouraged a 'catalyst' role for teachers and a more active and responsible role for pupils within the classroom.

Policies outlined in official statements, however, rarely receive complete translation to the actual activity of members and the school did not entirely reflect the policy of social and curricular integration. There were evident limits to the degree of openness in the organisation and classroom practices throughout the school. Subject boundaries continued to exist in certain areas—particularly the high status subjects—and the examination syndrome (CSE and GCE) continued to exert pressure to adhere to a syllabus (whether or not mode 3). Framing and classification, it might be said, were weakened but not weak (cf Bernstein, 1971).

Yet in Humanities lessons there was a degree of openness which warranted comparison and contrast with conventional practices. These lessons saw the fullest expression of the official policy in the routine and practical organisation of the classroom.

## Humanities Lessons and the Open Classroom

Humanities lessons were mixed ability and taught in open-plan classrooms by teachers operating in teams. The open-plan classrooms held from 60 to 80 pupils with the teachers working in teams of three, both in the planning of the syllabus and within the open-plan classrooms during lessons. This situation was one immediately recognisable as novel and offered a marked contrast with the situation in the vast majority of classrooms. Though open-plan classrooms have become familiar in primary classrooms and there have been some experiments with team teaching,[4] neither has become a regular feature of the secondary school classroom and both can be regarded as aberrations of the normal context for teaching and learning.

The classroom innovations in these Humanities lessons were complemented by curricular innovations. The Humanities course integrated English with Community Studies—both of which could be taken at CSE and GCE O level—and to this extent offered a move in the direction of an integrated curriculum. There was a definite attempt to weaken the boundaries between the two subjects, aided by the team basis for planning and presenting the course which brought members of staff from different discipline backgrounds together to plan the syllabus and present the material in the classroom. 'Lead' lessons, where the whole class was taught together by one or more of the team members, were generally for the purpose of introducing a new topic in the course. For the rest of the time the pupils split up into three sub-groups (with one of the staff being primarily responsible for each) where there was strong emphasis on resource-based methods of individualised learning. Most of the pupils' lesson time, indeed, was devoted to individualised styles of learning with the teacher operating as facilitator rather than instructor.

The pupils were encouraged to adopt a self-motivated and self-disciplined approach to their work and were given a degree of freedom to move
about the open-plan unit, to discuss the work amongst themselves and
to sit where they chose, with the ethos being very much that of the
'progressive' classroom (cf Bennett, 1976; Gross, *et al.*, 1971). The staff
aspired to a 'catalyst' role and, reflecting Kohl's (1970) vision of the
'open classroom', sought to achieve a non-authoritarian relationship
with pupils, a relationship using conviviality and friendliness in the classroom to foster a collaborative rather than didactic approach to teaching
and learning.

In sum, an integrated curriculum with mixed-ability classes taught
by teams of teachers in open-plan classrooms served to distinguish the
context from the conventional situation and, combined with the non-
authoritarian 'catalyst' role aspired to by staff, the context can be considered, with some justification, to be an example of a relatively open
classroom.

## Strategies and Experience of the Open Classroom

Experience of the open classroom need have no direct or concomitant
effect on the strategies of pupils or teachers. Both parties bring to the
situation a host of expectations and meanings based on current and
previous experience of classrooms and it is extremely unlikely that any
of the participants would be willing or able to divest themselves of
these orientations when operating in the open classroom unless they
came to regard the situation as routine and normal. Neither pupils nor
staff, however, spent a substantial portion of their school day in the
open classroom. Of the 33 periods a week, pupils spent six in the Humanities lessons and most staff spent less than half their timetabled periods
in the Humanities situation. As a result, for these pupils and staff the
Humanities lessons still constituted something of an abnormal situation.
Quite apart from their previous experience in conventional settings,
neither pupils nor staff at the school currently experienced open classrooms as the norm and it is reasonable to suppose that the strategies
they used were still heavily influenced by their experience of the closed
classroom. The Humanities lessons, therefore, although going some way
towards giving an example of open classrooms, were unlikely to provide
a full exegesis of the strategies possible within, or appropriate to, the
open classroom context.[5]

The abnormality of the situation provided pressure to reconstitute
conventional strategies within the new situation. For their part, the
staff exhibited this drive for continuity by implementing a subtle

'closure' on the openness of the classroom. The three sub-groups into which the class generally divided when 'lead' lessons were not in progress allowed individual teachers to be identified as responsible for a specific group of pupils and consequently reinstituted a significant feature of the closed classroom within the Humanities situation. These sub-groupings also provided an effective limit to the extent of choice available to pupils in terms of seating. With just rare exceptions, pupils were expected to remain somewhere within the sub-group and, in practice, did not generally sit with another teacher's group.

The situation in the Humanities lessons, then, was one which reflected many of the basic principles of open schooling and thus lent itself to comparison with conventional secondary school classrooms, but the comparison was limited by the fact that the open classroom context was experienced by pupils for less than one fifth of their timetable and staff for between one quarter and one half of theirs. The inertia of experiences and meanings gained in the closed classroom consequently influenced the participants' interpretation of events in the open classroom and restricted the extent to which strategies appropriate to the open classroom became evident. They were obscured by an attempt to normalise the situation in terms of experiences elsewhere and attempts to effect a closure on the situation.

Notwithstanding these practical limitations to the openness, however, the situation was markedly different from the conventional closed classroom and there was still a degree of openness which distinguished these Humanities lessons from the norm. The movement of pupils and staff about the open-plan unit and the degree of observability allowed by the classroom setting was significantly different from that afforded by the closed classroom. There was little of the 'privacy' associated with the conventional classroom, a fact reflected in the extent of movement in the classroom and contact between pupils and between staff during lessons. In sum, the Humanities lessons in the Leicestershire community college provided a move along the continuum to open schooling sufficient to warrant juxtaposition with the conventional classroom situation and sufficient to expose, albeit in limited fashion, the impact of new contexts upon the strategies adopted in the classroom.

## Classroom Control and Pupil Strategies

Different settings evoke different behaviour from those who interact within them and the classroom has been regarded as a unique setting incorporating its own set of pressures on the activity of pupils and teachers. Delamont (1976), in pursuing the point, has argued that the classroom situation engenders a struggle for power between the participants—each having opposed interests in the order of the classroom. She describes the situation in a chapter evocatively titled 'Let battle commence: strategies for the classroom'. As she acknowledges, such a view of the classroom as a battlefield—or at least a zone of conflict in which there exists a precarious truce (Waller, 1932)—is not a recent development but is an understanding of the classroom which has become well established in the literature. It is a view which reflects the reality of the classroom experienced by both pupils and teachers, a reality in which the struggle for control is a relentless battle of wits.

This view is not without its limitations, for certainly the routine activity in classrooms depends on some appreciable level of co-operation and compliance on the part of the pupils to the power exercised by teachers, yet it has the advantage of drawing attention to the negotiated element of activity in classrooms. It is patently absurd to consider classrooms as settings in which social order is by fiat and where pupils accede to the every word of the teacher. To a greater or lesser extent, the social order of the classroom is a negotiated phenomenon with pupils and teachers adopting strategies which promote their particular interests. Teachers have a vested interest in retaining control of the classroom—or at least the appearance of control (Denscombe, 1977, 1979)—and pupils, for their part, seek to impose their will on the progress of the lesson by adopting their own strategies designed to gain control of the situation (Delamont, 1976; Doyle, 1979; Jackson, 1968; Woods, 1978a, 1978b).

The basic situation within which pupils operate, however, is one where their activity is almost inevitably a *re*action to events. The situation in classrooms is one which institutionalises the authority of teachers to guide and control events and requires pupils to react, in whatever manner, to a situation not instigated by them. As Jackson (1968) has observed, one of the major features of the hidden curriculum to be learnt by pupils is that there is an unequal distribution of power in classrooms. Pupils, he argues, need to learn strategies which allow them to cope with this situation and he identifies the 'strategy of detachment' as the basic means used by pupils to accommodate the hazardous inequality of power in classrooms. Such a strategy, however, assumes a large degree of acquiescence to the situation on the part of the pupils and potentially underestimates the extent to which pupils might seek to challenge the imposition of control by teachers. It emphasises acquiescence at the expense of the involvement of pupils in negotiating the grounds on which that control will exist.

Yet pupils are not without interests, power and influence in the negotiation of classroom control. They can, and do, regularly seek to avert attempts by staff to impose a teacher version of order in the classroom and have at their disposal certain means, arising specifically within the classroom context, that can be used to counter teacher strategies for control. Ironically, they have at their disposal the very strategies employed by teachers in their quest for classroom control.

Pupils, ever adept at recognising and coping with the hidden curriculum of the classroom, can exploit the teacher strategies and use them to their own ends – the aim of gaining some influence over the conduct and progress of classroom events. This is a point well illustrated by the case of the teacher strategy of 'flirting'. Noted by Woods (1977) as a significant strategy available for teachers in their attempts to gain control in the classroom, flirting:

> is a widely used technique, especially by male teachers with female pupils. Since sex is one of the most prominent interests of the more rebellious girl pupils, it can be a great aid in securing their goodwill and co-operation. (Woods, 1977, p. 283)

Those teachers who used flirting as a strategy, however, would presumably not be immune to its effects and might be the prime targets of flirting when used as a counter-strategy by pupils. The young male staff, in particular, might find themselves the target for flirting by fourth- and fifth-year girls. The strategy, that is, because it is essentially an interactional phenomenon and a two-way process, has the potential to be cunningly exploited by the party it was intended to control – to be adopted by the recipients and redirected in order to serve their own purposes in the negotiation of classroom affairs.

Whatever the extent of pupil influence, however, it clearly takes the form of a *re*action to a situation not entirely of their own making and one in which they suffer a lack of institutionalised rights. Much of their activity, in consequence, takes the form of *counter-strategies* through which teacher strategies can be baulked and through which acquiescence to teacher control can be traded-off against aspects of lessons which pupils find preferable. Pupils can, for instance, use counter-strategies to negotiate the amount of work they do in lessons and the nature of the behaviour deemed acceptable within the classroom situation.

## Noise and Pupil Strategies

The existence of pupil counter-strategies is illustrated by the case of noise in classrooms. As argued elsewhere (Denscombe, 1977), teachers exhibit some preoccupation with noise and generally devise strategies to control noise in lessons. Their concern to control noise has some educational basis—for certainly pupils might be distracted from their work by high levels of noise—but their concern also results from the connotations of noise for control of the classroom. As Kohl (1970, p. 84) has observed:

Perhaps noise suggests lack of control and thus activates the authoritarian's fear of his not being in command.

Any strategies which teachers adopt in their attempts to control noise and thus protect the impression that there is control in the classroom, however, have some special significance for pupils. They open up for pupils a whole array of counter-strategies which can be used to challenge the control of the teacher and assert their will on the progress of the lesson. Pupils in closed classrooms are adept at generating noises which are intended to annoy the teacher and disturb the flow of the lesson. More than any other tool at their disposal, noise provides pupils with a means for countering the control instituted by teachers. Yet, as a strategy in the classroom, it arises precisely as a *counter* to the teacher invoked pressure to maintain quiet orderliness in the classroom. If teachers were not concerned to prevent noise, the strategy would become irrelevant because it would not provide a challenge to anything relating to classroom control.

In the open classroom, Kohl (1970) observes, the amount of noise generated in lessons almost inevitably rises. Increased pupil interaction cannot help but create higher levels of noise than a situation where the teacher is the only member of the classroom who can legitimately initiate talk and where the teacher is the only member who can legitimately move around the room.

For the teacher who attempts to introduce the open classroom into a school which is predominantly traditional, this extra noise can pose particular problems, as Kohl is quick to recognise. It can be misconstrued as a sign of a lack of control and is likely to invite hostility from those who regard it as a threat to the authority of the teacher. But, where the situation is more conducive to open classrooms—as at the Leicestershire community college—the significance of any extra noise for the competence of staff was countered by the observability which accompanied team teaching in open-plan classrooms. Because teachers worked alongside each other, frequently entering and leaving areas used by colleagues, they had less need to worry about whether the amount of noise might be interpreted by 'outsiders' as indicative of a lack of control. People could see what was going on and did not need to resort to informed guesswork.

Certainly, the general level of noise in the open-plan units was higher than elsewhere and there was an appreciable tolerance of noise. Radios were occasionally switched on during lessons and, though pupils were usually asked to switch them off, it brought no immediate caustic response from the staff. And though staff sometimes called for 'more work and less chat', pupils were not generally prohibited from talking to each other during the course of a lesson.

There were, of course, practical limits to the level of noise allowed in the classrooms which both teachers and pupils readily acknowledged. For the staff, the concern arose particularly when they wished to address their sub-group because, even if their groups were attentive, the other two sub-groups in the open-plan unit could cause enough noise to drown the teacher's words. Not surprisingly, then, one of the main curbs on noise arose when one of the three teachers tried to speak to his/her group — the other teachers typically responding with comments to their own group such as:

All right, cut the noise down a bit. Jim's trying to talk to his group and they can't hear him if you don't shut-up a bit.

Pupils, themselves, suffered from the noise created by other groups and claimed[6] that it interfered with their concentration on work. They indicated that there was more noise in the open-plan classrooms and, whilst many regarded it as just an incidental feature of the particular lesson, others attributed specific causes to the noise and regarded it as an indictment of the Humanities situation:

The open-plan classroom is quite good. I like it when we can all work together as one big group, but there can be quite a lot of noise.

I think that the volume of noise should be kept lower, so that you can concentrate better. Thus your work will be better.

In open classrooms there is more noise but in conventional classrooms you can concentrate because the teacher only has one class to keep quiet. But there is two other classes to keep quiet in open-plan classrooms.

The main sorce [*sic*] of noise in open classes is mainly students, although teachers do distract us sometimes when they are talking.

When you are listening to your teacher you can hear the other two still talking and it can put you off.

In an open-plan classroom you get more noise which breaks your concentration and you lose where you are when people start talking to you.

For some pupils noise interfered with their concentration on work and they identified two main sources. Firstly, the pupils in other groups whose talking could distract them and, secondly, from the talking of the other teachers whose instructions to their groups were audible through-out the classroom. Yet, despite such interference experienced by some members of the class, there continued to be a high tolerance of noise which distinguished Humanities lessons from more conventional sit-uations—a tolerance which stemmed from the combination of three factors: i) the progressive ambience of the staff; ii) the situation of team teaching in open-plan classrooms which largely negated the subtle implications of noise for teacher control; and iii) the amount of inter-pupil contact and pupil movement around the room regarded as accept-able and/or necessary.

The explanation of this tolerance, however, is possibly of less import-ance than the impact it had on the pupil strategies. Effectively it neg-ated the pupil strategy of noise. No longer were whispered conversations a source of annoyance to teachers. No longer could pupils hope to chal-lenge the progress of the lesson by interrupting with coughs and sneezes of exaggerated proportion, or any other form of sudden or surreptitious noise. *The relatively high tolerance of noise in Human-ities lessons effectively cancelled out and rendered redundant pupil strategies for control which utilised forms of noise.* Notably absent from the lessons were the tried and tested genre of pupil strategy based on the creation of noise.

Clearly, the changed context of the open classroom had the potential to alter pupil strategies by rendering them inappropriate and useless in the negotiation of classroom control. In the situation where teachers were less disposed to regard noise as a threat to the appearance of class-room control and where there was a generally greater tolerance of noise as a routine feature of the classroom, pupils became deprived of a well established counter-strategy and means of negotiation for control of the classroom. Where teachers no longer sought to assert control, pupils could no longer challenge.

As Hargreaves (1976) has argued, however, progressive teaching methods do not entail the absence of teacher control. Greater tolerance by teachers for certain features of classroom behaviour does not herald the abdication by teachers of their control function. Instead, the progressive methods consist of new and more subtle forms of control which, in turn, necessitate the use of new strategies by pupils. Pupils, alert to the hidden curriculum in its new guise, can avail themselves of the new forms of teacher control as a new means for countering the teacher strategy — as a means for asserting their influence on the situation and coping with the demands placed upon them in the lesson situation. So, while one door closes, another opens.

### The Strategy of Friendliness

A commitment to non-authoritarian relationships between staff and pupils is an essential feature of the open classroom (Kohl, 1970). In principle this was accepted at the Leicestershire community college (Rogers, 1971) and, in practice, there was some evidence of a move in that direction. Staff referred to 'students' rather than 'pupils' and there existed a conscious attempt to break from the pupil/teacher divisions of conventional schooling. Teachers, for instance, encouraged the pupils to refer to them by their first name, the canteen facilities were shared by staff and pupils, and the staff room was not treated as the private and exclusive domain of the teachers.

Now, whilst it would be misleading to suggest that fundamental aspects of the teacher/pupil dichotomy had been broken, there was a concerted attempt to reduce its more obvious manifestations. In the classroom this was apparent in the forms of relationship which developed between staff and pupils. Teachers in the Humanities lessons sought to avoid the pitfalls they attributed to authoritarian modes of teaching not merely by encouraging the use of first names but by fostering an atmosphere of friendliness and conviviality in the classroom — and it was evident that the pupils recognised and responded to this atmosphere. Pupils regarded the Humanities lessons as more relaxed and friendly, and felt that their relationships with the staff were more cordial than in other lessons.[7]

> The teachers are better than at my last school because they try to be friendly and don't shout so much.

> In Humanities they are easier than in other lessons. They treat you more like adults and you can reason with them.

You can chat with the teachers and they are easier to get along with than in other lessons.

Such an atmosphere of friendliness could feasibly result from the personal preferences of the staff and be nothing more than the product of a 'good relationship' between pupils and teachers. Our point, however, is that this atmosphere was not entirely an unplanned and fortuitous product of personal and personality factors but was, to some extent, consciously engineered by staff as a means to an end. Quite apart from the dispositions of pupils and teachers, that is, friendly relations in the classroom had the facet of being a classroom strategy aiding teacher control of the situation. Far from friendliness signifying the abdication of control, it provided teachers with a means for eliciting particular modes of behaviour—a means for motivating pupils to work hard and behave well—so that there were very good practical reasons for wishing to generate an amicable atmosphere in lessons.

A prominent survival strategy (for teachers) is to work for good relations with the pupils, thus mellowing the inherent conflict, increasing the pupils' sense of obligation, and reducing their desire to cause trouble. (Woods, 1977, p. 281)

As a control strategy, friendliness was particularly well suited to the open classroom context because it provided teachers with a means of control which had no recourse to heavy-handed or authoritarian styles. Superficially, at least, it relied on personal relationships rather than institutional power as the source of control and thus fostered the impression of collaboration in the organisation of classroom events. Friendliness, when successfully operated as a classroom strategy by teachers, allowed a subtle mode of control which shrouded the institutional disparities of power between staff and pupils and was particularly useful in the context of the open classroom where the teachers sought to minimise the appearance of authoritarian teaching styles.

In the Humanities lessons, friendly relationships were facilitated by two sub-strategies both, again, well suited to the open classroom context. These sub-strategies involved the use of 'cultural identification' and 'humour'.

Cultural identification, used as a classroom strategy, relied on the possibility of establishing a sympathetic rapport between staff and pupils through emphasising shared aspects of their respective lifestyles. Two features of Humanities lessons aided this strategy: first, a number of teachers in the teams were young and could hope to draw on some common interests and second, the Humanities course itself involved Community Studies with units based on subjects such as 'families and children', 'adolescence', 'education' and 'beliefs'. In many instances the staff could emphasise the similarity between themselves and the pupils and, even where the topics did not engender cultural identification as similarity — most obviously in the 'education' unit — they still enhanced the extent to which the interaction between staff and pupils could draw on personal identities. Staff had added opportunity to present themselves as 'real people' with social lives and experiences having much in common with the pupils — neighbourhood, local football, tastes in music, films, clothes, etc. They could readily draw on these shared interests and experiences to promote the course and to gain the involvement of pupils. Cultural identification allowed a point of contact and communication between the teachers and the pupils, and provided a resource upon which teachers could draw in terms of their efforts to control the class.

This resource was used and refurbished particularly when humour was involved. Humour has a special significance for classrooms and can be used in many ways by staff to produce the kind of relationships and atmosphere in the classroom which are deemed desirable (Stebbins, 1979; Walker, *et al.*, 1973; Walker and Adelman, 1976; Walker and Goodson, 1977).

As a social control mechanism, the use of humour is well known to teachers, with sarcasm and irony being well established features of teacher talk in the conventional classroom. Pupils can be 'punished' and brought into line by the cruel wit of the teacher and can be embarrassed into acquiescence with the teacher's version of the classroom situation (Woods, 1975). Sarcasm or the use of embarrassment provides teachers with a strategy which aids classroom control but, because the humour tends to be at the expense of one or more of the pupils, it is a strategy ill-suited to the demands of the open classroom. It is something of a one-sided humour which demonstrates and recreates the institutional divide between teacher and pupil in the classroom. It is a humour whose poignancy for authority relations in the classroom is unlikely to escape the attention of those who are the 'butt' of the joke — a point equally applicable for the staff. Humour in the classroom which is at the expense of the teacher has the potential to challenge the institutional authority relations and to threaten the teacher's control of the setting (cf Willis, 1977). Where pupils exclude teachers from participation in the humour and/or treat teachers as the object of humour, it is likely to be interpreted as a direct challenge to the teacher's authority and as a further expression of the social gulf between teachers and pupils in classrooms.

Humour in the open classroom cannot afford to be of such a variety. It cannot be at the expense of either party because it would necessarily expose the divide and militate against the collaborative ethos of the lessons. Rather, in the open classroom, the kind of humour needs to be that which reinforces friendliness and thus needs to be of a kind which is mutually conceived and in which neither party consistently 'suffers' the humour.

This is not to say, however, that humour in the open classroom ceases to have any appreciable control function because humour also has the potential to foster an atmosphere of 'fun and conviviality' (Walker, *et al.*, 1973). It can help to create a friendly atmosphere in the classrooms and allow teachers to be privy to the kind of personal information about pupils which they might not glean under less relaxed circumstances. Obviously, it is this kind of humour which is more appropriate for the open classroom, and in the Humanities lessons the humour certainly appeared to be of this kind. The staff spent time in joking relationships with pupils, using the humour to enhance the atmosphere of friendliness and collaboration in the classroom, and relied on humour to gain information and put points across to pupils in a way which did not rely on authoritarian commands.

But, of course, as a means of establishing a desired classroom situation, humour also had the potential to be employed by pupils as a method of asserting their influence on the situation. Like other teacher strategies, friendliness (incorporating cultural identification and humour) lent itself to use as a counter-strategy. Pupils could exploit the strategy and turn it back on itself in order to exert some degree of pupil control in the classroom and effectively challenge any autocratic rule by the teacher(s).

It was particularly interesting to observe how pupils used this counter-strategy when receiving individual attention from teachers. During lessons teachers generally moved from pupil to pupil (or groups) on a rota basis so that each individual or group received some personal attention during the course of the lesson. It was in these personal inter-action situations that friendliness, humour and cultural identification became particularly apparent—not simply as a means of teacher control, but also as a pupil counter-strategy for averting threatening situations and diverting the teacher's focus of interest.

> **teacher** Robin, you owe me some work. You still haven't handed in the last unit.

> **pupil** Well, I had to go out last night . . .
> **teacher** That's no excuse . . .
> **pupil** No, well . . . it was football . . . City, you know.
> **teacher** That's hardly the point . . .
> **pupil** Have you seen them recently? They're coming on quite good now. You know . . . they've got a lot of young lads in the side . . . good they are.
> **teacher** Yes, I hear the average age of the team is twenty or so.
> **pupil** Makes you too old, doesn't it . . .
> **teacher** Cheek. I've got a few years left in me yet.
> **pupil** Why, where do you play? Must be goalkeeper at your age.
> **teacher** Well, actually, if you must know . . .

Humour, as it occurred in the Humanities lessons, evidently had uses for both parties. It provided teachers with a means for establishing more intimate relationships with the pupils whilst, at the same time, allowing pupils to circumvent awkward moments. But, as a counter-strategy, it should be noted, pupils did not use friendliness and humour as a direct challenge to the authority of teachers. As a counter-strategy, humour appeared to have short-term aims of averting, avoiding and redirecting teachers' attempts to control rather than providing a fundamental challenge to the authority relationship: it was used by pupils as a parry rather than a counter-thrust.

Such counter-strategies were useful for pupils not only in avoiding awkward moments. They could also be used to provide a 'legitimate' respite from the rigours of work. Where pupils could conjure up a humorous interlude, either in small groups or in the larger units, pupils could generate for themselves a situation in class where there was no onus on them to be working. Creating a joke, therefore, provided pupils with a means for negotiating their involvement in work.

This, again, was well illustrated in the Humanities lessons when staff talked to individual pupils about their work. The interaction rarely attracted the attention of others in the classroom but, if the interaction produced some humour or laughter, those pupils nearby tended to get themselves involved. The numbers of those involved seemed to grow quite rapidly and, what often started as a private joke, had a tendency to increase in scope very quickly if laughter was heard. It might be argued that this snowballing effect was a response to the interruption suffered by the other pupils, but in the Humanities lessons there appeared to be a desire to become actively associated with the humour. Additional quips would be offered from those outside the original group and the 'ripple effect' sometimes caused the teacher to intervene to restore some sense of decorum.

Quite apart from the issue of pupils having their concentration broken, and quite apart from the pupils' genuine like of humour, the rapid spread of a humorous interlude in the open classrooms seemed to owe something to a pupil strategy for negotiating a legitimate pause from work and acceptable reason for breaking up the smooth flow of the lesson. The humour, in other words, could be used by pupils as a means for influencing the progress and conduct of the lesson.

Yet, whether humour was used to avert teacher control or to provide a respite from work, it appeared to depend on a level of friendliness and conviviality specifically associated with the open classroom. The open classroom, indeed, was more conducive to the use of humour as a counter-strategy by pupils than other settings simply for this reason.

### Indulgence

The same might be said for the teacher strategy of indulgence. Not only was it a strategy more readily associated with the open classroom but it, too, provided pupils with the basis for exerting influence on classroom proceedings. Indulgence is a teacher strategy in which pupils are allowed to go beyond normally accepted bounds of behaviour and where teachers decline to enforce general classroom rules. As used by Woods (1977), such indulgence is applied by teachers to the behaviour of the whole class, but it is worth noting that indulgence can be just as applicable to the behaviour of individual pupils within a class who, for whatever reason, come to be regarded as a special case and worthy of special treatment.

In a general sense, it has been observed that teachers do not always intervene when interruption occurs. On occasion they foresee that the intervention would cause a greater disturbance than was warranted by the initial disruption, or they might see the intervention as exacerbating the situation (Hargreaves, *et al.*, 1975; Stebbins, 1971). Teachers are occasionally prepared to indulge forms of behaviour, especially where they take into account the identity of the perpetrator of that behaviour. Teachers respond to behaviour by taking into account who was involved and what would be the likely outcome of remedial action applied to this particular pupil. And where they come to regard the behaviour as 'normal' for the particular pupil, there is a tendency to indulge the behaviour and cease attempts to remedy the normally unacceptable behaviour.

Certainly, instances of indulgence existed in the Humanities groupings.

In a fifth-year group, one boy spent the majority of his time walking between the three groups talking to other pupils. His marginality in the class was classically symbolised by the coat which he always wore despite the warm classroom. In the open-plan units movement around the class was not prohibited, but there were tacit amounts of movement deemed appropriate. In every sense, the movement of this pupil contravened this tacit rule, for his classroom presence was typified by movement around the room with occasional sorties to his desk rather than vice versa. On his travels the pupil stopped with groups of pupils, chatted with them, walked off with pens and rulers and created interruptions for the groups he visited. The indulgence with which this behaviour was treated was the product of both teacher and pupil strategies. Accounts of the situation by the teachers drew attention to the fact that movement, *per se*, was not prohibited in the classroom and that this particular boy had learning difficulties which would probably become behavioural problems if he were made to stay in one place. They also noted the general pleasantness of his character.

Looked at from the pupil's point of view, his success in countering normal modes of control by teachers stemmed from the combination of a number of factors. Had the staff attempted to force the pupil to stay in one place it might have provoked the kind of confrontation which could expose the essence of power relations in the classroom and explode the 'façade' of friendliness. The staff not only disliked confrontation of itself, but were aware of the broader implications for the tenor of the whole classroom. Added to this problem was the fact that he was regarded as a likable fellow—much in the style of the 'amiable idiot'. Yet this pupil's use of the indulgence strategy exhibited some considerable sophistication. When talking to a small group of pupils he provided for them a source of brief respite from work but his interruptions were essentially temporary; after a short time he would move on to disturb someone else.

From the point of view of the other pupils, then, his wanderings were more of a relief from work than a hindrance to it. Even when he walked off with someone's pen or ruler, he exhibited a delightful sense of timing in giving it back just before the protestations of the owner became serious enough to attract the attention of the teacher(s). This pupil, then, exemplified the manner in which indulgence could be used to avoid work and how it relied on an ambience of friendliness and good humour in the classroom.

## Pupil Strategies and the Open Curriculum

Negotiating involvement in work was aided by another feature of the open classroom. In the open classroom a greater degree of control over the curriculum by pupils was regarded as a positive advantage and something to be actively sought through the design of the course. This aspiration was evident in the Humanities course which proposed that, within each unit, the emphasis which a pupil placed on any particular topic was to be largely a matter of choice so that pupils could effectively devise a course geared to his/her own interests.

> The course is arranged as a sequence of ten units. In each unit a topic is taken as a subject of study and as a basis for various forms of expression, factual, critical and creative. . . . you may enquire into other aspects of your own or your teacher's choice. (Humanities course guidelines)

The *quid pro quo*, however, was that pupils could use this freedom to their own ends. They could, for instance, manoeuvre the teachers into dealing with topics on the basis of interest rather than any intended educational value. Now, whilst the two need not be mutually exclusive (and a strong lobby would argue that they are essentially supportive and reinforcing) the point is that such teacher strategies ran the risk of being used by pupils as a means for subtly altering the content of the course and imposing their own version of what the course should deal with—a version which might not reflect what the teachers had intended. It enhanced the possibility that pupils could focus on matters of interest to themselves and militated against the imposition of topics by the members of staff. Yet, quite apart from the leeway afforded pupils by the very nature of the course, the set-up provided a further strategy.

The relative openness of the curriculum provided a strategy for gaining control over the amount of work which was done by facilitating, if not promoting, discussion between pupils. The very interest and relevance of the topics, combined with a teacher tolerance of talk in open classrooms, allowed pupils to engage in 'legitimate' course-based discussion which in more conventional circumstances on less pupil-centred topics might be regarded as 'idle chatter'. Notwithstanding the potential pedagogic advantages accruing to relevant and interesting material, from the pupils' point of view it blurred the boundaries between 'proper work' and 'having a chat' in a way which could be exploited in the negotiation of work.[8]

**teacher** Jean, Allison, you've been doing a lot of talking. Get on with some work.

**pupil a** We're talking about the work.

**teacher** I've heard you chatting about clothes . . .

**pupil a** Yes, well that's it isn't it . . . we're talking about fashion. It's part of the unit.

**teacher** Still sounds like chat to me. Anyway how much have you written. It's got to be written down for the units . . .

**pupil b** But we've got to discuss things first.

Because conventional methods of distinguishing between work and non-work became less appropriate in the Humanities lessons, pupils had at their disposal a means for negotiating with teachers about the amount of work they did — a means specific to the open classroom situation.

The response of pupils to this new found curricular freedom, however, did not generally reflect the aspirations of open classrooms. Bringing with them the legacy of closed classroom instruction (with imposed syllabus and more rigid channeling of curricular knowledge) the reaction of pupils was to use the leeway as a means for negotiating or avoiding work rather than making educational work more interesting and relevant. The adaptation of a potential in the open curriculum in this manner clearly stemmed from the ghost of the closed classroom in which educational work is laborious rather than creative and was indicative of the way in which counter-strategies owed something to the closed classroom experience. Indeed, the fact that teacher strategies and pupil strategies existed at all in the Humanities lessons drew attention to the two 'limiting factors' on the open classroom context. Firstly, that both staff and pupils retained the legacy of experiences in closed classrooms, and hence engaged in negotiation about the amounts of work to be done rather than relying on self-motivation and self-discipline by pupils with a 'catalyst' role being attempted by teachers. And, secondly, the persistence of the strategies demonstrated that there remained a battle of wits for control of classroom events despite the aspirations of open schooling subscribed to by the staff. They had yet to achieve non-authoritarian relationships with the pupils.

## Summary and Conclusions

It has been argued that the strategies adopted by pupils and teachers in classrooms are context specific and that, although the closed classroom provides the normal context for such strategies, alternatives to this setting warrant attention.

Humanities lessons in a Leicestershire community college provided such an alternative. These lessons provided an opportunity to study the effects of an open classroom situation on the strategies used by pupils and teachers—a setting characterised by open-plan classrooms, team teaching, integrated subjects, emphasis on resource-based methods and aspirations to non-authoritarian relationships between staff and pupils.

There were, of course, limits to the openness, limits which owed much to the inertia of expectations held by pupils and teachers. Since neither spent a greater part of their classroom time in the open classrooms there was a tendency to re-establish expectations based on the closed classroom experience and attempt to normalise the situation with reference to current and past experience of other classrooms. In practice, therefore, features of the closed classroom were present in the Humanities lessons.

Though this subtle closure affected the extent to which comparison was possible, it did not prevent the Humanities situation being sufficiently different from the conventional context of secondary classrooms to warrant comparison and contrast. There were still certain behaviours which were significantly altered by the new context—strategies whose presence or absence could be explained by the variation in context between open and closed classroom.

Noise, for instance, had a significance in closed classrooms which was not apparent in the open classroom. Teacher attempts to control noise in closed classrooms, it was argued, constituted a strategy to signify general classroom control, but thus lent itself to counter-strategies by pupils for whom the use of subtle modes of noise could challenge the appearance of teacher control and reassert their influence on the progress of the lesson. Such counter-strategies, however, became largely redundant in the open classroom where the general level of noise was increased and teachers exhibited a greater tolerance of noise. In general, noise appeared to be a problem in the open situation only to the extent that it posed learning difficulties and was divested of its control connotations by the fact that the proceedings in the classroom were no longer 'private' but were regularly observable to those in the team and to other colleagues. For pupils, the significance of noise was restricted accordingly to its implications for concentration on work, and noise held little significance for pupils as a counter-strategy to teacher control. In fact, the absence of pupils' counter-strategies of noise can be attributed directly to the specific context of the open classroom.

The context, however, also fostered certain counter-strategies less readily associated with the conventional situation. The counter-strategy of friendliness was one. In the Humanities lessons there was an increased emphasis on self-motivation to work and on non-authoritarian relationships between pupils and teachers, and there appeared to be a generally relaxed and friendly atmosphere in the classrooms. Certainly, the pupils were aware of a difference between the Humanities lessons and more conventional lessons, regarding them as both more friendly and more relaxed.

This ethos of friendliness, however, did not herald the abdication of control by the teachers (cf. Hargreaves, 1976; Leacock, 1969; Sharp and Green, 1975) but entailed an alternative mode of control strategy by teachers. But, like any control strategy adopted by staff, it opened up forms of counter-strategy for use by pupils. In their attempts to assert influence on proceedings in the classroom and in their negotiation of classroom control, pupils could avail themselves of the opportunity afforded by the teacher strategy of friendliness and use it as a means for challenging teacher definitions of appropriate pupil behaviour and teacher definitions of appropriate curriculum content. In particular, pupils in the Humanities lessons could use humour in the classroom to limit the control of the teachers and negotiate the amount of work they did in class.

It was also evident that the open classroom lent itself to the use of indulgence as a teacher strategy and pupil counter-strategy. Where pupils could establish for themselves an image of incorrigibility they could negotiate modes of behaviour which contravened the generally applicable standards of behaviour within classrooms. Pupils could 'get away with' doing little work or disturbing other pupils by exploiting a strategy which was more appropriate to the open classroom than the conventional situation.

And pupil control of the curriculum, an explicitly preferred feature of open classrooms intended to encourage self-motivation and self-disciplined attitudes towards work, provided another strategy for pupils to use to negotiate with staff over the extent of control and amount of work to be undertaken in class.

The open classroom, in sum, was a context which invited a specific set of strategies. Although the extent to which these were manifested was limited by the willingness and opportunity of participants to 'normalise' the setting through closures, the classroom strategies of pupils and teachers still bore testimony to the novel influence of the open classroom situation. In particular, attention has been focused on the way in which certain counter-strategies for pupils can be made re-dundant in the context of the open classroom, illustrated by the case of

noise, and how certain strategies become more evident in the open classroom, illustrated by the case of friendliness. These examples reinforce
the conviction that advances in the study of classroom strategies need
to take account of the context specificity of strategies and the potential
of alternative physical and institutional contexts to influence classroom
behaviour.

## Notes

1. D. Hamilton, 'Correspondence theories and the promiscuous school:
problems in the analysis of educational change' – contribution to the Oxford Conference on 'Teacher and Pupil Strategies'.

2. Although the community college promoted the use of the term 'college',
the elements that were studied were comparable with secondary education rather
than further or higher education. It should thus be recognised as a 'school' situation
and not confused with other sectors of education. The term 'student' was similarly
encouraged but in this chapter reference will be to 'pupils' to avoid any confusion
that could arise through the use of the term 'student'.

3. A form of comprehensive education was introduced in Leicestershire during
the 1950s and was heralded as an example of progressive and innovatory education.
Accounts of the inception and implementation are to be found in Mason (1970)
and Holmes (1972). Bernbaum (1972) has argued that Leicestershire's reputation
for innovation serves to attract teachers with a predisposition to change and foster,
thereby, continuing innovations within the schools.

4. Such evidence as exists bears testimony to the scarcity of serious experiments
in, and research into, team teaching in Britain. See for instance Freeman (1969),
Forward (1971), Lovell (1967), Worrall, *et al.* (1970), University of Exeter (1968).

5. As Doyle pointed out in his paper to the Oxford Conference on 'Teacher
and Pupil Strategies' ('Student management of task structures in classrooms'),
pupils attempt to avoid ambiguity and re-assert normality in the classroom situation
and we should not be surprised, therefore, if both pupils and teachers appear to
resist serious challenges to their normal understanding of the situation.

6. The Humanities lessons at the school were observed over a period of two
years. After the first year of observation (and interviews with staff) a pilot questionnaire was distributed to 60 pupils which sought their opinions on the Humanities
situation. An open-ended format was employed. On the basis of the comments and
observations of pupils a further limited option questionnaire was administered as
part of the Humanities course unit which dealt with social research. This latter
questionnaire included further space for wide-ranging comment and was answered
by over 200 of the pupils. It served as the basis for further discussion with pupils
on the topic as well as computer analysis of the relationship between pupil attitudes
and aspects of classroom experience.

7. This view of Humanities lessons was particularly evident in the case of
pupils whose previous school had been a more authoritarian regime, but was still
apparent for those from more progressive schools. The comparison also held
between Humanities lessons and the rest of the pupils' current school timetable.

8. Such a manoeuvre would fit Woods's (1978b) typology as part of 'open
negotiation' about schoolwork between teacher and pupils.

# References

Bennet, N. (1976) *Teaching Styles and Pupil Progress*, Open Books, London

Bernbaum, G. (1972) 'At the School Level', in *Case Studies of Educational Innovation*, OECD

Bernstein, B. (1967) 'Open Schools: Open Society?', in *New Society*, 14.9.67

Bernstein, B. (1971) 'On the Classification and Framing of Educational Knowledge', in M.F.D. Young (ed.), *Knowledge and Control*, Collier Macmillan, London

Delamont, S. (1976) *Interaction in the Classroom*, Methuen, London

Denscombe, M. (1980) *The Social Organization of Teaching*, Leicester University; unpublished Ph.D. thesis

Denscombe, M. (1979) 'Keeping 'em Quiet: the Significance of Noise for the Practical Activity of Teaching', in P. Woods (ed.), *Teacher Strategies*, Croom Helm, London

Doyle, W. (1979) 'Student Management of Task Structures in the Classroom', paper presented at the Conference on Teacher and Pupil Strategies, St Hilda's College, Oxford

Forward, R.W. (1971) *Teaching Together*, University of Exeter, Institute of Education (Themes in Education no. 27)

Freeman, J. (1969) *Team Teaching in Britain*, Ward Lock Educational, London

Gross, N., *et al.* (1971) *Implementing Organizational Innovations*, Harper and Row, London

Hammersley, M. (1974) 'The Organization of Pupil Participation', in *Sociological Review*, vol. 22, no. 3, pp. 355-68

Hannam, A. (1975) 'The Problem of the "Unmotivated" in an Open School: a Participant Observation Study', in G. Chanan and S. Delamont (eds.), *Frontiers of Classroom Research*, NFER, Slough

Hargreaves, A. (1976) *Progressivism and Pupil Autonomy*, University of Leeds; Sociology Occasional Paper, no. 5

Hargreaves, D., *et al.* (1975) *Deviance in Classrooms*, Routledge and Kegan Paul, London

Holmes, B. (1972) *Leicestershire Plan: United Kingdom*, OECD

Jackson, P.W. (1968) *Life in Classrooms*, Holt, Rinehart and Winston, New York

Kohl, H. (1970) *The Open Classroom*, Methuen, London

Leacock, E.B. (1969) *Teaching and Learning in City Schools*, Basic Books, New York

Lovell, K. (1967) *Team Teaching*, University of Leeds; Institute of Education Occasional Paper, no. 5

Mason, S. (1970) *In Our Experience: The Changing Schools of Leicestershire*, Longmans, Harlow

Rogers, T. (1971) 'Looking to the Future', in T. Rogers (ed.), *School for the Community*, Routledge and Kegan Paul, London

Sharp, R. and Green, A.G. (1975) *Education and Social Control*, Routledge and Kegan Paul, London

Stebbins, R.A. (1971) 'The Meaning of Disorderly Behavior: Teacher Definitions of the Classroom Situation', in *Sociology of Education*, pp. 217-36

Stebbins, R.A. (1980) 'The Use of Humour in Teaching', in P. Woods (ed.), *Teacher Strategies*, Croom Helm, London

University of Exeter (1968) *An Experiment in Team Teaching*, Institute of Education, Themes in Education, no. 6

Walker, R., *et al.* (1973) *Teaching That's a Joke*, CARE, University of East Anglia

Walker, R. and Adelman, C. (1976) 'Strawberries', in M. Stubbs and S. Delamont (eds.), *Explorations in Classroom Observation*, Wiley, London

Walker, R. and Goodson, I. (1977) 'Humour in the Classroom', in P. Woods and M. Hammersley (eds.), *School Experience*, Croom Helm, London

Waller, W. (1932) *The Sociology of Teaching*, Russell and Russell, New York

Willis, P. (1977) *Learning to Labour*, Saxon House, Farnborough

Woods, P. (1975) '"Showing them up" in Secondary School', in G. Chanan and S. Delamont, *Frontiers of Classroom Research*, NFER, Slough. Also in *The Divided School*

Woods, P. (1977) 'Teaching for Survival', in P. Woods and M. Hammersley (eds.), *School Experience*, Croom Helm, London. Also in *The Divided School*

Woods, P. (1978a) 'Relating to Schoolwork; Some Pupil Perceptions', in *Educational Review*, vol. 30, no. 2, pp. 167-77

Woods, P. (1978b) 'Negotiating the Demands of Schoolwork', in *Journal of Curriculum Studies*, vol. 4, pp. 309-29

Worrall, P., *et al.* (1970) *Teaching from Strength*, Hamish Hamilton, London

# 4 ROUTES TO RIGHT ANSWERS: ON PUPILS' STRATEGIES FOR ANSWERING TEACHERS' QUESTIONS

Margaret MacLure and Peter French

## Introduction

Quite recently question and answer exchanges between teachers and pupils have provided a focus of attention for sociologists working within the classroom tradition, a focus we consider entirely justifiable on the grounds that asking pupils questions constitutes a crucial mechanism by which teachers monitor both the efficacy of their own teaching, and the competencies of their pupils (Pate and Bremer, 1967).[1]

For us the most exciting outcomes of the work in this area so far are the detailed accounts of the socio-cultural resources which pupils must bring to bear in successfully interpreting and answering a teacher's question (see Mehan, 1974; Hammersley, 1977). Of the accounts available, that provided by Hammersley (1977) is perhaps the most rigorous and exhaustive in its treatment of the issues involved, and as it was against the background of this particular work that the present exercise took place, we shall begin by summarising the points from it which bear relevance to this chapter.

Starting from the observation that all questions will admit of more than one answer which would in some abstract, a-contextual sense, fulfil the informational requirements of the question, and thus be recognisably valid or 'true', Hammersley poses a problem facing the recipients of questions: that of determining *which* answer formulation will be most relevant to this particular occasion. As he subsequently points out however, in *most* actually occurring instances of questioning, this 'problem' is readily soluble for recipients of questions, as they may, through the set of reflexive questions *Why* is *he* asking *me this*?, arrive at an assessment of the interests and relevancies of their interlocutors, and use this as a basis for formulating their answers.

However, as Hammersley goes on to argue, in the case of pupils as the recipients of teachers' questions, these usual procedures for establishing what may be of relevance to the questioner are rendered ineffective. Since teachers, for the purposes of assessment, typically ask questions to which they already know the answer, the identification of questioners' motives and 'problems' can be of little use to pupils in searching for answers: the pedagogic 'motivation' holds generally for *all* teacher questions, and the questioner has no real 'problem'. Therefore the questions *Why* is *he* asking *me this*? are unlikely in any particular instance to yield useful clues as to what, specifically, the teacher expects the pupils to answer, and they must look for clues elsewhere.

In terms of Hammersley's model, the clues to which the child must orient in order to produce an acceptable answer are 'embedded in the way in which the situation they face as pupils is organised' by the teacher (1977: p. 78), and if the pupil is to discern these clues, he 'must conform to his teacher's definition of the situation' (1977: p. 83), in the sense of 'tuning in' to the assumptions and concerns which underlie the lesson-as-talk so far.

It was against the background of this model that we began to examine the answers to teachers' questions which pupils produced in our infant classroom recordings: in particular those question and answer exchanges in which pupils' answers were negatively evaluated by the teacher. Examination of a large number of such exchanges suggested to us that some of the strategies pupils operate to produce answers might be totally independent of the teacher's definition of the situation, and hence indifferent to the clues which the lesson embeds.

Furthermore, as we shall argue with reference to the transcript at the end of the chapter,[2] such strategies are quite capable of yielding 'right' answers.[3] However, before proceeding to outline these strategies, it must be stressed that we do not envisage them as the sole, or even the most prevalent, means by which infant pupils generate answers: the most we shall claim for our analysis is that it provides an orderly and rational account of wrong answer production, as well as a possible account of how *some* right answers may come into being. In this sense then, we intend our analysis to complement, rather than to replace, Hammersley's model.

## Alternative Strategies for Answer Production

A first and very obvious strategy which pupils can use to provide an answer is simply to repeat the candidate answer of another pupil. Mehan (1974) has called this strategy 'imitation'. There are many such repetitious stretches in the transcript: for example *grass* at lines 22-3; *walking on / to walk on* at 24-32; *ducks eggs* at 62-5. It is interesting to note that such repetitions can be remarkably impervious to negative evaluation from the teacher, or at least lack of positive evaluation. The examples in this transcript are relatively short, but nevertheless, they are done despite a noticeable absence of positive feedback by the teacher, and despite

clear evidence from the video and audio recordings that they were
audible and probably attended to. In other recordings there are much
more extreme and extended examples: for instance in one discussion
concerning garden tools, where the teacher is holding up a picture of a
pair of secateurs and asking the class to identify them, ('cutters' turns
out to be the word she is looking for) there are 15 audible tokens of
*pliers* and *clippers* produced by different children in the face of negative
evaluation, before the sequence is terminated by the production of the
looked-for response. These observations indicate a considerably lower
immediate effectivity for teacher evaluations than has been suggested
(cf. e.g. Sinclair and Coulthard, 1975), and lend weight to our argument
that pupils are not always attuned to the teacher's definition of the situation, as mediated through her system of negative and positive options
for feedback.

A second strategy available to pupils is to retrieve items which have
previously been introduced into the discourse, usually by the teacher.
We have an example in this transcript at lines 40 and 42 where the pupil,
in response to the teacher's question *what do you think hedges are useful
for?*, replies *corn*. It would be difficult to impose retrospectively an interpretation on this utterance which would make it count as a valid answer,
despite the fact that the teacher treats it as a face-value (though wrong)
attempt to answer her question within its frame of relevance (line 43
*hedges are useful for corn?*). However we can note that the item 'corn'
was elicited by the teacher at the beginning of the discussion (line 7) in
the description of the painting which provided the starting point of the
session, and can hypothesise that the pupil had retrieved it at this point
as an attempted answer. Similarly, at a later point in the session, where
the teacher holds up a picture of pigs under a tree and asks *what trees
are they under?*, a child answers *hawthorn tree* (lines 245-6). Looking
back to line 156 we can see that *hawthorn* was introduced in reference
to the berries which had been shown in service earlier that morning. Of
course we have no way of verifying our analysis of the origins of these
answers: they might have been generated by some other means. However,
the prevalence of such instances of reoccurrence of previous items through
out the data we have so far examined, argues for more than coincidence.
That pupils should operate with the expectation that what has been said
before might be relevant to what is going on now as a resource for answering is by no means surprising. It is an expectation that is fostered through
the organisation of the situation, in the division of school knowledge into
subject matter, in the way teachers formulate and engineer topics, and
locate interactions by reference to pictures, books, objects of interest.

Hammersley (1977), analysing a piece of classroom talk involving older pupils, observes that retrospective-prospective interpretation (cf Garfinkel, 1967; Cicourel, 1973) is a major resource by which pupils finally arrive at a right answer. However, we can see that the sort of retrospective retrieval we have identified here is markedly different from that general interpretive procedure whereby adult interactants maintain a sense of social order by construing the sense of current utterances in the context of earlier remarks, and anticipate that later utterances will remedy the vagueness or problems of current ones. In order to employ *occasion relevant* retrospective-prospective interpretation, it is necessary to select, from the (continually added to) body of preceding events, just the one(s) crucial to the current concern. This entails not only perceiving *that* many events in the ongoingly created discourse are interrelated, but also *how* they relate to one another. For the pupils we have observed this second competence is frequently not in evidence. The domain of the preceding discourse clearly is treated as a pool upon which to draw for answers, but, in ignorance of the particular relationships in which present and past events stand, the assumption is simply that, as in popular fiction and drama, all events are integral to the plot. If the pupils do not actually know what the teacher's plot is, there can be no way of knowing *how* events interrelate, and therefore no principled (from the adult perspective) ground on which to do retrospective searching.

However, such 'unprincipled' searching could also result in right answers. By monitoring past items, it is possible that pupils might retrieve them in appropriate places, despite the fact that their retrieval would not be instigated by identification of their relevance to the matter in hand. The issue of whether *blackberries* at line 191 was a fortuitous retrieval from 139-41, and *acorns* at 257 from 172-4 retreats from investigation.

There is, however, a large body of pupil answers which cannot be interpreted as the product of such simple retrieval strategies. In these cases, we suggest that, when pupils do not have the requisite knowledge of the matter in hand, they draw upon their stock of typical classifications of objects and events into well-defined classes, and locate answers within these general, a-contextually available categorisations. This is done by orienting to some item presented in the question as a superordinate term for a class of items, and selecting possible answers in terms of their membership of that class. We have in mind examples such as the following:

(1)   166   T: What is the squirrel looking for?

        167   C: Nuts

        176   T: Any other nuts Karen?
        177   C: Coconuts

(2)     220   T: Here's some birds you don't see very often
        221        Can anybody tell me what they're called?
        222   C: Parrots

In each case, the answer can be heard as a member of a class of items
whose superordinate class-name is instanced in the question: nuts—
coconuts; birds you don't see very often—parrots. To this extent the
answers articulate with the questions. And it should be noted that, in
the case of the sequence from which example (1) was taken, there are
two other, *right* answers to the same question—i.e. of what sort of nuts
squirrels look for—namely *acorns* (172-3) and *hazelnuts* (180) which
could be products of *exactly the same a-contextualised categorisation*
performed upon the item 'nuts', rather than of the pupils' real knowledge
of what sort of nuts squirrels like.

We can see how these latter answers happen to fall within the domain
of valid answers by looking a little more closely at the logical structure
of wh- questions, from the adult perspective. All wh- questions in fact
require a categorisation operation to derive their answers. As we have
suggested elsewhere (French and MacLure, 1979) one way of concept-
ualising this is to say that wh- questions require, as their answer, a value
for the variable presented in the question, where the set of valid answers
is the set of possible values $1, \ldots \ldots \ldots n$ for that variable. Now if we
look at the wh- question of example (1) above:

*What sort of nuts*? (i.e. is the squirrel looking for: cf. line 171)

we would suggest that, from the adult perspective, the range of valid
answers to the question is a *sub-set* of the larger, general set of things
which count as nuts. This becomes clear if we paraphrase the above
question, analysing it into two components:

of the class of objects, 'nuts'/what sort do squirrels look for.

where the first component identifies a general class $(1, \ldots \ldots \ldots n)$ of
items 'nuts', and the second defines the range of possible values as a sub-
set $(j, \ldots \ldots \ldots n\text{-}l)$ of the items comprising that general class.

Schematically:

$$(1, \ldots (j, \ldots \ldots n\text{-}1) \ldots n)$$

If we imagine the collection of items of which the general class $(1, \ldots \ldots n)$ 'nuts' is comprised to include at least, say:

(coconuts, acorns, hazelnuts, peanuts, . . . . . )

then the range of possible values $(j, \ldots \ldots n\text{-}1)$ defined by the topically relevant second component will be the sub-set of items within the inner brackets, as follows:

(coconuts, (acorns, hazelnuts, . . . ) peanuts, . . . . )

and those which lie *outside* these inner brackets will be *invalid* answers. Now it will be clear that any child who, operating only by generalised classification, successfully selects a member of the class 'nuts' *which also happens to fall within the inner brackets* will be heard to have produced a right answer (and of course should the selected class member fall outside those brackets, to have produced a wrong one).

In the examples referred to above, the general class of items selected by the pupils coincided with the general class referenced in the teacher's question, accounting for the partial overlap which provided for the possibility that some pupil selections from within the class fell within the range of valid, and in this case acceptable, answers. At other points, however, pupils perform rather less felicitous categorisations, taking as the basis for their search classes of items which do *not* correspond to the general class-term on which the wh- question is predicated, and which do not provide for the possibility of valid or acceptable answers. The following is one such example:

(3)  56   T:   What about animals like rabbits squirrels hedgehogs
               insects butterflies
     57        What are hedges useful for for those animals?
     58   C:   Birds
     59   T:   Birds
     60        Can use hedges.

In so far as we can bring our componential paraphrase to bear on such an unwieldy question, we would suggest its proper division to be something like:

| of the class 'things hedges are useful for' | what are they useful for for animals (like rabbits, squirrels, hedgehogs, insects, butterflies). |

That is, the generalised class is the uses of hedges, and it is their uses for animals which delimits its range:

$$(1, \ldots (j, \ldots \ldots n\text{-}1) \ldots n)$$

| For animals | Things hedges are useful for |

However, the pupil does *not* orient to the generalised class referenced by the question—i.e. 'things hedges are useful for'—as the set from which to select answers, but instead orients to the item 'animals' as a class and selects the class-member 'birds', perhaps seeing as an invitation to do so the teacher's parenthetical enumeration of co-class members. In this case, the general class referenced by the question is clearly not available to most of the pupils as a resource for locating answers—note that the question 'what are hedges useful for?' has already been in play for some time and has resulted in few acceptable or valid answers.

Obviously, children can only mobilise those class-membership categories which are already known to them and when, as here, the general class referenced by the question is unavailable, they will select *other* items for the construction of classes.

It should also be noted that the teacher *accepts* the answer *birds* as a relevant answer, despite the fact that on any epistemological grounds it is an invalid one. Such occasions underscore the fluidity of interactants' criteria of relevance and topicality, and the readiness on the part of the speakers to hear answers as relevant in terms of their own questions.

Categorisation operations provide still more resources for the generation of answers. In the example

(4)    21    T: What do you think hedges are useful for?
       22    C: Grass

we can make sense of the pupil's answer—i.e. hypothesise as to the origin of its production—by hearing it as a co-class member with the item *hedges* of some superordinate class, say 'plants' or 'countryside greenery'. As opposed to the previous examples, the answer is not located as a member of a class whose name is explicitly mentioned in the question (e.g. *nuts – coconuts*; *animals – birds*), but rather as a co-class member *with* the item presented in the question in terms of some constructed, implicit class:

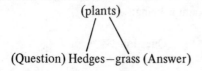

(plants)

(Question) Hedges – grass (Answer)

We are aware that, in attributing to the pupil the construction of an implicit class, within which the referents of both question and answer can be related as co-class members, we might be seen as reading coherence into the data as a product of our own interpretive procedures, in the terms of Sacks's 'hearer's maxim' which states that:

> If two or more categories are used to categorise two or more members of some population, and those categories can be heard as categories from the same collection, then: hear them that way. (1972: p. 333)

However, the analysis has at least the merits of accounting for the coarticulation of *hedges* and *grass* in a non-random way, and may stand, we think, in the absence of a better attempted explanation of the origins of the answer, in the light of evidence elsewhere in the transcript of categorisation as a pupil's resource for answering. In addition, we can adduce the evidence, both from our own acquaintance with pre-school interaction (see below) and from Sacks's (1972) analysis, that doing and hearing categorisation is a skill which children acquire long before they go to school.

A further answering resource results from a *combination* of categorisation operations and the retrieval of past answers from other pupils, resulting in a type of 'cohort production' (Mehan, 1974). That is, pupils can take previous candidate answers and, instead of simply repeating them, perform some categorisation operation to derive a different, related answer. Some of these examples have been referred to already, to make another point. For example, the sequence of 'animal' responses from 79 to 109 can be seen as a cohort production where each pupil (after the first one) instances a co-class member on the basis of one or more preceding answers.

Another method is to locate the superordinate class-term from which to select members in a preceding answer, rather than in the question itself. Thus at 63 the answer *ducks* can be heard as a member of the class 'birds' — an answer produced shortly before at 58. It is interesting to observe how items which were located as members of some superordinate class can thus become *themselves* the superordinate class-name from which further answers are selected as class members, the hierarchy of progression in the above example being:

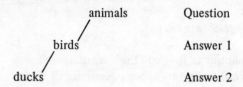

|  |  |
|---|---|
| animals | Question |
| birds | Answer 1 |
| ducks | Answer 2 |

As a final point in relation to categorisation strategies, note that, at one point in the transcript, the teacher herself seems to demonstrate awareness that children generate answers on the basis of untopicalised categorisations, by taking steps clearly to delimit the range of items from which answers must be selected:

(5)    134    T: What are some of the fruits that grow in autumn?
        135        On the hedges
        136        On the hedges
        137        Not on the trees now
        138        On the hedges

This can be read as an attempt to pre-empt classification on the basis of the general class 'fruits', rather than the restricted range within the inner brackets:

$(1, \ldots (j, \ldots \ldots n\text{-}l) \ldots n)$ Fruits
        Fruits on
        hedges

To conclude the analysis of children's answering strategies, we wish to make the point that several of the methods we have identified for producing answers are, significantly, *not* tied to the enactment of teacher-pupil interactions, but are also prevalent in the data we have on adult-child interaction in the home with much younger children. This is significant as a further argument against theories which attempt to explain the *entire* dynamic of pupil participation as the product of conformity to teachers' definitions and criteria. It does not lie within our brief to carry out here a comprehensive comparative analysis with pre-school interaction. Therefore we include just one, very revealing, snatch of conversation between a 30-month-old child and his mother which shows, we suggest, how children as young as this can generate answers to questions in the absence of any criterion of epistemic truth, accuracy, relevance, etc., by operating upon abstract classes.[4]

(6)  (About to begin drawing)
  1  M: Are you doing the elephant or not?
  2  C: Yes
  3     I'm doing a elephant
  4  M: What colour?
  5  C: Red
  6  M: You don't do elephants red
       ...
  7  C: No it's blue
  8  M: You don't do elephants blue either
       ...
  9  C: No it's purple
10  M: You don't do elephants purple
       ...
11  C: Yes it is purple
12  M: What?
13  C: It is purple
14  M: No it's not purple
15  C: It's white then
16  M: It's not
17     Shall I tell you which colour?
18  C: What is it?
19  M: Grey
       ...
20  C: And colour
21  M: What?
22  C: Grey and colour
       ...
23     Grey and colour

From data such as these then, it seems that children begin school life with resources for answering which can serve them in the novel situations they encounter. This fact alone should make us wary of pre-analysing school discourse *only* in terms of constraints and priorities filtering down from the social and pedagogic concerns of the teacher—an assumption by no means peculiar to normative structuralist paradigms (cf. e.g. Edwards, 1976). Indeed it appears from the present transcript that the degree of teacher control over the discourse may be somewhat weaker than has previously been assumed. If we take, for example, lines 24-32 which were discussed under the strategy of 'imitation' we may reiterate that one striking feature is the extent to which one pupil will replicate the answers given by another pupil across the teacher's unfilled feedback 'slots'.

## Conclusion

We shall finish with two qualifications to our analysis. The first concerns the nature of our data. Concentrating, as we have, solely on the infant classroom, it might be felt that we are attempting to generalise findings from one special educational context to others. This is not the case. In the absence of any data we remain neutral on the question of whether or not the particular strategies we have outlined here will provide comparable insights into teacher-pupil question and answer exchanges in the later years of schooling, although it is perhaps worth mentioning that Young (1976) has suggested (without going into the evidence) that right answers produced by secondary school pupils stand in no homological relation to cognitive routes.

Our final point concerns the extent to which these strategies may be in operation *within* infant classrooms. On this issue we shall reiterate the qualification we made at the outset: that whilst the analysis may provide a rationality for many wrong answers which would otherwise be regarded merely as failed attempts to conform to the teacher's definition of the situation, the efficacy of these strategies in terms of *consistently* producing right answers would seem extremely suspect.[5] In light of this then, the analysis is not intended to represent the exclusive or even the predominant methods by which infant pupils produce right answers to teachers' questions. At best, we would advance the account as a complementary addition rather than as an alternative to Hammersley's model.

*Acknowledgements*: We would like to thank Bob Dunstan, David Hustler, Martin Montgomery, Gordon Wells and particularly Martyn Hammersley for their comments on an earlier draft of this paper. We have not always followed their suggestions.

## Selected Excerpts from an Infant School Discussion Period

Transcription conventions:

| | | |
|---|---|---|
| T: | | Speech from Teacher |
| C: | | Speech from Child (unidentified) |
| Ch: | | Speech from two or more children at once |
| $C_1$: | | (Subscript) Identifies particular child on second or subsequent occasion of speech |
| ( ) | | Observer comments on activity |
| ⟨ ⟩ | | Tentative interpretation |
| —— | | (Underlining) Overlap of speech between adjacent utterances |
| *** | | Indecipherable utterance |
| | | Initial of child's name is used when he/she has been nominated by name by teacher. |

| | | |
|---|---|---|
| 1 | T: | Now some very good children have been doing some painting this morning |
| 2 | T: | I'd like to tell you about it |
| 3 | | We can use it afterwards |
| 4 | | But I want it to go in the book corner in the hall first of all |
| 5 | | The green round the edge is the hedge (pointing to painting) |
| 6 | | The yellow is the field of golden . . . |
| 7 | Ch: | Corn |
| 8 | T: | And it's beautiful |
| 9 | | It's growing at the moment |
| 10 | | But in this field there's nothing growing |
| 11 | | The earth is bare |
| 12 | | It's a ploughed field |
| 13 | | All right |
| 14 | | Afterwards when we've finished with it in the book corner in the hall |
| 15 | | We can have it to play with our farm on |
| 16 | | Can't we? |
| 17 | Ch: | Yes |
| 18 | T: | We can play with our farm on this |
| 19 | | Two fields |
| 20 | | And hedges all the way round |
| 21 | | What do you think the hedges are useful for? |
| | | (T goes off to put the painting in a corner) |

| 22 | C: | Grass |
|----|-----|-------|
| 23 | Ch: | Grass |
| 24 | $C_1$: | Walking on |
| 25 | $C_1$: | Walking on |
| 26 | $C_2$: | To walk on |
| 27 | $C_2$: | To walk on |
| 28 | T: | Hedges aren't made of grass |
| 29 |  | No |
| 30 | $C_3$: | To walk on |
| 31 | $C_3$: | To walk on |
| 32 | $C_3$: | To walk on |
| 33 | T: | If you've got an answer will you put your hand up |
| 34 |  | Go on (to child sitting near front of class) |
| 35 |  | To the back |
|    |  | (3 secs) |
| 36 | T: | Matthew what do you think hedges are useful for? |
| 37 | M: | <u>Corn</u> (quietly) |
| 38 | T: | <u>Stand up Craig</u> please and move |
| 39 | C: | Stand up (to Craig) |
| 40 | M: | Corn |
| 41 | T: | Can't hear you Matthew |
| 42 | M: | Corn |
| 43 | T: | Hedges are useful for corn? |
| 44 |  | No |
|    |  | (2 secs) |
| 45 | T: | Karen |
| 46 | K: | So's things can't get out |
| 47 | T: | So the things can't get out |
|    |  | (3 secs) |
| 48 | T: | Stop the animals getting into the cornfield to eat all the corn wouldn't it? |
| 49 | Ch: | Yes |
| 50 | T: | And if you've got cows in the field it would stop the cows from getting out |
| 51 | C: | Stop all the animals from getting out |
| 52 | T: | Stop all the animals from getting out |
| 53 | $C_3$: | Uh– |
| 54 | T: | Yes |
| 55 | $C_3$: | I know |
| 56 | T: | What about animals like rabbits squirrels hedgehogs insects butterflies |

(T is some distance from group, putting the painting away) *(note appears beside lines 26–27)*

|     |                  | (3 secs)                                      |
| --- | ---------------- | --------------------------------------------- |
| 57  | T:               | What are hedges useful for for those animals? |
| 58  | C:               | Birds                                         |
| 59  | T:               | Birds                                         |
|     |                  | (1 sec)                                       |
| 60  |                  | Can use the hedges                            |
| 61  | $C_3$:           | For God                                       |
| 62  | C:               | Duck's eggs                                   |
| 63  | $C_3$:           | Ducks                                         |
| 64  | $C_4$:           | Duck's eggs                                   |
| 65  | $C_4$:           | Duck's eggs                                   |
| 66  | T:               | What's the hedge used for?                    |
| 67  | C:               | ****                                          |
| 68  | C:               | The birds can make homes in                   |
| 69  | T:               | Yes                                           |
| 70  |                  | Good                                          |
| 71  | $C_3$:           | I know                                        |
| 72  | T:               | The birds can make homes in the hedges        |
| 73  |                  | What else?                                     |
| 74  | $C_3$:           | Nests                                         |
| 75  | T:               | Nests                                         |
| 76  |                  | Yes                                           |
| 77  |                  | Those are the birds' homes                    |
| 78  |                  | What else can live in hedges?                 |
|     |                  | (3 secs)                                      |
| 79  | C:               | Foxes                                         |
| 80  | T:               | Foxes                                         |
| 81  |                  | They live in holes under the ground           |
| 82  |                  | Under trees                                   |
| 83  |                  | Or under hedges                               |
| 84  |                  | Yes                                           |
| 85  | C:               | Um . . .                                      |
| 86  |                  | How about moles?                              |
| 87  | T:               | How about moles                               |
| 88  |                  | A good one Paul yes                           |
| 89  |                  | Debbie                                        |
| 90  | D:               | Rabbits                                       |
| 91  | T:               | Rabbits                                       |
| 92  |                  | Yes                                           |
| 93  | C:               | Badgers                                       |
| 94  | T:               | Badgers                                       |

| 95  | T:               | Lovely |
|-----|------------------|--------|
| 96  |                  | Sean |
| 97  |                  | Sit properly love  (not addressed to Sean) |
| 98  |                  | Louise |
| 99  | L:               | Mouse |
| 100 | T:               | Mouse yes |
| 101 |                  | You get fieldmice and dormice and harvest mice |
|     |                  | (3 secs) |
| 102 | C:               | Um . . . |
| 103 |                  | Hedgehogs |
| 104 | T:               | Hedgehogs |
| 105 |                  | Good |
| 106 | $C_3$:           | I know one |
| 107 | $C_3$:           | I know one |
| 108 | T:               | You know one Sheila ($C_3$) |
| 109 | $C_3$:           | A duck |
| 110 | T:               | Ducks |
| 111 |                  | Well they usually live near water don't they |
| 112 | $C_3$:           | And they can fly |
| 113 | T:               | They could use a hedge for shelter if it was near the |
|     |                  | water |
| 114 |                  | Craig |
| 115 | Cr:              | When I went out I found a mole under a hedge |
| 116 | T:               | You saw a mole and a hedgehog |
| 117 |                  | Well here's a book about looking (holding up a book) |
| 118 |                  | All put your hands down now please |
| 119 |                  | In autumn time what would happen to the hedges? |
| 120 | $C_3$:           | ⟨Squirrels wake up⟩ |
| 121 | $C_3$:           | ⟨Squirrels wake up⟩ |
| 122 | $C_3$:           | And it would blow away |
| 123 | T:               | The hedges would blow away |
| 124 |                  | No |
| 125 | C:               | Get cold |
| 126 | T:               | The hedges would get cold? |
| 127 |                  | What's happening to the trees in autumn? |
| 128 | $C_3$:           | All the leaves will <u>fall off</u> |
| 129 | T:               | <u>The leaves</u> fall |
| 130 |                  | What happens to hedges in autumn? |
| 131 | Ch:              | The leaves fall of |
| 132 | T:               | The leaves can fall |
| 133 |                  | What's growing on the hedges in autumn? |

| 134 | T:      | What are some of the fruits that grow in autumn? |
|-----|---------|--------------------------------------------------|
| 135 |         | On the hedges |
| 136 |         | On the hedges |
| 137 |         | Not on the trees now |
| 138 |         | On the hedges |
|     |         | (3 secs) |
| 139 | C₅:     | Blackberries |
| 140 | C₂:     | Blackberries |
| 141 | T:      | Blackberries |
| 142 |         | Good |
|     |         | (2 secs) |
| 143 | C:      | Buttercups |
| 144 | T:      | Buttercups |
| 145 |         | No |
| 146 |         | It's fruits that grow |
| 147 | C:      | Berries |
| 148 | T:      | Berries |
| 149 |         | Good |
| 150 |         | What berries has Miss ——— shown you in service? |
| 151 | C:      | Red berries |
| 152 | T:      | Rose . . . |
| 153 | Ch:     | Hips |
| 154 | T:      | And the . . . |
| 155 |         | Haws of the hawthorn |
| 156 | Ch:     | Hawthorn |
| 157 | T:      | Good |
| 158 |         | Nuts  (holding up picture in book) |
| 159 |         | Lots of food for the animals |
| 160 |         | This is a book called 'What to Look for in Autumn' |
| 161 |         | Put your hands down while I show you a few things |
| 162 |         | What have we got on the cover?  (holding up front of book) |
| 163 | C₃:     | Squirrels |
| 164 | T:      | Squirrels |
| 165 |         | Hands up if you know |
| 166 |         | What is the squirrel looking for? |
| 167 | Ch:     | Nuts |
| 168 | T:      | I said hands up |
| 169 |         | I didn't say call out |
| 170 |         | Paul |
| 171 |         | What sort of nuts? |
| 172 | P:      | Acorns |

| 173 | C: | Acorns |
|-----|-----|--------|
| 174 | T: | Acorns |
| 175 | | Yes |
| 176 | | Any other nuts Karen? |
| 177 | K: | Coconuts |
| 178 | T: | Not coconuts |
| 179 | | No |
| 180 | C: | ⟨Hazelnuts⟩ |
| 181 | T: | Hazelnuts that grow on the hazel tree |
| 182 | | There's a lot of those on the hedges |
| 183 | | Right |
| 184 | | Here's a picture on this page of when the harvest's being gathered |
| 185 | | There's the stacks of corn in the field |
| 186 | | Oh and the pigeons love to eat this seed |
| 187 | Ch: | **** |
| 188 | T: | This little animal you see a lot |

(BREAK IN TAPE)

| 189 | T: | Ah    (holding up picture in book) |
|-----|-----|--------|
| 190 | | Here's some birds having a lovely feast |
| 191 | Ch: | <u>Blackberries</u>    (all shout out) |
| 192 | T: | <u>There's some</u> *** |
| 193 | | ⟨That's⟩ food for the birds and the bees |
| 194 | | There's a bee there having a lovely feast |
| 195 | C: | Where? |
| 196 | C: | There |
| 197 | $C_5$: | Me and my dad we go down in *** |
| 198 | $C_5$: | We go down in the woods |
| 199 | $C_5$: | And ⟨then⟩ we pick the blackberries |
| 200 | T: | This is a picture in September |
| 201 | | It's gone past the time for this now |
| 202 | | But in this field they're growing hops |

(SECTION OF TRANSCRIPT OMITTED)

| 215 | T: | Here's something that the hedge is useful for |
|-----|-----|--------|
| 216 | | ⟨Birds⟩ are using it for shelter |
| 217 | | Sheltering under the hedge Richard |
| 218 | $C_3$: | Shelter |

| 219 | T: | You see them |
|-----|-----|-----|
| 220 | | Here's some birds you don't see very often   (holding up picture of pheasants) |
| 221 | | Can anybody tell me what they're called? |
| 222 | $C_2$: | Parrots |
| 223 | $C_6$: | Parrots |
| 224 | C: | Parrots |
| 225 | T: | No |
| 226 | | They're not parrots |
| 227 | $C_3$: | /kətuz/ (=cockatoos) |
| 228 | T: | Cockatoos |
| 229 | | <u>No</u> |
| 230 | $C_3$: | <u>Peacocks</u> |
| 231 | $C_3$: | Peacocks |
| 232 | C: | Peacocks |
| 233 | C: | Peacocks |
| 234 | T: | Pheasants |
| 235 | $C_3$: | <u>Peacocks</u> |
| 236 | T: | <u>Pheasants</u> |
| 237 | $C_3$: | <u>They look like peacocks</u> |
| 238 | T: | <u>They live in the country</u> |
| 239 | | They like living in cornfields |
| 240 | C: | I seen them in my garden |
| 241 | | I caught him |
| 242 | T: | Now |
| 243 | | On this page |
| 244 | T: | The pigs are under their favourite tree |
| 245 | | What tree are they under? |
| 246 | C: | Hawthorn tree |
| 247 | C: | Oak <u>tree</u> |
| 248 | T: | <u>Oak tree</u> |
| 249 | | <u>Good</u> |
| 250 | | Why is it their favourite tree? |
| 251 | C: | 'Cos if it's rain—if it's raining they'll get wet |
| 252 | T: | <u>David sit down love</u>  (to another child) |
| 253 | | If they're raining they won't get wet |
| 254 | | No |
| 255 | | It's their favourite tree because of the food that falls to the ground for them |
| 256 | | What falls to the ground off the oak tree? |
| 257 | C: | Acorns |

| 258 | C:  | Nuts                                   |
|-----|-----|----------------------------------------|
| 259 | C:  | Nuts                                   |
| 260 | T:  | /ei/ – (starts to say 'acorns')        |
| 261 | Ch: | Acorns (all shout out)                 |
| 262 | T:  | Yes                                    |
| 263 |     | And pigs like rooting around for the acorns |

(DISCUSSION CONTINUES)

## Notes

1. Throughout this chapter we use the term 'teachers' question' to refer only to what Labov and Fanshel (1978) have called the 'Request for Display'. Requests for Display differ from other questions in that 'A already has the information' the question requires, but 'the request is for B to display whether or not he has the information, and the information requested is actually the state of B's knowledge' (1978: p. 79).

2. The transcript upon which this chapter is based is one of a lesson involving an infant school teacher and a class of 30 five-year-old children. The lesson was video-recorded as part of the follow-up phase of the Bristol Longitudinal Study of Language Development: 'Language in the Transition from Home to School', supported by grants SSRC 4541 and Nuffield SOC 290. This research is directed by Gordon Wells.

3. Throughout this chapter the terms 'right answer' and 'wrong answer' are defined consequentially: a pupil's right answer is one which is positively evaluated by the teacher, a wrong answer is one which is negatively evaluated.

4. We are indebted to Martin Montgomery at the University of Bristol School of Education for the use of this data.

5. That this is the case is attested by the fact that children *do*, cognitively speaking, grow up.

## References

Cicourel, A.V. (1973) *Cognitive Sociology*, Penguin, Harmondsworth

Edwards, A.D. (1976) *Language in Culture and Class*, Heinemann, London

French, P. and MacLure, M. (1979) 'Getting the Right Answer and Getting the Answer Right', to appear in *Research in Education*, November

Garfinkel, H. (1967) *Studies in Ethnomethodology*, Prentice Hall, New Jersey

Hammersley, M. (1977) 'School Learning: the Cultural Resources Required to Answer a Teacher's Question', in P. Woods and M. Hammersley (eds.), *School Experience*, Croom Helm, London

Mehan, H. (1974) 'Accomplishing Classroom Lessons', in A.V. Cicourel, H. Jennings, K. Jennings, K. Leiter, R. Mackay, H. Mehan and D. Roth, *Language Use and School Performance*, Academic Press, New York

Pate, R.T. and Bremer, N. (1967) 'Guided Learning through Skilful Questioning', *Elementary School Journal*, 67.8

Sacks, H. (1972) 'An Initial Investigation of the Usability of Conversational Data for Doing Sociology', in D. Sudnow (ed.), *Studies in Social Interaction*, Free Press, New York

Sinclair, J.McH. and Coulthard, R.M. (1975) *Towards an Analysis of Discourse*, Oxford University Press, London

Young, M.F.D. (1976) 'The Schooling of Science', in G. Whitty and M.F.D. Young (eds.), *Explorations in the Politics of School Knowledge*, Nafferton, Driffield

# 5 DEVIANT LABELLING IN SCHOOL: THE PUPILS' PERSPECTIVE

## Cathy Bird

This chapter is concerned with the pupils' perspective of deviant labelling in schools. It questions a number of assumptions made by labelling theorists about the amplification of pupils' deviant behaviour.[1] Following Becker, labelling theory would suggest that

> social groups create deviance by making the rules whose infraction constitutes deviance, and by applying these rules to particular people ... deviance is not a quality of the act the person commits, but rather a consequence of the application by others of rules and sanctions to the 'offender'. The deviant is one to whom that label has been successfully applied; deviant behaviour is behaviour that people so label.[2]

This concept of deviance has been transposed into the school setting by a number of writers, in an attempt to understand the amplification of deviant behaviour in schools.[3] The assumption has been that deviant behaviour may be the result of teachers consistently labelling pupils as deviant. Following this labelling, pupils may internalise the labels and embark on deviant careers.

These studies[4] have been principally concerned with the social re-action to the act of deviance and the treatment of the labelled deviant by the labeller. They have failed to incorporate the context of the labelling into their analysis[5] and have assumed a certain consistency of labelling by all teachers in all contexts of the school. My work in a large comprehensive school has shown that consistent deviant labelling rarely occurs. Consequently, pupils do not internalise the deviant labels that may be assigned to them and rarely embark on deviant careers.

Because the context of the labelling process has important implications for the consistency of that labelling, an analysis of context provides a basis for looking at the pupils' perspective of deviant labelling in schools. Many pupils see deviance in relation to specific teachers in certain contexts. Many others are unaware of teachers' labels because of the inconsistency of application and because many pupils are absent from the classroom, or the school as a whole, for long periods of time.

94

In certain circumstances, labels may become consistently applied through the institutionalised reinforcement of the label by certain structures in the school. While pupils see behavioural labels as specifically related to certain teachers in certain contexts, academic labels, reinforced by structural and administrative procedures in the school, are more generally accepted and internalised by the labelled pupils.

The following work draws on preliminary fieldwork carried out in a number of comprehensive schools in outer London. The research forms part of a larger fieldwork programme concerned with disaffected school pupils in outer London schools. The majority of fieldwork relevant to this paper was carried out in one large comprehensive school. Coney School is a purpose-built community school in outer London. It has over 1,500 pupils and between 70 and 80 staff. During the years 1977 to 1979, many staff in the school were interviewed and involved in informal discussions concerning difficult children and the problems that teachers face in teaching them. During 1978 to 1979, a group of 'difficult' fifth-year girls were interviewed in depth about their experiences in the school. While accepting that the interview situation has a number of inherent problems, in that it forces both teachers and pupils alike to assimilate and organise previously unthought-out ideas, the interviews have provided useful and revealing details about the processes of labelling in schools and the pupils' perspectives of these processes.

## The Importance of Context in Deviant Labelling

### 1. *The Changing Context of Teacher/Pupil Interaction*

In a modern comprehensive school, a teacher may see between 150 and 300 pupils during his working week. A pupil may be taught by up to 15 teachers during that same period of time. Classes change every hour or so and a teacher may be faced with a new teaching group and another classroom every time the bell rings for a new lesson. Because of these limitations on continuous teacher/pupil interaction, the actual amount of time available for a teacher to build up any kind of relationship or establish a label for a specific child is limited.

Many teachers accept this as a fact of life and some may use it as a means of explaining why they do not get involved with individual pupils on anything more than a teaching basis. They can arguably legitimate this in terms of the perceived constraints inherent in their teaching situation. As one teacher explained

One of the problems is that we are so busy and have so many children in the classroom that we just haven't got time to see every individual child. The actual amount of time a child gets in a lesson is pretty minimal . . . the school really is too big. If a child is a problem, it is time consuming finding out why . . . and it just takes too long to deal with any individual child.

Many teachers only applied deviant labels to pupils at times of crises in the classroom. This labelling tended to be very individualised with teachers labelling pupils in certain ways in certain lessons. Because of the limited time available for teacher/pupil interaction and the constantly changing context of that interaction, the teachers based their labels on previous knowledge of similar deviant acts, rather than on previous personal knowledge of the child. Unless a child misbehaved consistently in one classroom with one teacher, or misbehaved in a similar way in a variety of places throughout the school with a number of teachers who were all labelling her in the same way, then the pupil was likely to see deviant labels as very inconsistent in their application. Hargreaves has suggested that

> If one particular label is repeatedly applied by a variety of teachers in a wide variety of situations, then at minimum, the pupil will be under no illusions with regard to the teacher's conception of him and part of the groundwork for the acceptance of the label by the pupil has been laid.[6]

While this is certainly true, the likelihood of one particular label being repeatedly applied by a number of teachers in a large comprehensive school is small, because of the individualised way in which teachers appear to label pupils.

It has been argued[7] that deviant labelling may become consistent through gossip in the staffroom. While agreeing in principle, it should be noted that a modern comprehensive school staffroom may have up to 70 staff in it at any one time. Friendship patterns do not normally extend to more than a fraction of the total staff. Unless a child presents such a problem that a teacher deliberately sets out to talk to all staff who teach that child, or a case conference is initiated specifically to talk about a child, then a teacher is likely to continue to see certain pupils in his own individual way.

The likelihood, then, of a variety of staff applying the same consistent behavioural label to one pupil is minimised because of the practical realities of a large school and the constraints of class size and time available for personal teacher/pupil interaction.

## 2. Contextual Rules and the Interpretation of Deviance

As the context of teacher/pupil interaction changes throughout the school day, so too do individual teachers' interpretations of deviant behaviour. Every location in the school is subject to a set of contextual rules, the infraction of which, constitutes deviance and influences the teacher's definition of deviant behaviour. As a pupil moves between lessons, subjects and teachers in the school, she is exposed to different interpretations of deviance and different thresholds of what constitutes deviant behaviour. For example, structural situations and subjects that present more constraining rules on pupils' activities are more likely to give rise to an increase in deviant labelling by teachers. As Sharp and Green point out

> The more elaborate the system of norms and rules which define acceptable pupil behaviour, the greater the possibility for pupils to transgress these institutionalised expectations and acquire a deviant status.[8]

A pupil has to come to terms with these different systems of norms and rules. In a lesson, she has to understand the teacher's individually imposed rules, the rules that relate to the subject being taught and the rules inherent in the structural situation in which the lesson is taking place. All three interact to provide a unique set of contextual rules specific to that context.

Because different teachers provide different interpretations of deviance, it is possible for a pupil who is defined as deviant in terms of the rules in one lesson to be accepting the rules of a different lesson. It is also likely that a pupil whose behaviour is consistent during the whole day is seen as deviant in one context, but not in another, because of the different rules that relate to the different situations in which she finds herself. Discussing the changing behaviour of one pupil, a form teacher explained

> Geography tends to capture children more because they can use colours and it's more varied. But this variation also causes problems. Suzanne has a problem in geography, it's one of the worst subjects as far as behaviour is concerned. In English, she doesn't muck about, I've not had one bad comment about her from the English Department, but then English is an easier subject for her, not so many things she

can do wrong.

Geography appeared to have greater possibilities for rule infraction, because of the larger number of contextual rules required for maintaining a level of behaviour, suitable for learning to continue in the classroom. The actual labelling of deviant behaviour was intimately connected to the contextual rules of the subjects in the school.

A pupil's perception of deviant labelling is therefore coloured by her understanding of what constitutes deviance in different subjects or lessons. A deviant label is seen as specific to a lesson and the contextual rules of that lesson and not to the school as a whole.

### 3. *Changing Types of Labels*

The actual labels that teachers use are also dependent on the institutional or classroom contexts in which the labelling occurs. The labels are intimately connected to the structural and administrative procedures for dealing with deviant pupils in the school. In a classroom, a teacher, usually seeing a pupil as a unique individual, may label that pupil in a crude way if a crisis arises that threatens the rules of the classroom. In this case, the teacher may have to make an immediate decision concerning the control and containment of that child. Procedures of action are usually limited by the structural and administrative constraints of the school. Similarly, the possible labelling of the problem child will also be limited by the same constraints.

In Coney School, the channels of procedure for dealing with deviant children were clearly defined. A child could be withdrawn from certain lessons, sent to another teacher or given some form of punishment. The procedures for punishment were well established. Initially, the pupil would be put on report or given a detention. If the deviant behaviour continued, the pupil was likely to be given the cane, suspended from the school for a certain period of time, or expelled. These clear procedures of action provided the teachers with back-up for their deviant labels.

The classroom teacher had only a limited number of procedures open to him following a crisis in the classroom. Apparently crude labels were formed at these times of crises as a response to the limited choice of action available to him. When the teacher was removed from any potentially threatening situation of deviance in the classroom, he was more likely to consider the pupil in her entirety and as a unique individual. Leisurely chat in the non-threatening atmosphere of the staffroom or a discussion of case studies at a case conference introduced more sophisticated categories into the teacher's vocabulary although these were still confined by the teacher's commonsense understanding of the procedures open to that child.

This movement, from hard crude categories to more sophisticated typing[9] gives rise to more inconsistencies in the labels that teachers apply to pupils. Understandably, this fluidity of movement helps to reduce the impact of deviant labels on pupils.

### The Pupils' Perspective

Previous studies of labelling in schools have tended to look at the pupils' reactions to labelling as if from a management perspective, providing the types of reasons that teachers would generate as a response to the question 'How do you think a pupil would react to a teacher's consistent labelling?' Hargreaves[10] discusses the factors which he feels may influence a pupil's acceptance of labels in the school and the consequences of that labelling. He suggests four factors which may influence a pupil's decision to accept a label: firstly, the frequency of the label; secondly, the extent to which the pupil sees the teacher as someone whose opinion counts; thirdly, the extent to which other teachers support the label; and fourthly, the public nature of that label. While these factors, undeniably have importance within the process of pupil reaction to labels in the school, they appear to present a teacher's interpretation of pupils' reactions rather than the pupil's own interpretation of deviance and deviant labelling.

Interviews and informal discussions with a number of fifth-year pupils showed that many pupils saw deviance as specific to certain lessons and teachers. Other pupils appeared unaware of the deviant labels that had been applied to them, especially those pupils who had rejected school as being of little significance and who spent little or no time in either lessons or the school.

### 1. *The Implications of Changing Context*

The group of girls in Coney School identified many inconsistencies in the way teachers reacted to them. Rarely did a girl think that all teachers considered her a problem all of the time. They would pinpoint individual teachers or subjects as being the main reason for their behaviour.

> Yes we do act up, but it's with individual teachers and you act up to them in their own way . . . It varies between lessons and who the teacher is. Some days, I'll be really polite and other days I'll be really bad and muck most of the lessons up.

Now, Miss P., she's someone who really doesn't like me. The thing is, I really don't like taking showers and I think up an excuse every week for why I won't have one. She gets really cross about it. Then there's Mrs. T., she takes me for typing, I always muck her about. She's thrown me out of the class twice . . . Now human biology, I do work hard in that, really hard. I never muck about, I just sit there and enjoy it because it's good.

Alternatively, they pointed to specific locations as giving rise to problems at certain times. For instance the lavatory at break time.

When Miss W. has been on duty, she only comes to the door of the toilets. She won't come right inside. She just stands there telling us all to get out. There's usually about twenty of us all sitting there smoking and listening to the radio. We're always getting pulled out, but we always go back, every break . . . Sometimes you can't even tell who's there because the smoke is so bad.

Pupils would consistently act badly in specific lessons or locations with certain teachers and they would recognise the fact that they were labelled as a nuisance in that context. However, they also recognised that they were not seen as a nuisance in another lesson with a different teacher. A pupil may act up to the label given to her in the first class and use it to impress her friends while remaining quiet and working hard in another lesson.

## 2. *The Implications of Changing Labels*

Having followed a group of girls over a year and a half of their schooling and watched their development during that time, it became obvious that teachers' labels were constantly changing in relation to any one pupil. Crises came and went and pupils' fame, in the eyes of the staff, often rose and fell. Pupils who were 'a problem' one term became accepted as normal pupils the next. Pupils moved in and out of a teacher's favour and rarely did they remain consistently out of all teachers' favour for long periods of time. This fluidity and change meant that many pupils were never fully aware of the label that may have been attached to them by certain teachers. As one girl explained in response to my question 'What do you think the teachers think of you?'

Well, it would depend on which teacher you were asking. You know it's a funny thing, 'cos last year I used to do geography. When I was

in the third year. And I never knew it, but I didn't get on with Miss D. I
didn't know I didn't get on with her, but me and Jane really used to
muck about in her lessons. We never used to say anything to her, so I
didn't realise that she really hated me. I was talking to these friends a few
months ago and they said 'We hear you don't get on with Miss D.' I said,
'How do you know that?' They said, 'Oh, she said to us that she doesn't
like you.' She was talking about the pupils who were her worst and she
said I was one of the worst pupils. I didn't know she felt like that about
me . . . I never said anything really to her, so I don't know why she
thought I was so bad.

This pupil was clearly surprised that a teacher had considered her to be
a nuisance during the previous year. During the current year she felt that
she had got on well with the same teacher and assumed that Miss D. was
also seeing her in a new light, as her behaviour was now improving. This
pupil had been totally unaware of the teacher's attitude towards her,
because deviant labels had only been applied at times of crises and in an
inconsistent manner. Crises in geography were now few and far between
and consequently, the girl was convinced that Miss D. now saw her as a
hardworking, 'normal' pupil.

### 3. *Bunking Off: In School and Out*

For many pupils, teacher labelling was an inconsistent phenomenon
because they were constantly absent from the context of the labelling.
The group of girls in Coney School rarely spent more than two or three
days a week at the school.

Not only did the school appear to represent a minor part of these
pupils' day, but the classroom represented an even smaller part. School
was not seen as a learning environment, but one in which to meet friends
and to have a good time. To this end, they stretched out their socialising
time in the school by arriving late for both school and lessons and by
deliberately missing lessons during the school day. For these pupils,
lessons appeared to be

. . . not important at all. What is, is having a laugh and meeting my
friends . . . I look forward to school because it's fun, rather than
because I've got to come and do lessons.

This point was reiterated by another pupil

. . . Lessons? They're not important at all. You know, you go to school for a laugh, and then you go into lessons and have a bit of a laugh in them as well.

The teachers appeared to form an insignificant role in these pupils' experience of the school day.

> **CB** How important are the teachers to you?
> **P** . . . Well, I don't know really. Not a lot I suppose. I think the teachers see you as someone in the class, someone to get on with lessons. If you're in a lesson then you're just one of a whole crowd.

One pupil, a truant, was asked what she liked about school. She explained that she thought school was good, she really liked it. It was, though, she explained, the lessons she did not like. In her mind, was a division between school as a place for socialising and school as a place for pupil/teacher interaction and learning. This division was recognised by many of the girls. During later interviews, when these girls had reached the fifth year, this division became even more obvious. Many of the girls were absent from school for long periods of time. Even when they were in school, they were rarely in lessons, but were wandering around the corridors or were in the canteen.

> But it's not really bunking off, is it? Because once you're in the fifth year you're not taking exams in lots of subjects so you don't bother to go to certain lessons. No, we're not really bunking, just not bothering to sit in the classroom. It doesn't feel like bunking. We don't even think about it and we certainly don't think about being caught. Now we've got the canteen, we all go down there . . . I mean, there's still lots of people around.

To these pupils, school appeared to form only a small part of their every day experience, taking its place with part-time jobs, socialising and home activities. Even when they were in lessons, they were faced with a new teacher and a new class group every hour or so. It seems realistic to suggest that as far as these girls were concerned, any form of teacher labelling was of little consequence, because of the limited time in which teacher/pupil interaction was occurring for them in the school.

For many pupils, then, deviant labelling is an inconsistent and often unimportant phenomenon in school. Rarely are labels generalised throughout all lessons with all teachers. Because of this, few pupils see labelling as a matter of concern. While pupils may accept that they are seen as problems by certain teachers in certain lessons, they do not internalise deviant labels and do not embark on deviant careers as a consequence of that labelling.

## Institutionalised Labelling

In certain circumstances, labels may become institutionalised by the structural reinforcement of those labels within the school. Once institutionalised, the labels may become more consistently applied and may lead to a more consistent response by the pupils.

Pupils were able to differentiate in their minds between academic and behavioural labels. While most behavioural labels were seen as inconsistent and related only to specific lessons, academic labels were seen as consistent over context and time. Unlike the behavioural labels, these academic labels had been internalised by the pupils.

Academic labels are institutionalised through their reinforcement of and response to the structural and administrative procedures of the school. Most comprehensive schools are specifically designed to deal with different ability levels through a system of streams and sets. The teachers also use academic labels as a means of pupil and group differentiation. It provides the teacher with a ready-made analysis of the expectations of any pupil's performance, which is ideally not expected to alter between contexts or over time. Academic labels are used continually within the school and may become routinised.

The group of girls in Coney School accepted the authority of the school in this process of academic typing. They had become initiated into teachers' definitions and understandings of the terms, and had to some extent internalised the academic labels that had been given to them, e.g, remedial, bright, intelligent. When these pupils were asked how they thought teachers saw them and whether teachers put pupils into groups in their minds, the pupils suggested only ability-type labels.

> **P** Well, they do. Bright ones over there, dim ones there and medium ones in the middle, things like that.
>
> **CB** Where do you see yourself fitting into that?
>
> **P** Oh, I'm one of the thick, stupid ones at the bottom.
>
> **P** She sort of separates out those who can do it and those who can't do it. If you're stuck with those who can't do it . . . you never get any further.
>
> **P** . . . Yes they're always helping the brainy ones and they're the ones who don't really need help. It's the stupid ones who need more help, isn't it?

P I mean, I'm in the pink band, that means I'm not very bright. The teachers tell you that. It's the same in all my lessons. You get split up into groups in the lesson, I'm always with the bottom ones.

It appeared that the pupils were reacting more readily to academic labels that were given to them by teachers. Consequently they were seeing themselves in certain ways because of that labelling. This was in direct opposition to the way the same pupils saw themselves in relation to behavioural labels. While they saw their academic level as a general condition, unchanged by context or teacher, they related their behavioural labels very specifically to contexts and points of time.

This distinction between academic and behavioural labels has a number of important implications. In the days of grammar and secondary modern schools, streaming was usually consistent throughout a child's school life. A child could be with the same peer group of a similar ability level for four years. The bottom stream of a school was seen to develop a delinquent subculture as a result of being at the bottom of the school.[11] The assumption was that academic and behavioural labels became one and the same thing. The bottom stream was seen as being thick, stupid and delinquent and the top stream as bright, intelligent and well-behaved. With the advent of mixed ability teaching, the likelihood of a school-based low ability delinquent group developing has been minimised by a decrease in the time that the less academic children are taught together as a group. Although many schools have non-examinable fourth- and fifth-year groups, the chances of the same group staying together for four or five years, as had been the case with the old secondary modern schools, has now been lessened.

This change may be significant in what appears to be a more individualistic approach to disruption in modern comprehensive schools. The group of girls in Coney School all constituted problems to teachers. They had become a close-knit group through a common rejection of the norms of the school. However, few of them had ever been in the same tutor group or class together. They had 'found' each other following their constant removal from classrooms and their use of the girls' toilets as a retreat for smoking and 'having a laugh'. Because they were of varying abilities, they rarely met in the classroom. They met together at break times or when they were bunking off from lessons. They would meet up in the canteen or the girls' toilets. They would disrupt certain lessons on an individual basis or cause a nuisance as a group during their periods of socialising outside the classroom.

Any suggestion of a low ability delinquent group did not occur in

Coney School. Every class had its 'clown', but misbehaviour was in no way related to low academic ability. While the class clowns often emerged together as social groups outside the classroom; inside, misbehaviour occurred on an individualised level. The labelling of this misbehaviour remained separate in the teachers' minds from labels related to academic standards.

## Summary and Conclusions

Continuous fieldwork in a large comprehensive school has shown that the pupils' perspective of deviant labelling is often different from that assumed in previous studies. The assumption has been that pupils are likely to take on a deviant identity and embark on deviant careers as a result of consistent teacher labelling. While not wishing to suggest that much of the previous useful work on labelling in schools is invalid, I feel that a number of important variables have been neglected. Because of changing contexts and inconsistent labelling, it appears that even the most problematic child does not pick up the signs of labelling from a teacher in any consistent manner. While she may accept and internalise an academic label, it is likely that a behavioural label is never applied consistently enough to influence a pupil in her course of action.

The results of fieldwork have led to a questioning of labelling theory as an explanation of deviant amplification in school. Firstly, because it appears that pupils may be unaware of deviant labelling because of limits on teacher/pupil interaction. This limitation is a consequence, both of the institutional routine of constantly changing teachers, classrooms and class groups during the school day, and through the process of bunking off lessons and school by many pupils.

Secondly, inconsistency of labelling allows many pupils to be labelled in a variety of ways, with the result that no label has a real chance of sticking over a period of time. Thirdly, pupils see behavioural labels as being specifically related to context and time. Pupils rarely see a deviant label as generalised over all lessons with all teachers.

Thus, a pupil's perception of deviant labelling is often one of ignorance, rejection or rationalisation of the label. Each provides added weight to a questioning of the assumption that pupils may achieve deviant identity as a consequence of teacher labelling. Obviously, the pupils' perspective of the process is complex and this chapter has only touched on some of the issues, but it does provide a basis for a further questioning of the use of labelling theory in the consideration of school deviance.

## Notes

1. For general discussion of the relationship between labelling and the amplification of deviant behaviour see Lemert (1967), Schur (1971), Rubington and Weinberg (1973). Also Becker (reprint 1971) and Goffman (1961).
2. H. Becker, *Outsiders: Studies in the Sociology of Deviance*, (Free Press, New York, 1963).
3. Most particularly by Hargreaves, Hester and Mellor (1975). For a useful summary of relevant literature concerning labelling and deviance in schools, see Hargreaves, Hester and Mellor (1975), ch. 2. For discussion of teacher categorisation of pupils, see Sharp and Green (1975), ch. 6. See also Hargreaves (1976) for details of pupil reactions to the labelling process in schools.
4. Ibid.
5. See Hargreaves (1977) for discussion of recent work on processes of typification (for example, Becker, 1952; Nash, 1973; Woods, 1976). Hargreaves points to a number of defects in these models, especially the contextual variations in typifications and the changes in typifications over time.
6. Hargreaves (1976), pp. 201-7, p. 202.
7. Ibid., p. 202.
8. Sharp and Green (1975), p. 129.
9. For useful discussion on different processes of typing of pupils, see Woods (1979), ch. 8.
10. Hargreaves (1976).
11. See Lacey (1970). Also Hargreaves (1967).

## References

Becker, H. (1952) 'The Career of the Chicago Public Schoolteacher', in *American Journal of Sociology*, 57, pp. 470-7.

Becker, H. (1963) *Outsiders: Studies in the Sociology of Deviance*, Free Press, New Yor

Becker, H. (1971) 'Social Class Variations in the Teacher-Pupil Relationship', in *School and Society: A Sociological Reader,* Routledge and Kegan Paul, London

Goffman, E. (1961) *Asylums*, Pelican, London

Hargreaves, D. (1967) *Social Relations in a Secondary School*, Routledge and Kegan Paul, London

Hargreaves, D. (1972) *Interpersonal Relations and Education*, Routledge and Kegan Paul, London

Hargreaves, D., Hester, S. and Mellor, F. (1975) *Deviance in Classrooms*, Routledge and Kegan Paul, London

Hargreaves, D. (1976) 'Reaction to Labelling', in M. Hammersley and P. Woods (eds.) *The Process of Schooling*, Routledge and Kegan Paul, London

Hargreaves, D. (1977) 'The Process of Typification in Classroom Interaction: Models and Methods', in *British Journal of Educational Psychology*, 47, pp. 274-84.

Lacey, C. (1970) *Hightown Grammar*, Manchester University Press, Manchester

Lemert, E. (1967) *Human Deviance: Social Problems and Social Control*, Prentice-Hall, Englewood Cliffs

Nash, R. (1973) *Classrooms Observed*, Routledge and Kegan Paul, London

Rubington, E. and Weinberg, M. (1973) *Deviance, The Interactionist Perspective*, Macmillan, New York

Sharp, R. and Green, A. (1975) *Education and Social Control*, Routledge and Kegan Paul, London

Schur, E. (1971) *Labelling Deviant Behaviour*, Harper and Row, New York
Werthman, C. (1963) 'Delinquents in Schools: A Test for the Legitimacy of Authority', in *Berkeley Journal of Sociology*, vol. 8, pp. 39-60
Woods, P. (1976) 'Pupils' Views of School', in *Educational Review*, 28, pp. 126-37.
Woods, P. (1979) *The Divided School*, Routledge and Kegan Paul, London

# 6 SCHOOL GIRLS' PEER GROUPS

## Robert J. Meyenn

## Introduction

Remarkably little research has been done on the experience of girls in school, despite a considerable growth in interest in recent years in within-school processes and particularly social relationships within schools. Work has mainly concentrated on teacher-pupil relationships, while pupil-pupil and teacher-teacher relationships have received attention in only a minority of studies. However, pupil-pupil relationships and peer networks[1] are a major component of a child's experience of schooling. In a recent study, Lomax (1978) concludes that, irrespective of 'adjustment' to school, peers are still the most important feature of a child's school experience. Parents and teachers continually acknowledge the importance and influence that a child's peers have in their orientation to and interpretation of school experience. A teacher in the school where this research was conducted illustrates this point when he is talking to me about a girl with whom he is spending a considerable amount of time counselling. 'I'm convinced it's not her, though, it's the company she keeps, particularly that—. Do you remember her? That's where the trouble lies.' (Field notes 21/4/78)

The studies in this area, in this country, have tended to focus on boys (Hargreaves, 1967; Lacey, 1970; Reynolds, 1976; Willis, 1977) or in a very few cases on girls (Lambart, 1976; Furlong, 1976) in single sex institutions, usually either secondary modern or grammar schools. A common characteristic of these studies tends to be the focus on the upper age range—boys and girls who are about to leave school or reach the statutory minimum leaving age. This is understandable as it is at this stage that the full effects of the school and school system can be observed and assessed, the pupils have received the full complement of state provided education. However, there are indications, particularly in the work of Willis and also in the work of Lacey and Hargreaves, that many of the features and outcomes that are observed and so avidly described at the end of a school career have their direct antecedents much earlier on in the school. Willis's 'lads' identify quite clearly the second year (age 12/13 years) as the crucial point when the 'lads' sort themselves out from the 'ear 'oles'.

The research reported in this paper was conducted in a 9-13 year middle school serving a new town estate in the Midlands and was carried out over a period of two years, 1976-1978. The research centres on the social relations and peer networks of one cohort of middle school boys and girls in their third and fourth years (ages 12 and 13). The cohort consists of four mixed ability classes and while data has been collected on all classes, an intensive in-depth study has been made on one of these classes. It is the material relating to the girls from this in-depth study that is presented here. The class, 4F, consisted of 16 girls and 15 boys and the data presented here was collected by participant observation, interviewing and sociometric techniques.

## Peer Groups as a Useful Concept

There has recently been a challenge, led by some interactionists, to the notion of peer groups and to their usefulness in the study and understanding of educational processes particularly that of classroom interaction. Furlong (1976) criticises the approach of both Hargreaves (1967) and Lacey (1970) because of their assumption that informal peer groups are the basis of pupils' social relations. Furlong (1976) claims that the approach has three major weaknesses — that 'interaction does not just "happen" in friendship groups but is "constructed" by individuals' (p. 161) and so pupil interaction will not necessarily include friends all the time. Furlong uses the term 'interaction set', in describing these fluid groupings, to mean those that share a common definition of a situation at a particular point in time, however short lived this may be. He points out that these common definitions may be communicated by smiles, nods, looks, etc., as well as verbally. Furlong's second criticism is that the norms and values of groups of friends are not necessarily consistent. 'It would be obvious even to the most casual observer of classroom behaviour that there is no *consistent* culture for a group of friends' (p. 161). Thirdly, he claims that the model posited by Hargreaves (1967) and Lacey (1970) based largely on the American small group social psychology, suggests that there is pressure on members of a group to conform to the group norms and values. In refuting this, Furlong (1976) argues that

> the culture is presented as an external reality, and social behaviour is shown not so much as an interaction between two or more individuals, but as one person responding to some reified group. The implication is that the individual has little choice in his actions as he is controlled by something outside him — the group. (p. 161)

In summary, Furlong claims that 'consistent groups do not exist in reality and observation has also shown that there is no consistent culture for a group of pupils' (p. 163).

Delamont (1976) calls for a less static concept than 'clique' when studying classroom interaction. She claims that the Hargreaves and Lacey categories of 'goodies' and 'baddies' are too simplistic and reveal little about classroom behaviour. Following Furlong (1976), she points out that even the most 'delinquent' pupils are well behaved and conformist in some circumstances and that even the 'model' conformist may 'get into trouble'. This point is also made by Willis (1977) and Lacey (1970) but while the 'lads' may sometimes act in a conformist way it is certainly not seen as being typical of their general behaviour.

This challenge raises two interrelated questions. Do peer groups exist, in this case among 12/13 year old boys and girls, as a social reality and secondly, is the concept of peer groups useful in aiding an understanding of school and classroom behaviour? Furlong and Delamont would argue that at least in the context of the classroom there are no definite groupings. The point that a certain degree of fluidity is present is taken and must be included in a model of pupils' social relationships as must the point that groups or more particularly individuals within groups are not always consistent in their behaviour and don't consistently adhere to group norms. However, peer group networks do exist in reality for some pupils, there are groups of pupils who interact more with each other than with other pupils in their class or year group and who exhibit relatively consistent patterns of behaviour particularly in relation to their orientation towards school and other pupils.

The 16 girls in 4F, the focus of this case study, were all members, and saw themselves as members, of a peer network. This, however, did not apply in the same way to the boys in 4F nor may it be the case for girls in other situations. It may well be that some pupils do not see themselves as members of distinct peer groups or others may indeed desire affiliation with a particular group and yet not be a member of that group. It is also possible that individual pupils who may be members of a particular peer group desire membership of another group but are prevented for various reasons from becoming members of that group. This reference group may have more influence on the particular pupil than that of the more immediate peer group. A possible example of this is that of Vera, a member of the 'quiet' girls, who indicated to me that she would 'quite like' to be friends with the 'science lab' girls and when completing the sociometric questionnaire revealed a desire for friendship with three of the 'science lab' girls in addition to the girls in the 'quiet' group.

It is important to recognise and distinguish between different types of interaction. Some classroom interaction is simply the result of pupils all being in the same class while the playground may be the arena for much more focused interaction. Interaction sets may well be a more common feature of forms of school organisation where there is constant change in the composition of class groups for different subjects. It may be that some interaction sets are a preliminary stage leading to more consistent patterns of interaction.

The 16 girls of 4F were all members of a peer group network. The importance of the peer group in the school lives of these girls which is argued and illustrated in this paper should not obscure, however, the importance of non group members, particularly 4F boys, and the girls in the other groups in influencing the patterns of interaction. This influence differed in strength between the groups. For example, the 'PE' girls were very much dominant in their relationships with the boys in 4F. If a 'PE' girl wanted to borrow a pen she would simply go up and take it from one of the boys and if the boy protested, he was ignored. Collectively in the playground if the 'PE' girls decided that they wanted to play with a ball they would go to the nearest boys' football game and take the ball. On the other hand, the 'quiet' girls were teased and harassed by the boys. Two of the girls particularly, Vera and Anne, were tormented constantly by the boys. As a consequence, the 'quiet' girls developed strategies to avoid the boys whenever possible.

### Girls and Peer Groups

The bulk of the research on peer groups has been conducted with boys and there does seem to be some doubt as to whether or not peer group networks are a phenomena in the social life of girls or whether the peer group is only a male phenomena. McRobbie and Garber (1976) attempt to explore some of the reasons for the absence of girls from the literature on peer group subculture which they feel is striking and demands explanation. When girls are referred to, it is usually in ways that 'uncritically reinforce the stereo-typical image of women' (p. 209).[2] Is it that girls are not present in youth subcultures or is their omission simply a product of the dominance of male researchers? McRobbie and Garber cite Willis, whose portrayal of girls is that of giggling sex objects, and ask the following questions:

Are they typical responses to a male researcher, influenced by the fact that he is a man, by his personal appearance, attractiveness, etc? Or are the responses influenced by the fact that he is identified by

the girls as 'with the boys' studying them and in some way siding
with them in their evaluation of the girls? Or are these responses
characteristic of the way girls customarily negotiate the spaces provided for them in a male dominated and defined culture? (p. 210)

In general, McRobbie and Garber feel that boys are much more likely
to take subcultural options than girls. So

> If subcultural options are not readily available to girls, what are the
> different but complementary ways in which girls organize their cult-
> ural life? And are these in their own terms, subcultural in form?
> (Girls' subcultures may have become invisible because the very term
> 'subculture' has acquired such strong masculine overtones). (p. 211)

It is a mistake to try to locate girls by indicating a presence or absence
of girls in the male subculture. More research is needed in the ways in
which girls interact with each other to see if girls possess a distinctive
subculture of their own. It may well be that girls' youth culture is similar in form, if not in activities, to that of boys. However, McRobbie and
Garber tend to agree with Jules Henry who, in describing the American
teenage experience, points out that:

> As they grow towards adolescence, girls do not need groups, as a
> matter of fact for many of the things they do more than two would
> be an obstacle. Boys flock; girls seldom get together in groups above
> four whereas for boys a group of four is almost useless. Boys are
> dependent on masculine solidarity within a relatively large group. In
> boys' groups the emphasis is on masculine unity; in girls cliques the
> purpose is to shut out other girls. (pp. 121, 122)

Lambart's 'sisterhood' provides us with perhaps the best example
of a girls' peer group. The group saw themselves very much as a group
and were seen by the staff as being a deviant group. They were not,
however, academically weak and in fact were 'keen' on school and were
in the middle or top groups for the various subjects. The norms of the
group prevented them from being too keen, all had 'a sense of fun
bordering on mischief' and seized any opportunity to disregard the rules.
The 'sisterhood' always ate their lunches together, met after school and
often helped each other with homework. All got 'good' 'O' level passes
in the end. Lambart claims that the sisterhood is of interest in that it
shows 'how factors determined both within and outside the school,

interacted through its formal and informal structures . . .' (p. 152).

Blyth (1960) in reviewing the literature on peer groups states 'girls' groups tend at all ages to be smaller and more intimate than boys' (p. 139). While Coleman (1961) found the structure of girls' peer networks to be much more elaborate and complex than that of the boys which seemed to be organised almost entirely around sport.

The 16 12- and 13-year-old girls who are the focus of this study, div-ided into four different groups (the 'science lab' girls, the 'PE' girls, the 'nice' girls and the 'quiet' girls)[3] and very definitely saw their groups as being a central and vital part of their school lives. There were no other girls outside of the four groups and all of the groups except the 'science lab' girls contained additional members outside of this class group. For all the girls these groupings remained constant for school activities wherever possible, and for some this grouping extended to out of school social life. While it was possible to sit in the classroom and observe inter-action sets which crossed the boundaries of these friendship groups (and which sometimes included the boys) the big majority of the interaction would take place within the peer group. In addition to Participant Observation methods, groups were identified by sociometric question-naires (see sociogram of 4F girls below), by interviews with the girls themselves and discussions with teachers. For the teachers, the 'science lab' and 'PE' girls were the most obvious and readily identified.

The sociogram is drawn from the combined data collected in response to three questions: a) Who do you usually play with after school?; b) Who do you usually play with in the playground?; and c) Who do you usually work with in class? Only mutual choices are plotted and these can be across any of the three questions (data sets).

For these girls it was groups rather than pairs that were the dominant form of social organisation. These groups were very distinct, clearly def-ined and different and were accepted and acknowledged by the girls them-selves, their teachers and were clearly obvious to myself as an observer.

The following, from an interview with two girls,[4] indicates clearly that the girls see themselves as part of a group and see the other girls as being members of groups that in some cases are very different from their own.

> **BM** So tell me again then, why being in your group is important to you.
>
> **Bessie** It's just knowing that you've got friends, being together. It's knowing that you're upper, you're head, you've got the authority and everybody grovels to you because you're the head girls.
>
> **Lorraine** It's not just that. You need friends. They're all groups of

## 4F Girls

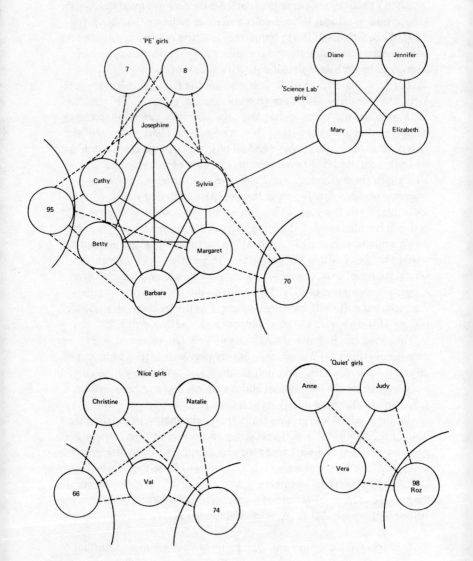

'PE' girls

7 8

Josephine

Cathy Sylvia

95

Betty Margaret

Barbara 70

Diane Jennifer

'Science Lab' girls

Mary Elizabeth

'Nice' girls

Christine Natalie

66 Val 74

'Quiet' girls

Anne Judy

Vera 98 Roz

KEY:

reciprocated choice between girls in 4F.

reciprocated choice with girls in another class.

little goody-goodies. There's groups just like us but they're goody-goodies, they'll do anything for the teacher. Like they're the library monitors for our class. They get all the jobs to do for Mr. Fisher, for all the teachers.

**Bessie** I mean goody-goodies. What springs to mind—Diane and Mary, Jennifer and Elizabeth, all this lot, you know. I mean, as soon as you say the word 'goody-goody', a picture appears.

For the girls their group of friends is vitally important and there are constant manoeuvres to make sure their group is together whenever possible.

**Diane** If we had to say somebody who was our best friend you wouldn't say one person. It would be all this lot.

**Jennifer** We always stick in a group.

**BM** What do the teachers think of your group?

**Elizabeth** We always . . . um . . . sort of . . . if we have to do a job it will be all of us to do the job.

**Diane** Like, if two of us are picked we go to the teacher and say '*please* let's do it together'.

**Jennifer** I had to go to the post office to get 50p worth of stamps and I asked if Diane and them could go too.

It can be seen from Diane's comment that the group is so important to the girls that it is inconceivable to just have one best friend. Any attempts to break up the group by other girls are resisted. The greatest 'disaster' that can befall a group is for another girl, or group, to take one of 'their' girls away from them. This fear is the source of much argument and causes a considerable amount of internal friction within groups. Accusations that 'you are taking her off us' are common. The following group of girls explained to me how they dealt with a threat such as this the previous year.

**BM** Could there be anyone else in your group . . . ?

**Diane** If they want to be in the group they've got to stop there and not try splitting us up. 'Cause sometimes . . . We did have . . . in our group once.

**Jennifer** Yes, we did once.

**Diane** And she tried splitting Jennifer away from us. So we said out she had to go.

Contrary to the findings of McRobbie and of Henry, girls in all of
the four groups seem convinced that it is better to be in a group rather
than to just have one friend.

> **Val** We all three of us sit on the same table in class.
> **Natalie** We just go in a group.
> **Val** We're just friends.
> **Christine** We're always in a group.
> **BM** So it's important to have friends.
> **All** Yeah.
> **Val** You're not supposed to just have just one friend. It's best to have more than one friend 'cause you get on better like that.
> **All** Yeah.
> **Val** 'Cause we're always arguing.
> **Natalie** 'Cause if you break friends you've got someone.
> **Christine** Yeah

At the very end of the year when the prospect of going to the high
school with its setting and streaming organisation loomed large, many
of the girls were somewhat concerned as to what might happen to their
groups. Three of the four groups felt that they would still be friends and
remain as a group but it might be much harder as they could be split up
a lot more and mixed with pupils from the other feeder school.

> **BM** Do you think you will stick together next year?
> **Josephine** Well, there is a chance, yes.
> **BM** What do you think, Cathy?
> **Cathy** I don't know really. It depends what forms we get put in, we will probably be split up.
> **BM** Is that the most important thing? Do you think the form you are put in matters, after all you can still meet in the playground and that sort of thing.
> **Cathy** Yes but we would not be as close because we would not be working with each other.
> **Margaret** I hope we will all be in the same class. There is more classrooms and there is the other school kids as well.
> **BM** And you think that will break your group up, do you?
> **Barbara** Yes, because . . . We might all be split up.
> **BM** And does that worry you that you might all be split up?
> **Josephine** No, not really. We will still be friends but we will not be as close as we are now because we will all be split up.

**BM** Do you think you will still see each other? Do you think you will be a group or pairs?

**Margaret** I think we will still be a group. Especially at breaks. We can still play a little bit and be with each other. Lorraine has left already. Lorraine lives at——now. She left yesterday. Judy is going to ——and Betty is going to —— so there is not going to be many of us left. So we might still be together but there is not going to be as many of us.

The girls here feel that if their group is broken up then it will be as a result of the pressures placed on it by the organisation in the new, bigger high school. If this did happen, then other groups would form to take its place.

One group, though, felt that the upheavals caused by the new organisation would probably lead to a change in the way their social relations were organised. That the breaking up of the group would lead to girls 'going round' in pairs rather than in a group.

**BM** So you think your group of friends will start to break up next year?

**Jennifer** Oh, yes. We are already starting to break up.

**BM** Why do you think that is?

**Jennifer** Because we all get on each other's nerves! We have been together too long. But on the last day we will be sorry to see each other go. I will cry, anyway.

**BM** So you think your group might start to . . .

**Jennifer** Yes. I don't think there will be another group, anyway . . . and I think people will pair off then.

**BM** Pairs rather than groups? Why is that?

**Jennifer** I just think three is a crowd and all this business. If you have a group and everybody's in a different group (school subject groupings) you never see them.

**BM** What do you think, Mary? Do you think there will be groups still at the (high school)?

**Mary** I think there might be the odd few groups but I think mainly one or two people together. I think the boys will go in groups. They are not in groups at the moment, except for a few.

**BM** You think it will be in pairs then. Why do you think that?

**Mary** I think it will be casual groups. Because you can't see each other when you are in groups. If you have just one mate you are going to stick with them most of the time, aren't you? You are not going to split off with them just to go in your normal group. To play at playtimes, you probably will want to stay with the friend you stay with all the time in the lessons.

**Jennifer** Unless you have got more than one friend in your group. And it is impossible to get back if you go off with another friend.

**BM** Why is it impossible?

**Jennifer** It just is.

**Mary** I don't think so.

**BM** Do you think you will form a group or will you just stick with a friend?

**Jennifer** I think I will have just one friend.

The comments of these girls, which were taken from an interview at the very end of the year, and which on the part of the girls are very much speculation and conjecture, do perhaps suggest that there may be a change in the nature of their social relationships when they move on to the high school. If, indeed, there was a movement from peer groups to pairs this would tie in with the research findings of McRobbie and Garber. This possibility can, at this stage, be only tentative and would need to be explored by further research.

My field notes are replete with observations of girls in groups in class, in the playground, coming to and going home from school, in the corridors, at the weekly lunch time disco, at sporting events and in the dining hall. These groups were consistently similar in their composition. In the staff room there was a lot of conversation among the teachers which indicated that they were aware of the various girls' groupings. Comments like 'you know Josephine's mob', 'the science lab mob', 'Betty and her lot' were commonly made in conversation or when recounting incidents.

### The Groups

There was some interaction between the four groups but this tended to be limited. One group in particular had very little contact at all with the others. Group boundaries were not rigid but remained relatively consistent throughout the final year of the middle school. There was, as briefly mentioned earlier, considerable internal fighting, in the case of one group this was often physical, with the girls 'breaking friends' with surprising (to me, at least) frequency and usually within a very short time making friends again. This appeared to be an ongoing feature of each of the girls' groups.

While each of the four groups had features in common, they also exhibited distinct and different patterns of behaviour, attitudes and orientation to school (culture). Each of the groups readily saw itself as being different and distinct and was identified by the teachers as being different. However, in attempting to describe and locate the groups the readily available models, based largely on boys, proved to be inadequate. Commonly, the majority of the studies of peer groups present a very polarised picture with some groups accepting the definitions offered by the school (the pro-school, conformist, 'ear 'oles') and other groups rejecting these definitions (the anti-school, non-conformist, delinquescent 'lads'). This may, to a large extent, be a methodological artefact. (See Hammersley and Turner in this volume for a much fuller discussion of this issue.) There seems to be an additional tendency to concentrate on, even celebrate, the most extreme of the anti-school groups. These groups are only one part of the total picture and if one is concerned to present more complete pictures and thorough analysis then the work of researchers like Willis (1977) must be complemented by studies which attempt to present a cross-section, or at least focus on, other parts of the cross-section. While we may have considerable knowledge of extreme anti-school groups, our knowledge of these groups in relation to the rest of their peers is negligible, our knowledge of pro-school groups is very limited and our knowledge of 'all those in the middle' is non-existent. Moreover, by characterising school pupils in this polarised fashion, considerable distortion must inevitably take place.

For girls of this age range, an at least equally significant dimension to that of pro/anti orientation to school would seem to be the degree of commitment to, and involvement, in 'teenage culture' elements of which, for these girls, were the wearing of make-up and jewellery, 'modern' dress and boyfriends. This dimension seemed to be salient in distinguishing one group from another but certainly did not run parallel to anti-school attitudes and postures as did the findings of Sugarman (1967) with boys. So, for example, the girls most likely to be described as pro-school express similar attitudes to the girls most likely to be described as anti-school in their opposition to the school's policy over the wearing of make-up.

I will take each of the groups in turn and present data from interviews with the four groups which illustrate similarities between the groups in areas such as: how their group of friends is an important factor in their school lives; the value of 'good friends' to get on with, play with, and have fun with; the importance of sharing and helping each other, and differences in areas such as: helping each other with homework; helping each other in tests; more general orientation to and behaviour in school; commitment to elements of teenage culture; and attitudes towards teachers.

Additional data is presented separately on the within group fighting and on one element of 'teenage culture', that of wearing make-up. Different groups' perceptions of each other are examined and there is preliminary exploration on the ability of two of the groups to manoeuvre and avoid being subjected to some of the school rules.

### The 'PE' Girls

The group was given this name by the PE mistress as many of the girls in the group are good at, and interested in, PE and games (see Note 3). This is the biggest of the groups with six of the girls coming from 4F and one girl from 4E. There were two other girls from 4A who were often, but not always, part of the group. Two of the girls were in top sets, the others were in middle sets (none were in the bottom sets). One girl had West Indian parents and another a West Indian father and an English mother. Both girls were born in this country. All the girls were physically more mature than the average fourth-year girl and, as a group, they were lively and friendly. There were a very 'noisy' group and seemed to be somewhat conspicuous both in lessons and around the school generally. They were very conscious and concerned with their dress and 'experimented' with the school uniform. Dresses had to be of a 'fashionable' mid-calf length. I was particularly intrigued by the shoes worn by the girls. The type of shoes worn changed three times during the fourth year. At the beginning of the year, they all wore black wedges and when I asked Josephine why they had to be black, she replied: 'I wouldn't be seen dead in brown shoes, sir!' This changed during the year to pumps and in the summer term to flat, open sandals. A conversation with Margaret indicated that they realised the transitory nature of peer fashion when she said to me: 'Me mum said to me this morning, "If I'd told you to wear those Jesus creepers (sandals) six months ago, you'd have screamed your head off at me"' (laughter) (field notes, June 1978).

The following are extracts from conversations with the girls which explore the characteristics of their group.

> **BM** What sort of person do you need to be in your group?
> **Betty** Not stuck up or anything.
> **Barbara** Not snobby.
> **Josephine** Modern clothes in it—we've all got modern clothes.
> **BM** What does that mean? I'm very ignorant. What does it mean . . . modern clothes?
> **Josephine** Knee length and high shoes and things like that.

**BM** So, you have to wear these, what do you call them, wedges?

**Josephine** You don't have to wear them, but . . .

**Sylvia** All of us have got them.

**Betty** Not quiet.

**All** No.

**Josephine** A good fighter. You've got to be a good fighter.

**BM** Who do you fight with?

(Laughter)

**Josephine** Boys, most of the time. You've got to be able to fight your own battles. Not a cry baby or anything.

**BM** What else?

**Sylvia** Like to mess about and like to get into trouble.

(Laughter)

**BM** You enjoy messing about—what does that mean? How do you mess around?

**Josephine** Talk in class an' do silly things—playing around.

**Betty** Listening to the radio.

(Laughter)

**BM** What, when you should be in class?

**Betty** We are in class and we are listening to it. We were doing it in music today . . . took it off us. You're not supposed to bring radios to school, though.

**Josephine** There's nothing else to do, though.

**Josephine** You've got to be agreeable.

**Betty** And be good friends.

**Josephine** Don't tell lies and we share things . . . most of the time . . . if we don't want to, we just run away and hide them.

**Josephine** Can tell them a secret and they won't tell anyone.

**Betty** Say you told them a secret and they went and told someone else, then we wouldn't be friends with them. Or told lies to us.

**Josephine** We all wear eye shadow but I don't wear nail varnish. I'm not allowed to wear any make-up. I put it on before I come to school, after me mum goes to work and me dad goes to work at quarter past eight, so I've loads of time to put it on. I'm not allowed to wear these (beads) but I put them on after.

**Josephine** Brush your hair in class. (Laughter) We're not allowed to do that and we always do it—turn round and brush our hair.

**BM** What else?

**Josephine** Eat in class. If we've got biscuits we share them all around, put them under the table or we have 'squabbles'. We put one (biscuit) in the middle of the table and put our hands under the table and say go!

**Cathy** We all go into dinner together. We're all together all of the time.

**Josephine** We share lunch, crisps and things and when it comes to dinner time we always say 'I'll have anything you don't want'. Everyone says that to the other person . . . they give you anything they don't want at the dinner table.

**Josephine** We play tricks on each other sometimes. Sylvia put salt in my water. (Laughter) I nearly killed her. I drank it straight down and spat it all back up.

**Cathy** We play tricks all the time.

**BM** What about school work—you've not mentioned that.

. . . We help each other.

. . . Yeah, we help each other.

**Barbara** We help each other in tests—give each other the answers.

**Josephine** We throw a piece of paper.

**Barbara** Or whisper it.

**Betty** Put it on your hands and show them.

**BM** Do you think this is all right?

**Betty** As long as we help each other, it's all right.

**BM** What about homework?

(Laughter)

**Josephine** We never do that. Only Sylvia does it.

**BM** So, only Sylvia does it. What about the rest of you, don't you get into trouble?

**Josephine** We do it at the last moment. Last week Sylvia was off ill and we hadn't done our science homework and she sent —— (her little sister) with a big piece of paper with all the homework on it. It said here's a piece of paper in case you haven't done your homework, 'cause she knew we wouldn't have done it.

**Betty** Not always. Sometimes we do our own.

**Josephine** I do me homework when I'm really bored, like Sundays I get bored. Sometimes on Sundays—like this Sunday, I did it.

**BM** Do you like school?

**Cathy** Yeah, it's OK. Better than at home, it's boring at home.
**Betty** Not much – I don't like the rules and the school uniform.
You get too much homework.
**Josephine** Bossy teachers.

From an interview with Sylvia's mother, it became clear that Sylvia was 'made' to do her homework by her parents. It is interesting to note the way in which Sylvia uses this as a group resource, i.e. by making her homework available. Thus she remains an acceptable member of the group even though in this area, at least, she does not conform to the general norms of the group.

For this group of 'PE' girls, 'fashionable' dress, make-up and jewellery are important. There's an emphasis on having a good time and playing practical jokes and it is important to be able to 'look after' yourself. Continuous attempts are made to 'get round' the school rules and there is much co-operation in helping each other cope with academic aspects of school life. There is a brief indication of the girls' dominance over the boys in the area of fighting and an interesting insight into the need for some girls, at least, to avoid parents in order to subscribe to peer group norms concerning the wearing of make-up.

### The 'Nice' Girls

This group consisted of three girls with two girls from 4D often joining in the group. The girls were of mixed 'ability' with one girl, Christine, in top sets for most subjects while the other two, Val and Natalie, were in middle and lower sets. The girls were quiet and friendly and somewhat unobtrusive. In the classroom they did not seem to intrude, nor were they conspicuous, and would hardly be noticed around the school. The girls did not seem to be interested in fashion or make-up and were physically less mature than the 'PE' or 'science lab' girls. They always met up in the playground where the main activity was standing around in their group and talking.

**BM** What's important about being in your group?
**Natalie** We all help each other with homework.
**Val/Christine** Yeah.
**Val** Say, like this morning, Natalie forgot her science homework and mine was a load of rubbish 'cause I'd been away. She copied mine and got the same. (Laughter) I got rubbish right through the page 'cause I'd been away.

**Christine** That's another reason why we all go round together, 'cause we all have a good laugh.

**Val** I tell the jokes—they laugh.

**BM** What do you talk about in the playground?

**Natalie** Talk about Mr. Fisher.

**Christine** He's everybody's hero.

**BM** You like Mr. Fisher, do you?

**Christine** Yeah, he's all right.

**Val** He's got such a big Adam's apple and me and Natalie couldn't stop laughing today about his Adam's apple. When he was talking it was going up and down.

(Much laughter)

**Natalie** He's always saying 'hello, darling' and that.

**BM** Is he?

**Natalie** I asked him for my science book the other day and he goes 'hello, darling, how are you?'

(Laughter)

**Natalie** Mrs. Davis says that he reckons all the fourth-year girls fancy him.

**BM** Do you three fancy him?

**All** No, not really. He's all right.

**Val** He's all right for a teacher!!

**Val** You must not be big headed or show off and things like that—must not take people off you. Sharing is important. We share our crisps and that and we share our lunches.

**BM** Do you help each other with your work?

- **All** Yeah

**BM** In what ways?

**Natalie** Telling the answers and all this.

**Christine** Like . . . um . . . someone is saying 'oh, I can't see your work, let me have a look, get your arm off'. Or you tell them the answers before you write it down.

**Val** I don't. I say, 'Christine could you help me on this question, please, I'm stuck' or something like that.

The 'nice' girls are primarily concerned with making their school lives as easy and pleasant as possible. They co-operate with homework and in school lessons but do not seem to be concerned to break the school rules and are certainly being 'well behaved'. There is little interest, at this stage, at least, in the aspects of teenage feminine culture of dress and make-up. Their attitude to their class teacher is one of acceptance of him as an authority figure – to be talked about and laughed about but in no way is his authority challenged nor is he seen in any way as an equal.

## The 'Quiet' Girls

This is an extremely quiet group of girls who are physically less mature than the 'PE' or 'science lab' girls and are socially unsure and uncertain. If they were sought out they would be very friendly, but they would initiate contact only in very rare circumstances. The three girls, Vera, Anne and Judy, were in 4F and they were often joined by Ros from 4A. The girls were in bottom sets for most subjects, except for Vera who was in a top set for English. These girls, like the 'nice' girls, did not seem to be interested in make-up or fashion. They spent their time in the playground talking and playing their own games, always near to the school building where they were 'protected' by the teacher or playground staff from interference by other groups of girls or the boys. This is in marked contrast to the 'PE' girls who endeavoured to get as far away as possible from supervision. Mr. Fisher, their teacher, described the girls in the following way:

They're a very quiet group. They stick together and I think they're very happy now that they've found sort of mutual friends because they could all be loners very easily but they all seem happy working together and they stick together and seem to go round quite a lot together.

**BM** What do you do together? How do you spend your time together?
**Vera** We usually do things like playing tig, tracking, or just messing about.
**BM** What are the important things about being in this group?
**Ros** We get more fun.
**BM** Don't be shy! Tell me why you like being in this group.
**Judy** It's just 'cause we're all friends.
**Vera** We play about and pretend to be dunces – point to our head and go 'derr'!
**BM** You were doing that the other day, weren't you? So, you pretend to be dunces?

**BM** What's this business, pretending that you're dumb?
(Laughter)

**Vera** Well, we're like dunces, we don't know our times tables and those things.

**Ros** In maths yesterday, we didn't know what our times tables was and we went — 'derr' — sixteen.

**BM** I see, this is like an 'in' joke in your group, is it? Do others have this joke?

**All** No, it's just us.

**BM** What sort of person are you in your group?

**Ros** Thick.

　　　(Laughter)

**BM** What does that mean?

**Ros** Sometimes we don't know our times tables.

**BM** You mean you're not clever at school?

**Judy** No, we're mostly in the bottom groups.

**Ros** We're all in the bottom groups except Vera.

**BM** Does it worry you?

**All** No.

**Ros** Sometimes they make fun of you, though.

**BM** Who?

**Ros** All the boys. We don't care, though, 'cause they're usually in the bottom groups as well!!

　　　(Laughter)

**BM** So, that's the important thing about your group.

**All** Yes, yes!

**BM** What else?

**Ros** Got to be able to run fast, as well.

. . . Got to be kind, as well.

**Judy** Yes, got to be imaginative.

**BM** Imaginative for what?

**Judy** Playing games.

**Vera** Crafty for things like tracking and things.

**BM** What else?

**Vera** Well, we have fun together.

**BM** What else do you do in your group?

**Judy** You have to lend things to each other.

**Ros** Giving each other crisps and that. It's only us two who usually bring our lunch and we share it with these two. Sometimes she'll bring a bag of crisps.

**BM** What other things?

**Vera** We usually lend out our things, like rulers, pencils, pens.

**BM** Do you share with other people?

**All** Oh, no!

**Vera** No. It's just us four.

**Ros** Usually I bring an apple and give everybody a bite.

**BM** What about school work?

**Vera** Oh, in maths . . . um . . .

**Ros** She usually helps me.

**Vera** If she leaves an answer out, I fill it in and tick it.

**BM** So you have a little bit of—sort of cheating, is that right?

**All** Yes. (Much laughter)

**Vera** The first time . . . I didn't realise that she wanted me to fill them in and she only got seven out of twenty. Ever since, I do now.

**Judy** We all help each other. In other subjects as well. We all sit together.

**Ros** Sometimes we help each other's homework.

**Vera** Well, if Anne hasn't done her homework, then I let her copy mine or Judy's. And in science, too, if they haven't quite finished, I let them copy . . . say, copy the labelling.

**Judy** Once Anne hadn't done her homework and she didn't know what to do and I told her what to put and she got more than me!

(Laughter)

**BM** Does it worry you that you're 'thick'?

**All** No! No!

**Anne** No.

**BM** Would you like to be clever?

**Vera** Well, yes and no.

**BM** What do you mean by that, Vera?

**Vera** Well, yes, I'd like to be clever so as . . . but I wouldn't like to be too clever . . . because it wouldn't be very fun together and it . . . er . . . we don't want to be too clever . . . er . . . well, you know what I mean. I can't really explain it in words.

**Judy** Sometimes, though, if you were clever and everything and you were in the top groups you'd always have homework and you can't play out.

**Ros** You have more fun when you're not clever.

For these girls, virtually their entire social life at school is conducted within the bounds of the peer group. They are certainly a very good example of the pervasiveness of the peer group in making the situation tolerable, even fun (Willis (1977); Cusick (1973)). They show no interest in teenage fashion, clothes or make-up and seem to have accepted and, indeed, made light of, their placement in the bottom groups. The acceptance of their 'thickness', even to the extent of playing games about it, had led to a complete inversion of official school attitudes towards academic learning. For these girls, it's more fun when you're not clever. Despite this inversion, these girls could hardly be described as anti-school or at least they don't fit the picture in the literature of anti-school groups. They certainly provide each other with considerable practical and moral support in coping with the demands of school work.

## The 'Science Lab' Girls

A group of four girls who looked after the science laboratory, particularly the animals, and who were all in 4F. They were a confident, outgoing group of physically and socially more mature girls and were seen by the staff as being popular and reliable. One girl, Diane, was in the top sets for all subjects and the other three, Mary, Jennifer and Elizabeth, were in a mixture of top and middle sets. They were seen by staff as being very academically orientated and pro-school. Like the 'PE' girls they were certainly fashion conscious and liked to wear make-up and jewellery. Most of their spare time was spent in the science lab as the officially designated science monitors. This involved the care and feeding of the laboratory animals. An interesting way in which they combined school duties with pleasure and their interest in animals and boys was the period when they were able to persuade several boys to dig worms for them in the lunch hour to provide food for the toads. Normally, these boys were passionately involved in lunch time football games.

> **BM** What do you do after school?
> **Jennifer** We went to Diane's house and um . . .
> (Laughter)
> . . . See, Mary's boyfriend is Derek and her boyfriend is Gary . . .
> **Jennifer** They went to Diane's house. Me and Mary went over in Mary's mum's car. She took us over there and . . . um . . .
> **Diane** We found that they were there.
> **Jennifer** We found that they had followed us and they were there.
> **Diane** In the half term holidays.
> **Jennifer** We sat there, listening to records and that. When Diane's mum wasn't in. Us and the two boys.
> **Mary** We played some games.
> (Laughter)
> **Jennifer** We had to chuck them out in the end.

**Diane** In case me mum came home.
**Jennifer** We played dares and that.

**BM** What is the most important thing about being in your group?
**Jennifer** To help each other a lot.
**Diane** Yeah, to help each other.
**Jennifer** To stick up for each other.
**Diane** Like, when I was in hospital, all that lot brought me cards and everything.
**BM** What sort of person do you have to be in your group?
**Jennifer** Reliable.
**Diane** Sensible.
. . . Reliable. Like, if someone asks you to come to their house, you've got to turn up.
**Mary** Like that. Like that. They don't do that, Josephine's gang don't. Like, last night Margaret was supposed to go to Betty's house and she didn't go.
**Elizabeth** You've got to be able to take a joke and that.
**All** Yeah.
**Jennifer** Not snobby. Sometimes we get called that if we get good marks in in our classes and that, and we all stick up for each other.

**Jennifer** We all share each other's dinner.
**BM** You all share dinners. You always bring a packed lunch?
**All** Yeah.
**Jennifer** She (Mary) started bringing a packed lunch and so I started to bring a packed lunch and so did she (Elizabeth).
**Diane** So I was the odd one out, so I started to bring a packed lunch.

**Diane** We all try to dress the same and that.
**Jennifer** I wore a green blouse yesterday, but I can't wear the same blouse twice. And she wore a green blouse the same as me.
**Diane** In the holidays, we phone each other up. I'll phone Mary up and say 'what are you wearing?' and she'll say 'a pleated skirt' and I'll put on my pleated skirt.
**Jennifer** She'll say 'are you wearing eye shadow?' and I'll say 'yes' so she'll put some on.
**BM** So you do everything the same?
**Diane** Well, with work, like, with our own topic, Mary and Elizabeth did trees together, but we did it on our own and shared a

few ideas.

**Jennifer** Sometimes we have different answers and sometimes we won't tell each other.

**Diane** Especially in important tests, we won't help each other. Otherwise, if—when we're split up at the high school and we can't help each other and then if we had a test, you'd be in a low group like . . . So important tests we don't help each other. But tests like one to ten tests, spellings and that . . . science. Especially spelling. Jennifer helped me with that 'cause I'm no good at spelling.

**BM** So you like school?
**All** Yeah.
**BM** So, what's important about school?
**Mary/Jennifer** It's your friends.
**Diane** And learning.
**Elizabeth** Yeah, and learning.
**Jennifer** We got a chance to group together doing hockey and all that. We go everywhere together. If she got run over, I'd cry my eyes out.
**Diane** Yeah.
**BM** What about you, Elizabeth?
**Elizabeth** Yeah, I like it.
**Diane** I like all of school. I don't like it when we have students come.

**Diane** We get on with the teachers very well.
**All** Yeah.
**Jennifer** 'Cause they treat us more grown up.
**Elizabeth** I think Mrs. Davis . . .
**Diane** Yeah, she treats you very grown up and I like that.

These girls present us with an example of a very tight group who do many things together, and rely on each other for support and who are very much involved in school and school activities. While they often help each other with the work, they have taken on the school's defin- itions of the value of learning and of individual competence and don't help each other in tests. Similarly, they are very much involved in teen- age culture with dress, make-up, records and boys an important part of their lives. They are aware of their good relationship with the teachers and the fact that they are treated 'like grown ups'. This relationship and their obvious (to the teachers) positive attitude to school enables them to avoid or not be subjected to some school rules.

## Internal Fighting

One feature which was common, and very obvious to the observer, to all groups—irrespective of their orientation, set placement, or involvement in teenage culture—was the amount of fighting that went on within each of the groups. Breaking friends which occurred after an argument which might be on one of a wide range of topics and making friends again was a continuing feature of all the groups. The breaking of friendships lasted anywhere from five minutes to a few days. During the entire fourth year the four groups under discussion remained the same and so none of these 'squabbles' resulted in groups breaking up. The following is from a discussion with the 'nice' girls.

> **BM** Do you spend most of your time in school together?
> **All** Yeah.
> **Natalie** Except when we break friends. (Laughter)
> **BM** What makes you break friends?
> **Christine** Just arguments 'cause we always argue about you're taking her off me so I'm not your friend.
> **Val** Just silly little things.
> **Christine** 'Cause we broke friends Monday night and we made friends yesterday (Wednesday) morning.
> **BM** What did you break friends on Monday night about?
> **Christine** Can't remember. Oh, yeah! It was about me and Natalie, we were arguing. She was saying that I was a big head and everything 'cause I got high marks.
> (Laughter)

Only among the 'PE' girls did this fighting become physical. The following from a group interview is part of a rather lengthy account of a well organised fight between two of the 'PE' girls 'supervised' by one of the girls' mother and father. One of the protagonists was of partly West Indian origin but from all accounts and from my observation colour did not seem to be a significant factor in the dispute. It was striking that no racial insults were used.

> **Josephine** While we were there, they went nasty against Margaret.
> **BM** Why?
> **Josephine** I don't know why. They just started calling her names and that sort of thing. They didn't want her around. And then I didn't

think it was fair, so I started playing with Margaret, and me and Margaret went to her house and then we were all shouting from her window and calling each other names. Betty asked me out for a scrap but I did not want it then. So I told her I did not want to then, so she says, have it on Sunday at three o'clock. I told my mum about it, about the fight, and she says okay you can have it then . . . when I came back they were all waiting at the corner for me, following me around, so I said to my mum I am going to have that fight now. She says all right and my dad says well, I am coming and I said why? And he said because I want to come and watch to make sure it is a fair fight. So he came up and he was just standing there with his arms folded while me and Betty had the fight, but Judy was going to join in; she was swearing and everything. And she says, if you don't kill her, I will! So my dad said just you try! And then she ran off. So it was a fair fight. My mum was going to help me but my dad would not let her—she loses her temper ever so easy!!! . . .

**BM** Who won in the end?

**Josephine** Me.

**BM** What happened? How did you fight?

**Josephine** Well, at the time I was sitting on top of her, smashing, well, punching her head. She just said she gave in!! My mum shouted don't. She said keep at it until she cries. I couldn't, though. I just can't. I can't do things like that.

**BM** Are you friends now?

**Josephine** Yes. We made up friendly afterwards, about three days later.

The 'PE' girls recounted several incidents where internal disputes had resulted in physical combat. Extreme though this 'contest' appeared to be, friendships were restored within three days. In general, the 'PE' girls' playing about in school and particularly in the playground were very physical in their contact with each other. Their play usually consisted of a considerable amount of 'rough and tumble' and, in this regard, they were usually able to out 'rough and tumble' the boys.

The description of the fight incident also provides a fascinating insight into the role of the parents in peer group affairs. The parents played a very definite supervisory role in connection with the fight. There seemed to be no unease on the part of Betty that Josephine's parents were there to see that it was a fair fight, nor did any of the other members of the peer group who were there to watch think it strange or unacceptable. Similarly, there seemed no reluctance on the part of Josephine to consult with, and indeed have involved in a supervisory capacity, her parents. This is in distinct contrast with Josephine's avoidance of her parents over the issue of wearing make-up and jewellery to school. Both the physical fighting and the wearing of make-up and jewellery would certainly been seen by the school authorities as anti-school and it is interesting that in this case the peer group norm of fighting your own battles is supported by Josephine's parents while the peer group norm of wearing make-up to school is discouraged by them and Josephine has to wait till they have gone to work before she dons her make-up and jewellery to go to school.

### Make-up and Jewellery

Both the 'PE' girls and the 'science lab' girls expressed resentment about the school's policy concerning make-up and jewellery. In fact, most resentment was expressed by the 'science lab' girls rather than as one might have expected by the 'PE' girls. (Neither the 'quiet' girls nor the 'nice' girls expressed interest, at this stage, in wearing make-up to school.)

The following transcript illustrates the strength of feeling of the 'science lab' girls concerning make-up and jewellery.

> **BM** What about make-up and jewellery?
>
> **Jennifer** Well, surely about earrings it is up to us. After all, they don't have to rush to hospital in pain. If we're going to get our ears ripped it's up to us. They say we have to wear studs and it is expensive for a pair of real silver studs. I am allergic to not-real gold. Sometimes I am, it depends on what sort of metal it is. Sometimes studs are expensive and my mum says she is not going to pay out that much money when I have got other earrings upstairs.
>
> **BM** So you think it is a bit unreasonable, do you?
>
> **Diane** Yes. And we are going to be allowed to wear make-up at the high school and considering we only got a week left.
>
> **BM** You think this is a bit unfair?
>
> **Mary** Yes. One thing that Mr. —— hates is about when you wear rings. I wore a little metal ring one day which I had forgotten to take off. And he shouted out in front of the whole class, 'will Mary get that ring off'.
>
> **Jennifer** He went mad.
>
> **Mary** I took it off and I went bright red, and I took it off but I put it back on again at lunch time.
>
> **BM** Is he the main one? What about the teachers?
>
> **Jennifer** Mrs. Davis takes my earrings off a lot, but I don't mind

because I said I would get a pair of studs. I did have a pair of studs but they are broken now. Uniform gets me mad as well. I think the uniform is stupid. What good does that do you? Some of the clothes that we have got at home, nice dresses, much better than this rotten school uniform. I hate it, I do; that is why I wear this.

**BM** You think that the business about uniform, especially jewellery and make-up, is a bit hard?

**All** Yes.

**BM** What happens to you when you wear make-up?

**Jennifer** He just goes at you. He nearly poked my eyes out. And he just said take it off.

**Mary** In class we just came into the classroom and he pulled us all out, didn't he? I was leaning over the desk and he could not see me and he goes 'Betty, come here. Get that off.' 'Jennifer come here, get that off.' Then he turned round and saw Diane and he said 'Diane, come here, get that off.' Then he goes 'Where is she?' Then he saw me and told me to get that off. He made us all go and get it off and when we came back he chucked us out.

**Jennifer** What is wrong with wearing make-up anyway? It makes you look nicer anyway. I mean, you look baby faced if you don't wear it too much. I mean, you have to wear a little bit of rouge or something, sometimes.

On the other hand, the 'PE' girls seem to be somewhat more accepting of the school rules concerning the use of make-up and the wearing of jewellery. It must be added, however, that even though they were more accepting, it didn't appear to prevent them from wearing make-up to school. The views of some of the 'PE' girls are expressed in the following:

**BM** Do you get into trouble for wearing make-up?

**Josephine** Well, not at school, no. I have been told to get it off once or twice.

**BM** Who by?

**Josephine** Mr.——(headmaster).

**BM** Tell me what happened.

**Josephine** Well, he comes up to you with a face like that. Squashes your eyes.

**Cathy** He is always doing that to Betty.

**Barbara** He always picks on her for that.

**Josephine** Mr. Fisher tells you sometimes and Miss Aldridge, she tells Betty.

**BM** And does Miss Aldridge tell you to get your make-up off, as well? Does that bug you?

**Josephine** Not really. I mean, we are not supposed to wear it so we should expect to get told off for wearing it.

The reactions of these two groups are interesting in that one may have predicted that the 'PE' girls would have presented some sort of a challenge to the rule concerning the wearing of make-up and jewellery in school because of a) their generally consistent attempts to break school rules whenever possible and b) their strong commitment to teenage culture. In this light, Josephine's comment is somewhat surprising, and indeed may not be typical of the whole group, or it may be typical of the more general stance adopted by these girls where they see school rules as being fixed by those with more power and which are there to be broken when possible. If one is 'caught' breaking the rules, some sort of punishment or correction is expected after which a new attempt against this or some other rule is launched. In some ways, for these girls being 'caught' or being 'told off' is part of the daily cut and thrust in the battle over school rules and so is to be expected.

The same line of argument cannot, however, be applied to the 'science lab' girls. As has been illustrated in earlier transcripts, these girls also have a strong commitment to teenage culture but, unlike the 'PE' girls, are very positive in their orientation to school and in their acceptance of school rules. Importantly, the teachers see these girls as being pro-school, mature and sensible. For these girls, commitment to and involvement in elements of teenage culture is very much a sign that they are 'growing up' and are becoming adults. In many respects, the staff of the school treat them in a 'grown up' manner and they are given considerable responsibility and so the refusal of the staff to sanction the wearing of make-up and jewellery, which to them is a very important sign of their growing up, is seen by the girls as being inconsistent and so is reacted against. So, for the 'science lab' girls their commitment to elements of teenage culture plus the, as they see it, inconsistent treatment meted out by staff results in this very strong reaction to staff attempts to prevent them from wearing make-up and jewellery.

## Perceptions of Other Groups

All of the girls were easily able to identify each other's groups and were able to describe the culture of the groups and the differences between them. In the following, the 'science lab' girls discuss the differences between them and the 'PE' girls.

> **Diane** Really, we don't get on that well with our class.
>
> **Mary** No, we don't.
>
> **Diane** 'Cause when we get good marks they (the 'PE' girls) all say teacher's pet and things like that.
>
> **All** Yeah.
>
> **Elizabeth** They're jealous of us.
>
> **Jennifer** We're not really all that cleverer than they. If they wanted to, they could do it.
>
> **All** Yeah, yeah.
>
> **Jennifer** They'd rather play with bits of paper and throw staples at people.
>
> **Diane** Yeah.
>
> **BM** It's their attitudes to school?
>
> **Mary** Yeah, that's it. They just mess about.
>
> **Elizabeth** They'd rather hang around ice skate rinks and things like that.
>
> **Diane** Well, they prefer to mess about at school and not to work and we don't.
>
> **Mary** Like, when we sit quietly and just do our work and they're making a noise and that.

This transcript clearly illustrates that the 'science lab' girls see themselves as different from the 'PE' girls. They recognise that they are more positive towards the academic orientation of school and that this is resented in some ways by the 'PE' girls. Interestingly, the 'science lab' girls see this as being their own fault and that if, *they wanted to*, the 'PE' girls could be as 'clever' as them. It is because they *prefer* to mess about while the 'science lab' girls *prefer* to get on with their work.

Two of the 'PE' girls discuss their group and the differences between them and the 'science lab' girls.

> **BM** Is your group the same sort of group as theirs (the 'science lab' girls) or are you different?
>
> **Betty** No, I think we're different 'cause they don't go round together at night and their mums don't allow them out to go to discos or anything. Jennifer's all right, her mum lets her go to discos but the others don't go.
>
> **BM** What ways, then, do you think your group's different to them?
>
> **Judy** They're just different.

**Betty** Well, they're always in the science lab, they're never going out.

**Betty** They're always trying to get round the teachers and everything. They're always teachers' pets, them four.
**Judy** We don't get on with the teachers. I think we probably get on with them sometimes.
**Betty** Yeah.
**Judy** Not all the time.
**BM** Why not?
**Betty** We're never doing no work. Most of them, they're always getting on with their work. We do sometimes, we have our working sessions but not all the time.
**Judy** We've got the best fighters, we're tougher than them.
**Betty** We don't have lots of scraps, but we like causing trouble.

**Betty** They're snobby. They're different – they just are.
**Judy** They like snobby boys. Really snobby. We don't, we just like normal ones that are like us.

Once again, it is obvious that the 'PE' girls see themselves as different in many respects from the 'science lab' girls. The 'science lab' girls are teachers' pets and always do their work, whereas they are less interested in work and more interested in 'messing about and causing trouble'. Even the boys they like are different. Betty's comment that it is the parents of the 'science lab' girls that contribute to these basic differences indicates that for some groups, at least, the peer group is subject to parental influence.

### Summary and Conclusion

The peer group appears to be the dominant organising principle in the social life of these 12/13-year-old middle school girls. The group of friends was seen as a central and vital part of at least their school lives. The bulk of interaction was, wherever possible, within the bounds of the peer group. With one group particularly, the 'quiet' girls, peer interaction was almost exclusively within the peer group.

The girls were involved in constant manoeuvres to keep the groups together, particularly as in the fourth-year groups were increasingly being split up by setting procedures. Groups of girls outside classrooms waiting for the rest of their friends were a constant and obvious feature. All of the girls were aware of the composition of the various groups and were able to identify very clearly the differences in attitudes, interests and behaviour between their group and the other groups.

Attempts to break up a group are strongly resisted and the threat that someone is taking a member of the group away from the group is the source of much of the internal tension found in all groups. These relatively stable and consistent groupings among the girls are also acknowledged by the girls' teachers and some of the more conspicuous groups are recognised by teachers throughout the school.

Most of the girls were adamant in their view that groups were a more satisfactory way to organise social relationships than were pairs. However, in some interviews at the very end of the fourth year, when most of the girls were feeling somewhat apprehensive about their transfer to the high school, a *few* of the girls suggested that perhaps this may change once they got to the high school and that pairs of friends may become the dominant form of social organisation among girls.

They felt that the organisational arrangements of streaming and setting at the high school would make it too difficult either to sustain the present groups or to form other similar groups. It may also be that, particularly as these suggestions came from some of the girls most involved in boyfriends, with the increasing involvement in boy/girl relationships that the group would lose its importance and, in some ways, may be inconvenient (see McRobbie and Garber, 1976).

There were differences in the culture of each of the four groups and each group did seem to exhibit a relatively consistent culture. This relatively consistent culture was recognised and identified by the girls themselves, by the teachers, by the other groups, and was certainly apparent to an observer. Some features, such as the importance of the friendship, fun and support offered by friends in the group, the almost continuous process of making and breaking friends, and the considerable amount of helping each other and sharing, were common to all groups. Other features, such as orientation to school, helping each other in tests, commitment to elements of teenage culture and relationships with teachers, tended to distinguish groups from each other.

Considerable difficulty was experienced in attempting to place these groups on a pro/anti-school continuum. In gross terms, some groups, when compared to others, were more positively oriented towards the academic values and the importance of learning promulgated by the school. But this form of classification presented problems, for example, in comparing the 'quiet' girls with the 'PE' girls. The 'quiet' girls were almost complete in their inversion of the value of academic learning and had developed rather elaborate mechanisms to cope with the demands of the school. On this criteria they would have to be classed as anti-school;

however, they were quiet, well-behaved, caused no trouble, said that
they were happy and even enjoyed school. The 'PE' girls, on the other
hand, were much more successful academically and yet they were very
robust in their rejection of, and reaction to, school rules and discipline;
they enjoyed 'messing about' and 'causing trouble'.

An, at least, equally significant distinguishing dimension among these
groups of girls is that of commitment to elements of teenage culture. In
contrast to the findings of Sugarman, with boys, this commitment to
teenage culture was not necessarily associated with anti-school attitudes
or poor school performances. Indeed, it was the most pro-school group,
the 'science lab' girls, as well as the most publicly anti-school group,
the 'PE' girls, that were most involved in elements of teenage culture.
Both groups reacted strongly against the school's attempts to prevent
them from wearing jewellery and make-up.

Similarly, it was these two groups who were most able to create space
for themselves to avoid school rules. The 'science lab' girls' work in the
science lab, for example, meant that they could, with a degree of impun-
ity, be late for (and sometimes not even attend) registration or assemblies.
The 'PE' girls, with their boisterous natures, their sense of fun and their
preparedness to 'try it on' either because of the sheer force of their personality as a group or because, perhaps, some teachers found it easier to
avoid confrontation over rule infringements with this group, were also
able to negotiate more space for themselves. An example of this is the
playing of radios which were banned in school.

One occasion when I walked into the fourth-year area (out of bounds
at break times) the 'PE' girls were all sitting around in a circle listening
to the radio. They told me that they were bored and had nothing to do,
so the teacher had said they could stay there. (Nobody else was allowed
in the area.) Not long after this, the 'science lab' girls told me how they
had been playing a radio in the rural science room and the deputy head
had seen them and hadn't said anything—just smiled. Both groups were
successfully able to negotiate the school rule about radios (see Cusick,
1973).

The peer groups were aiding, supporting and reinforcing the process
of stratification. There was evidence in all groups of varying degrees of
'collective efforts' in the doing of work in school, homework and in tests.
There were, however, important differences in that the 'science lab'
girls clearly saw the 'need' for individual competence if they were to be
successful in the academic school system. They realised that they 'had to
be able to do it themselves' and that they were in competition with each
other, and so at times would definitely not show each other answers.

There was certainly a large degree of mutual support, but this only went as far as to help each other in 'small one to ten tests' or with spelling.

In the other groups, this awareness of the need for individual competence was not present, except in isolated individuals and then for different reasons. Getting the work or the homework done was what was important. Collective support and help in tests was provided wherever possible, particularly in the case of the 'quiet' girls and the 'PE' girls. The 'quiet' girls were, in fact, able to explain to me the elaborate systems they used to help each other in tests. The girls saw nothing wrong in this 'cheating' and, particularly in the case of the 'PE' girls, saw helping each other as the important factor. The peer group for these girls acted as a buffer against the academic demands of the school.

There seems to be fluidity within the groups in the sense that no clear leader or role of leader emerges (unlike Whyte's Street Corner boys or Willis's 'lads'). It may be that equality of status is a feature of girls' peer groups. It certainly would appear to be a prominent feature or at least aspiration of the women's movement. It is, perhaps, possible that this may be related to the 'caring', 'supportive' role of women in our society, i.e. the girls' peer groups may act as a particular kind of socialising agency within capitalist societies that produces women who find it difficult to or prefer not to compete with men. The exception to this in terms of the peer groups here examined would be the 'science lab' girls and one might speculate about their future roles, both in the family and within the occupational structure. They might be more competitive, independent and autonomous.[5]

The peer group networks appear to considerably reinforce the performance hierarchy particularly because of the clear way in which each group sees the performance of others. We have the pathetic and disturbing example of the way in which the 'quiet' girls have accepted their placement in the bottom sets and the definition that they are 'thick' to such an extent that they see this as being preferable and indeed 'more fun'. The 'science lab' girls see themselves as positively oriented to learning and academic achievement and because of this, and their hard work and good behaviour which has brought them success and 'good reports', other groups are jealous and call them names such as 'teacher's pet'!

The 'science lab' girls see the 'PE' girls as being just as 'clever' as them but not succeeding to the same degree because of their own unwillingness to do so. The 'PE' girls on the other hand see the success of the 'science lab' girls as a result of their being 'snobs' and 'teacher's pets' and argue that they are more interested in having fun and 'causing trouble'.

The continual interaction and reinforcement of attitudes within the group plus the explanation of the academic success or failure of other groups results in a locking-in process which is continually reinforcing the performance hierarchy and the processes of stratification within the school and this, of course, may relate to later placing within the occupational structure.

## Notes

1. The importance of peers is, of course, built into subculture, e.g. Hall and Jefferson (1976) and interaction, e.g. Goffman (1976, 1972) theories.

2. See discussions by Sharpe (1976), Mitchell (1971), Rowbotham (1973) on these typical images of women.

3. The 'names' of the groups are largely my own. The name 'PE' was used by the PE mistress to describe this group of girls, the 'science lab' girls are so called because they were the science lab monitors and spent most of their time 'working' in the science lab. The words 'nice' and 'quiet' are words which were used generally by teachers to describe the girls. It must be pointed out, however, that the girls themselves did not use these names as in any way identifying features of their groups. The girls themselves do not use any single name or characteristic to identify the four groups.

4. Bessie and Lorraine were from another class but were members of the 'PE' girls' group.

5. The perspectives in this paragraph have been prompted by comments from Kristine Mason.

## References

Blyth, W.A.L. (1960) 'The Sociometric Study of Children's Groups in English Schools', in *British Journal of Educational Studies* (May)

Coleman, J. (1961) *The Adolescent Society*, Free Press, New York

Cusick, P.A. (1973) *Inside High School: The Student World*, Holt, Rinehart and Winston, New York

Delamont, S. (1976) *Interaction in the Classroom*, Methuen, London

Furlong, V. (1976) 'Interaction Sets in the Classroom: Towards a Study of Pupil Knowledge', in M. Hammersley and P. Woods, *The Process of Schooling*, Routledge and Kegan Paul, London

Goffman, E. (1972) *Interaction Ritual*, Penguin, Harmondsworth (first published in 1967)

Goffman, E. (1976) *The Presentation of Self in Everyday Life*, Pelican, Harmondsworth (first published in 1959)

Hall, S. and Jefferson, T. (1976) *Resistance Through Rituals*, Hutchinson, London

Hargreaves, D.H. (1967) *School Relations in a Secondary School*, Routledge and Kegan Paul, London

Henry, J. (1963) *Culture Against Man*, Random House, New York

Hollinghead, A.B. (1949) *Elmtown's Youth*, John Wiley, New York

Lacey, C. (1970) *Hightown Grammar*, Manchester University Press, Manchester

Lambart, A. (1976) 'The Sisterhood', in M. Hammersley and P. Woods (eds.), *The Process of Schooling*

Lomax, P. (1978) 'The Attitudes of Girls to Different Aspects of Their School Experience', *Educational Review*, vol. 30, no. 2, June

McRobbie, A. and Garber, J. (1976) 'Girls and Subcultures: An Exploration', in S. Hall and T. Jefferson (1976)

Mitchell, J. (1971) *Woman's Estate*, Pelican, Harmondsworth

Reynolds, D. (1976) 'The Delinquent School', in M. Hammersley and P. Woods (eds.), *The Process of Schooling*

Rowbotham, S. (1973) *Woman's Consciousness, Man's World*, Penguin, Harmondsworth

Sharpe, S. (1976) *'Just Like a Girl', How Girls Learn to be Women*, Pelican, Harmondsworth

Sugarman, B. (1967) 'Involvement in Youth Culture, Academic Achievement and Conformity in School', *British Journal of Sociology*, vol. xvii, no. 2

Whyte, W.F. (1955) *Street Corner Society*, University of Chicago Press, Chicago

Willis, P. (1977) *Learning to Labour*, Saxon House, Farnborough

# 7 INITIAL ENCOUNTERS IN THE CLASSROOM AND THE PROCESS OF ESTABLISHMENT*

Stephen J. Ball

The ethnographic paradigm of classroom interaction research is now a well-established element of the sociology of education in Britain. There are now several collections of papers which represent the development and current state of work in this area (Chanan and Delamont, 1975; Stubbs and Delamont, 1976; Hammersley and Woods, 1976; Woods and Hammersley, (1977) as well as Delamont's (1976) exemplary introductory text. Most of the work, from the ethnographic paradigm, included in these various contributions to the field is founded to a greater or lesser extent upon a theoretical perspective derived from symbolic interactionism, although phenomenological and ethnomethodological perspective have also made themselves felt (e.g. Torode, 1976, 1977; Cicourel, *et al.*, 1974; Payne, 1976). However, despite the growing body of empirical work on classroom interaction and the concomitantly increasing amount of theoretical commentary, surprisingly little attention has yet been given to the evolutionary and developmental nature of teacher-pupil relationships in the classroom setting. The tendency has been (with one or two exceptions in the American literature) to treat and portray classroom relationships as fixed and static patterns of interaction within which teachers and pupils select strategies or act out the constitutive rules or procedures which serve to structure this interaction. Little attention has been given to the ways in which strategies are tested or rules established and in my view this has tended to inhibit the development of a coherent formal theory of classroom interaction. In part, I want to argue, this state of affairs is an artifact of the nature of classroom interaction research itself and the constraints upon it. The problem is that most researchers, with limited time and money available to them, are forced to organise their classroom observation into short periods of time. This usually involves moving into already established classroom situations where teachers and pupils have considerably greater experience of their interactional encounters than does the observer. Even where the researcher is available to monitor the initial encounters between a teacher and pupils, the teacher is, not unreasonably, reluctant to be observed at this

*I am indebted to Richard Tudor, Tony Bailey, Barry Cooper, Martyn Hammersley and Peter Woods for their comments on previous drafts of this paper.

stage.

But the reasons for the teacher's reluctance are exactly the reasons why the researcher should be there. These earlier encounters are of crucial significance not only for understanding what comes later[1] but in actually providing for what comes later. However it should also be said that even in cases where the researcher is able to be present during these initial encounters, his conceptual and empirical grasp of the observed situation at this stage, if it also happens to be the start point of a research project, may be so underdeveloped as to render the complexities of these encounters virtually unintelligible.

Whatever the reasons for this neglect of initial encounters, and there may be other factors which I have overlooked,[2] it seems to me that this has resulted in an unfortunate distortion in the representation of classroom relationships in interaction research. As Hammersley (1978) puts it:

> We have studies of teacher strategies and of pupil strategies but nothing as far as I am aware on patterns of relationships between the two beyond the vague notion of negotiation.

In this chapter I want to take up the vague notion of negotiation as it illuminates initial encounters between teachers and pupils in the classroom and in particular what I shall refer to as the 'process of establishment'. This is defined as an exploratory interaction process involving teacher and pupils during their initial encounters in the classroom through which a more or less permanent, repeated and highly predictable pattern of relationships and interactions emerges.

The data on which this largely exploratory chapter draws comes from two different sources and is of two distinct kinds. The greater part of the data on which the initial formulation of the chapter was based is taken from a participant observation study of a comprehensive school which was in the process of introducing mixed-ability classes to replace a system of banding (Ball, 1978). This includes classroom observation and transcript notes and the associated comments of the pupils and teachers involved. The second source of data is a small-scale interview study of PGCE students who were encouraged to describe their initial encounters with classes in their teaching practice.

### First Encounters

The theoretical position in which this chapter is embedded is Mead's symbolic interactionism and specifically Blumer's (1969) formulation of this. A single quote (also quoted in the introduction to *The Process of Schooling* Reader, Hammersley and Woods (1976) will probably serve to illustrate the particular focus with which I am concerned. Here Blumer (1969) stresses the importance of realising and retaining the emergent and negotiative character of social interaction and concentrating upon processes and experience rather than structures and roles.

> Rather than viewing behaviour as a simple 'release' from a pre-existing psychological structure (such as drives, personalities, emotions or attitudes) or as a consequence of an external coercion by social 'facts' (cultures, structures, organizations, roles, power), the interactionist focusses upon emergence and negotiation – the processes by which social action (in groups, organizations or societies) is constantly being constructed, modified, selected, checked, suspended, terminated and recommenced in everyday life. Such processes occur both in episodic encounters and in longer-lasting socialization processes over the life-history.

What Blumer's work suggests, particularly in terms of episodic encounters like lessons, is the particular importance of the initial meetings between actors for the negotiation and emergence of social perspectives, and patterns and routines of social interaction. It is during these initial encounters that the negotiation of social parameters in the classroom setting is exposed to view in a way that they are not in later lessons. And one crucial aspect of this is the gathering of information on both sides.

Obviously it is often the case that both teacher and pupils can anticipate their initial encounters in a number of ways. Both carry with them previous experiences of classrooms and possibly specific information about each other from other sources and these are important as Goffman (1959) stresses

> Information about the individual helps to define the situation enabling others to know in advance what he will expect of them and what they may expect of him. Informed in these ways, the others will know how best to call forth a desired response from him.

However it was apparent from interviews with pupils, teachers and student teachers that a great deal of information relevant to the classroom, both for the pupils and the teacher, is actually gleaned from face-to-face contacts.[3] In practice, for the pupils, this involves such things as the level of noise the teacher will tolerate; the method that they are allowed to use in addressing him or her or attracting his or her attention; the amount of work demanded of them and the level of risk involved in this;[4] the acceptable form of presentation of work and numerous other features of the teacher's organisation and management of the classroom. Indeed a teacher will begin to give out cues and information to the pupils the moment he or she walks into the classroom—by style of speech, accent and tone of voice, gestures and facial expression, whether he or she sits behind the desk at the front or walks up and down and talks to pupils privately. As Garfinkel (1967) suggests 'members of a society do interpretative work on the smallest and most fleeting fragments of behaviour'. As yet however, we know little about the social knowledge that pupils employ in recognising these cues as relevant or the interpretative procedures employed in making sense of them.

It was clear both from my observation and interview data that these initial encounters were recognised both by teachers and pupils as a distinct phase in the history of their interaction. For example:

It's depressing to know that whenever you have a new class that for the first few lessons you're going to have fun and games until you show them who's boss. (Maths teacher)

They're scared they don't know who you are, then they find out you're not a Harry Jones [teacher renowned for being very strict with pupils] or you haven't got the charisma of David Lortimer [teacher renowned for having excellent relations with pupils]. (English teacher)

**SB** What happens usually when you have a new teacher?
**Band 2 pupil** We're nice to him the first day then real horrible, you have to get used to him first.
**Band 2 pupil** The boys muck about to see if they can get away with being stupid.

From the pupils' point of view these initial encounters necessitate a testing out of the new teacher. This normally involves two stages, the first is a passive, and in a sense, purely observational stage. This is indicated by the first pupil quoted above, 'we're nice to him the first day', and was noted by all the student teachers I interviewed. For example:

In the first lesson they were very quiet. (English student)

They're quiet at first because they don't know where they stand.
(Geography student)

As a general statement the rowdiest forms are quiet in the first lesson.
(Physics student)

This stage in the development of their relationships with pupils was
referred to by some teachers and students as 'the honeymoon': it rarely
appeared to last beyond the first lesson. Hargreaves (1975) refers to this
as the 'Disciplinary Illusion'. After this the second stage is embarked
upon, which usually involves at least some pupils in being 'real horrible'.
This is when the pupils are actually involved in what Wadd (1972) refers
to as 'elementary escalation', playing up the teacher.

... to see if the teacher is prepared to defend the authority he is
seeking to establish.

This stage of testing out through playing up the teacher is evident in the
following observation notes collected in an early lesson of a new school
year involving a religious studies teacher and a third year, band two class.
The class arrives in groups of four or five over a two or three minute
period. The teacher is already in the classroom and is standing at the
front of the room with her arms crossed. She is pointedly 'waiting' for
the class to arrive and to pay attention. Teacher:

You're taking a long time to settle down. (This descriptive comment
is clearly intended to reduce the volume of the noise being made by
the pupils, and to indicate that the teacher wants their attention. This
is the function of the teacher's talk here.)

Two boys, Keith and Charlie, are being particularly noisy and there is
considerable confusion, Keith and Charlie are talking out loud and
making comments across the room ignoring the teacher. The teacher
shouts at the class to be quiet and then immediately sends Charlie out.
The class is then threatened with 35 minutes detention and the amount
of noise decreases considerably. Keith is now reading as instructed, but
he seems intent on annoying the teacher. He turns round in his chair
again and waves out of the window. The teacher again addresses the
class as a whole.

I'm very annoyed with you and I shall show you how annoyed I am by punishing you.

Keith begins to do some work but is still making noises in his throat. He is going as far as he can, pushing the teacher to the limits of her tolerance, the teacher's response is to delineate the steps towards that limit.

> That's your last warning Keith, any more and you shall be in detention.

He tests and pushes and she lays down the rules. What is expected, what is allowed, what is not, Keith is moved to the front, he is now quiet. The teacher calls for silence.

> I'm not satisfied with the standard of work, anyone who talks will be in detention for an hour tomorrow night.

The teacher asserts herself gradually and imposes her definition of the way the classroom should be, over the attempts to assert an alternative definition by some of the class. Her expectations of work and behaviour are made very clear. But the class were alert to the way in which she would treat Keith and Charlie, their behaviour tending to respond to the way in which these two were handled. When Keith is finally subdued the teacher is able to impose an unbroken rule of silence on the whole class.*

It is interesting to note that this pattern of information gathering and testing as observed and noted by the present writer in a British comprehensive school is almost exactly paralleled by Doyle's (1979) analysis of American classrooms based upon his observation of student teachers. Several points seem worth picking out. For example he notes the same two stage process whereby playing up or misbehaviour, what Doyle refers to as 'behaviour tasks', are manifested only after a preliminary period of quiescence.

> After a brief period of hesitancy, behaviour tasks were usually initiated frequently over the course of the first day or so after the student teacher assumed the teaching role in the classroom. Many of these behaviour tasks, which varied over a fairly wide range, appeared to

*From my observations of this class group in other lessons and interviews with the pupils it was clear that Keith and Charlie based their social identities upon their roles as disrupters in the classroom. They derived status from their classmates in this way, by engaging in a continuing series of clashes with their teachers.

function as active tests of the ability of the student teacher to man-
age classroom routines and rule systems.

Furthermore, as in the lesson described above, Doyle found that rules
or prohibitions uttered by student teachers were invariably subjected to
testing out in practice.

Verbalized rules were seldom accepted at face value. In almost all
cases, students sought empirical evidence that the student [teacher]
would actually follow routines and enforce rules. Behaviour tasks are
an especially useful way for students [pupils] to obtain such evidence.

Finally, again as in the lesson described, Doyle also found that
participation in this testing out process tended to devolve to a few pupils
only in any class. The teacher's responses to these few however in the
public arena of the classroom may serve as indications to all the
pupils in the class for their future behaviour.

It is important to emphasize that in nearly all situations only a few
students participated in behaviour tasks, at least initially. Moreover,
it was not always clear that a particular behaviour task was a deliberate challenge to the student teacher's managerial skills. But classrooms
are very public places and students often appeared to take advantage
of all behaviour tasks to measure a teacher's classroom abilities. Some
students, in other words, seemed to rely on others to test the rule
system.

The pupils' information gathering and 'testing out' of the teacher may
be considered conceptually as having two major purposes. Firstly the
pupils find it necessary[5] to discover what parameters of control the
teacher is seeking to establish over their behaviour. So for instance:

I'm new and they know it and I think they're trying it on. I expect
to have some problems in the first year, but I think they're pushing to
see how far they can go. (Probationary English teacher)

It may be that the kinds of expectations evident in this comment have
their own impact on classroom relationships by self-fulfilment in the strategies that teachers employ in anticipation of or in response to certain
types of behaviour. This possibility seems even more explicit in the following remark:

I know I expect some kids to be charming and interested and others to be difficult and very much a confrontation situation and I am very tight when I go in there. (Probationary History teacher)

Secondly, as noted above, the pupils find it necessary to explore in practice whether or not the teacher has the tactical and managerial skills to defend the parameters he or she is seeking to establish. So for instance, as one 'successful' teacher explained:

They know exactly where the red line is, and what will happen if they step over it, both in terms of work and behaviour. And I like this group. (Maths teacher)

It is important though to bear in mind that the relationship between the theory and practice of control is not always a simple one. Some teachers, and many student teachers, attempt deliberately to avoid imposing parameters of control on their pupils and seek instead through establishing personal relationships to have the pupils exercise self-control in the classroom. Other teachers who do seek to impose parameters of control on their pupils find that they lack the appropriate tactical and managerial skills to do so. For example Kounin's (1970) study of discipline and classroom management discovered a close connection between the effectiveness of teachers' 'desists', that is control statements, and their 'withitness', and 'transition smoothness', ability to deal with 'overlaps' and provide a variety of work tasks for pupils, and monitoring and management of movement in the classroom. That is to say, those teachers who demonstrated skills in these areas proved to be more able to respond appropriately and effectively to the 'deviant behaviour' of their pupils than those who did not. As Doyle (1979) notes, 'students [pupils] appear to respect what might be called "tactical superiority"'. Thus the outcomes of the pupils' 'testing out' of their teachers are by no means a foregone conclusion. The outcome depends upon the nature of the teacher's response to the pupils' actions. From my observations it was evident that taking no action at all, or getting angry and losing self-control, or showing signs of confusion on the teacher's part, all typical of the inexperienced student teacher, demonstrated the kind of lack of tactical skill that would be taken advantage of even by pupils in the most pro-school oriented classes. The subsequent nature of the classroom relationships established between teacher and pupils and the nature of the pupils' behaviour, especially the amount of disruption and 'deviant behaviour', is highly dependent upon and emerges out of these processes of information-exchange and test and response in these initial encounters. Clearly this proposition is basic to the ubiquitous 'start as you mean to go on' and 'go in hard and ease off later' folk remedies for the beginning teacher (see Marland, 1975). Hargreaves (1975) notes that

> . . . most experienced teachers insist that the teacher must, if he is to survive, define the situation in his own terms at once. Basically this initial definition is not so much a statement of the rules that will govern the class, but rather a clear indication that the teacher is completely in charge and not to be treated lightly.

Hargreaves goes on, in considering classroom discipline, to discuss the long-term establishment of a completed body of classroom rules in some detail. This, he says, 'takes some weeks to establish because the rules must be created and always clarified in relation to concrete incidents where the rules are applicable.'[6] Once they are established and routinised the social parameters of teacher-pupil interaction are less readily accessible to the researcher, as noted previously. Once routinised: 'Action becomes a symbolic medium. The occurrence of particular actions, and perhaps even more their absence, communicate messages.' (Hammersley, 1979)

## Defining the Situation

I now want to go on to address two of the issues that seem to me to be raised by the discussion so far. Firstly, how can we make sense of the processes outlined above, in terms of symbolic interactionist theory? And secondly, why do these processes occur anyway? That is to say, how can we explain why the pupils find it necessary to identify and test out the parameters of control that their teachers seek to establish in the classroom? It may be that one answer will suffice for both questions.

Initial encounters between teachers and pupils in the classroom are it would seem problematic definitional situations *par excellence*. The mode of definition which is of concern here is what Stebbins (1977) refers to as *habitual personal definition*.

> the same category of situation holds roughly the same meaning for a particular class of actors participating in it, but in which each individual participant is more or less unaware that people like him who are having the same kinds of experiences elsewhere define them the

same ways.

It is important to recognise the relevance of Stebbins's use of the phrase 'roughly the same meaning' here, we have already touched on some sources of diversity in the action orientations and the predispositions that different teachers carry with them, but aspects of the surroundings – and other environmental/institutional factors: class size; age and status of pupils; form of grouping (streamed, setted, mixed-ability, etc.); length and timing of lesson (note the interpretation of the teacher of 4B last two periods on Friday afternoon mentioned below); lesson topic; resources and materials to be used and location (particular strategies may be adopted for lessons timetabled in the assembly hall, canteen or cloakroom) – can all contribute to definitions which are personally and situationally unique. As Stebbins (1977) outlines, the teacher's definition of the situation is a process involving perception of others and reflexive 'looking glass' perceptions of self. It is 'a synthesis, interpretation and interrelation of salient predispositions, intentions and elements of the setting'. For the pupils' movement from lesson to lesson may require considerable adaptation and flexibility in terms of the diversity of the rules of behaviour and performance expected or demanded by the teachers. Hargreaves *et al.* (1975) faced this problem in attempting to establish a typology of classroom rules in their study of deviance in classrooms.

> . . . there are some general rules that are 'generally accepted' even though they are not written down. But these fuse into the individual preferences and judgments of teachers, who vary in what they will 'have' or 'stand for' or 'tolerate' within their classroom over which they exercise a legitimate authority.

However, it would be oversimplistic to interpret the adaptation of pupils to different classroom settings solely as a methodological process of learning and accumulating 'facts' about the classroom. It is more realistic to see this 'social knowledge' of the classroom as 'knowledge of relevance'. It is not a matter of learning situational/contextual rules, but forgetting for the moment transcontextual ones, whittling down a stock of knowledge to a core of relevant and/or acceptable strategies. From the pupils' point of view the action limitations of the classroom situation are virtually unknown in the lesson of a new teacher. Despite the traditional and institutional authority of the teacher as major significant other in the classroom[7] and the provision of institutional rules of behaviour, the interactional detail of classroom conduct is broadly left to the individual teacher to establish. As Waller (1932) points out, when a teacher faces a new class he faces an undefined situation:

> ... and it is part of his job to impose his definition of the situation upon the class quickly, before any alternatives have an opportunity to be considered.

This definition of the situation is essentially a process. To quote Waller again:

> It is the process in which the individual explores the behaviour possibilities of a situation, marking out particularly the limitations which the situation imposes on his behaviour, with the final result that the individual forms an attitude toward the situation, or, more exactly, in the situation.

Clearly this process of defining the situation may be seen to relate to the information gathering and testing out by pupils described above. However, this does not necessarily reaffirm Waller's conflict model of the classroom. It is misleading to assume *sui generis* that the testing out by pupils of their teachers engenders a challenge to the definition of the situation that the teacher is seeking to establish. For some pupils 'testing out' may be important in that it enables them to acquire the knowledge necessary for them to conform, for instance knowledge of their teachers' conventions, for attributing 'achievement', 'success' and 'good behaviour'. They are concerned to know the teacher's conception of the classroom, in the sense of being able to perform competently within it, rather than to challenge it. Indeed even in the case of the lesson quoted earlier it is possible to suggest at least four interpretations of the pupils' actions.

a) The pupils were seeking to arrive at a competent interpretation of the meanings of the situation held by the teacher.
b) The pupils were seeking to negotiate a mutually acceptable and congruent definition of the situation.
c) The pupils were attempting to challenge the teacher's competence or right to assert her definition over certain significant sub-sets of the classroom situation. (E.g. who has the right to initiate talk.)
d) The pupils were attempting to challenge the teacher's competence or right to assert her definition over any aspect of the classroom situation.

In part at least the likelihood of one or other of these interpretations being correct will depend upon the previous educational careers of the pupils involved, and of the teacher, and thus the attitudes and purposes carried by the participants into the new classroom situation. Nevertheless in all of these cases (except perhaps the first) the teacher's competence, what Wadd refers to as 'personal power', will have a crucial bearing on the definitional consequences. So too will the extent of the pupils' commitment to and sharing in the long-term purposes of the teaching encounter, in whatever way they perceived them. While the status of teacher presents the incumbent with a certain degree of official legitimacy problems always revolve around the individual teacher's ability to 'bring it off' in the interactional sequences of everyday classroom life. While, as we have seen, the first lesson may be conceded by the pupils, the emergent social orderings appear to rely heavily upon how the teacher actually handles or manages his or her relationship with pupils during these preliminary interactions.

Clearly then there is always the possibility that the defining process of mutual testing, cue-reading, elaboration and modification may lead to an outcome that is satisfactory to neither teacher nor pupils. For example a colleague described to me his strategy for dealing with 4B, last two periods on Friday afternoons, as 'playing for a draw'. As Stebbins (1977) illustrates, definitions are tried out by participants and then accepted, rejected or modified in response to the reaction of others in the negotiation process.

However the definition of the situation is of further relevance and importance in the classroom in regard to the possibility of the pupils being able to predict and routinise patterns of interaction. As I see it one of the major functions of the pupils' testing out of teachers is a guidance to the evaluation and selection of future possible actions. Pupils are concerned to know in advance what the teacher's reaction will be to certain types of behaviour. Will deliberate disobedience (or failure to hand in homework, or 'doing poor work') incur the teacher's wrath; involve a minor dressing down, being told to 'stop it', being sent out of the room or to the headmaster, being put on detention, given lines or will it be ignored. On the basis of this kind of anticipation of the teacher's response the pupil is able to weigh up the amount of satisfaction to be obtained from the commission of a 'deviant' act against the dissatisfaction likely to be involved in the teacher's response to it, if any. This may in fact account for pupils' often stated preference for 'strict' teachers.[8] Strictness usually also provides for a highly structured and therefore a highly predictable situational definition.

Indeed beyond this, in general terms, Gergen (1968) argues that personal consistency is a quality of person that is broadly supported by the values of Western culture. He reports evidence from laboratory experiments which demonstrates that consistent persons are liked by others, while inconsistent persons are disliked.

However, the teacher's control of the pupils is not the only aspect of classroom interaction that requires the negotiation of definitions. Whereas control may be regarded as a persistent and background feature of the classroom setting, the organisation of learning by the teacher is often more prominent. The well-worn example of discovery learning provides many illustrations of this. In Doyle's (1979) terms the task accomplishments associated with discovery learning 'task structures' confront the pupils with high levels of risk and ambiguity compared with the task accomplishments associated with more straightforward 'memory task structures'. Doyle (1979) found that pupils who were confronted with potentially high risk, high ambiguity, learning situations adopted various interaction strategies to resist or reformulate these 'task structures'. In other words the pupils attempted to resist or renegotiate aspects of their teachers' definition of the situation.[9] And this resistance to risk-laden learning situations is not restricted to the school pupil, university students and teachers on in-service courses also, in my experience, actively seek to renegotiate 'task structures' with their tutors. So then equally in terms of 'task structures' what actually comes to pass in the classroom, may be seen to be the outcome of the relative capacity of the different actors to establish their definition of the situation over and against the definitions held by others. A further example of the role of the pupils' definitions of the situation, in terms of the legitimate use of authority by teachers, is provided by Werthman's (1963) study. Werthman was able to demonstrate the importance of the pupils' interpretations of teachers' activities as a basis for an organised and rational set of responses to the teachers' assignment of grades. Snyder (1971) also illustrates, in the case of college students, the ways in which students found it necessary and useful to employ strategies of manipulation and negotiation in order to cope with their undergraduate workload. The student

. . . is forced to make judgements about what is relevant; he develops a method of study and fixes a way of budgeting his time. But it may also foster a sense of gamesmanship and make the encounter between student and professor a competitive rather than a cooperative one. (Snyder, 1970)

In terms of both control and 'task structure' once the establishment is completed[10] it will be maintained and reproduced by the actors' shared expectations of the situation. However the network of interdependency that is embodied in the situation will in itself be moving and changing over time, 'the association of people is necessarily in the form of a process in which they are making indications to one another and interpreting each other's indications' (Blumer, 1969). All actions have their intended and unintended consequences in this process and teacher-pupil relationships in the classroom may be expected to evolve and change over time as a result. The tentative and precarious nature of social order in the classroom, which is most apparent in initial encounters, is never totally suspended since the teacher will be continually testing inferences about the pupils' responses. However this natural form of group life, of designation, interpretation and redirection, is different in kind from the exploratory gestures and reactions evident in the process of establishment itself.

It is difficult to describe and account for the significance of establishment without accentuating the normative and authoritarian aspects of defining the situation that are involved. However in general terms it is *not unusual* that the traditional and institutional authority of the teacher will serve to legitimate his or her normative practice and his or her definition of the situation, to the pupils. It is *not unusual* for pupils to accept the teachers' definition of the situation. The problem is that it is the 'conflict model' of teaching, referred to previously, that is most commonly employed in observers' accounts of classroom processes. Its generality and appropriateness are assumed but not proven. This may be related to the problem of order that is fundamental to almost every sociological theory, and this is of course exquisitely vital to the understanding of life in classrooms. Several studies have addressed this question directly, Torode and Nash (both 1976) for instance, but the tendency has been to start from the problem of disorder and work back from there. The unusual is deployed as typical and, perhaps as a consequence, the typical remains unexplored. One of the reasons for this state of affairs is undoubtedly that many of the studies thus far available on the classroom interaction of teacher and pupils have tended to focus upon the interesting, but untypical, perspectives of anti-school pupils in their latter years of schooling (cf. Furlong (1976), Gannaway (1976), Birksted (1976), and Willis (1978)) Epistemologically this may be related back through the theoretical antecedents of much of the contemporary work on classroom interaction, Mead, Blumer, Becker, etc., to the work of the Chicago School, from whence the 'underdog perspective' is derived. A concern with the disenfranchised and alienated derived from this theoretical tradition melds well with the empirical tradition of mainstream sociology of education which concerns itself with explaining the failure of the working-class pupil.

In making reference to and use of this body of literature it is all too easy to forget that these cases may not be normal or representative. (See Hammersley and Turner in this volume.) In its crudest form the 'conflict model' merely sees the classroom regime as a matter of a single competition for ultimate supremacy, and this seems inadequate to explain or illuminate the primary school classroom; the first-year classroom in the comprehensive school; the top stream classroom; the O-level classroom; or the sixth-form classroom. 'The marshalling and developing of familiar themes' (Willis, 1978) in these particular circumstances require a more sophisticated and subtle model of explanation. I am not trying to suggest that teachers' and pupils' interests are always complementary. I would agree that this is unlikely in the classroom given the range of different interests on both sides and the large number of pupils involved in most cases. And indeed the absence of overt conflict cannot be taken to mean that interests are complementary, it is more likely to mean that a working consensus has been negotiated. My criticisms are of the assumed ubiquity of conflict in much of the writing on classroom interaction and the often unexplicated nature of situations and incidents identified by observers as representing conflict.

Thus, to return to my major concern, while I want to argue that teaching is normally 'done' on the basis of the communal features of everyday life in classrooms and 'picks its fruits', I would also argue that the convenience and comfort of this intersubjective state is often necessarily suspended in initial encounters.[11] The naively assumed and implicitly reaffirmed *sense* of community that *is normally* a part of everyday life in classrooms, *is normally* unavailable to teacher or pupils in their initial encounters. The classroom *is normally* a social environment where violations in the communicative and interactive process are assumed to be minor or unimportant and easily remediable (cf. Hargreaves, *et al.*, 1975), it is an optimistic environment. The initial teaching encounter is however, more often than not, a pessimistic environment.[12] The 'until further notices' that hold together the social patchwork of classroom life cease to be routine, or have not yet become routine. Distrust in the 'we-ness' of interaction becomes the order of the day, or disorder of the day, and it is intersubjectivity that provides the 'surprises'. The nature of the other is radically problematic here, that is to say the ratio of *assumption* to *appraisal* in the we-relationship and the *sense* of community in the classroom is shifted dramatically towards *appraisal*.

The initial encounters are necessarily situations of *performance* – participation on the part of the teacher (and perhaps as suggested earlier by some of the pupils too) and this is most evident in the deliberateness and reflexivity of involvement in these lessons. This deliberateness and reflexivity is particularly clear in the diaries kept by student teachers.

I felt a bit out of my depth – and in conflict internally, because I didn't want them to be totally silent or have to keep nagging at them. But I did want them to get down to some proper work. Conflict also re the learning situation, because I wanted them to choose what they'd do, but they were totally unable to behave while two groups did a bit of drama. In the end we wasted the whole lesson. Right at the end I broke – I told them I wouldn't tolerate so much noise, and said that if anyone didn't want to learn they should say so and leave the lesson. I promised dire, unknown, evil punishments if I didn't get order and quiet next lesson. I sent John out during the lesson and I had a word with him afterwards on his own; he promised to behave. Someone even came in because they were being so noisy – I felt I may be losing my self confidence. (PGCE English student)

Initial encounters, then, constitute pessimistic social environments that necessitate, or are conducive to, the continual reflexive calibration of the congruence between the self and others. The doing of teaching requires the establishment of a communal we-relationship between teacher and pupil. I am saying that in initial encounters the teacher may find that the thesis of 'the natural attitude of everyday life' is empirically refuted (for some teachers or in some schools or certain classrooms it may be constantly refuted), although its reaffirmation is likely to be always more readily available to the 'strict' teacher (cf. Furlong and Gannaway). Even here though a *sense* of consociality in the classroom must be achieved and appraised. It cannot be assumed.[13]

## Notes

1. See Walker and Adelman (1976) for an account of the culture of the classroom which illustrates this.

2. Another simple and rather facile reason for this neglect of initial encounters might be the fact that the school year begins in September but the university year does not normally commence until October.

3. As Hargreaves, *et al.* (1975) have pointed out the classroom is just one of several social arenas 'at school' in which the pupils must become competent by

constructing appropriate modes of interaction. The corridor, the assembly, the dinner canteen, and perhaps most of all the playground, require exploration and adaptation by the pupil. The focus of this chapter is however, limited to the classroom and to the specifics of particular classrooms. It is not concerned with what is held in common between classrooms in a single institution but rather with what is idiosyncratic and therefore difficult for actors in different classrooms.

4. Doyle (1979) in his paper discusses the importance of changes in pedagogy for pupils in terms of the increased 'risk' involved. That is the increased possibilities of failure that are inherent in those forms of learning where the stress is upon understanding rather than memorisation.

5. There are a number of studies which explore the primacy of the teachers' ability to control in the dynamics of classroom interaction. Furlong, Gannaway and Nash (all 1976) all stress in particular the importance of the pupils' perceptions of their teachers in this respect. However it may be that in certain circumstances 'control' is superseded by or subordinated to other factors, for example in my own research I came across a group of fifth-form pupils who were primarily concerned with 'respect' that they 'tested for' in their initial encounters with teachers.

6. This chapter is asking 'how are rules established between teachers and pupils?' but it is also possible, and at some stage necessary, to examine 'the rules for establishing these rules' which underlie the processes and experiences addressed in this chapter.

7. For some pupils obviously there are other significant others to whom they refer when making decisions about ways of behaving in the classroom. But I would want to argue that in the typical classroom the teacher remains the *major* significant other, if only inasmuch that decision-making on the pupils' part will take the teacher into account, albeit as a negative reference point.

8. Nash (1976), Gannaway (1976) and Musgrove and Taylor (1969) among others have demonstrated, via widely differing techniques, the preference of pupils, of all kinds, for 'strict' as opposed to 'soft' teachers.

9. This resistance to potentially high risk 'task structures', especially in school, can be related to the instrumental and essentially alienated orientations of pupils towards their academic labour and its products.

10. The process of establishment may be regarded as completed at some stage in as much as it is recognised as a distinctive and identifiable phase in the history of teacher-pupil interaction in the classroom by the teachers and pupils themselves. The tentative and exploratory nature of interactions in this phase are regarded as qualitatively different in kind from later interactions.

11. The formulation of this concluding section draws upon a theoretical argument outlined by Martin Pollner in an oral paper delivered at a Schutzean Studies *ad hoc* group meeting at the 9th World Congress of Sociology, held at the University of Uppsala, Sweden, 8-13 August 1978.

12. This pessimism was clearly expressed in almost every one of the student teacher interviews I conducted and is also apparent in the comments of the probationary English and History teachers and the Maths teacher and the pupils quoted above. However one documented exception to this is the 'optimistic compliance' noted by Woods (1979) in the case of first-year secondary school pupils.

13. This is an assumption often made by student teachers when they make their first forays into the classroom, an assumption that seems to lead inevitably to chaos and recriminations.

# References

Ball, S.J. (1978) 'Processes of Comprehensive Schooling: a Case Study', unpublished D.Phil. thesis, University of Sussex

Birksted, I. (1976) 'School Performance: Viewed From the Boys', *Sociological Review*, vol. 24, no. 1, pp. 63-77

Blumer, H. (1969) *Symbolic Interactionism: Perspective and Method*, Prentice-Hall, Englewood Cliffs

Chanan, G. and Delamont, S. (1975) *Frontiers of Classroom Research*, NFER

Cicourel, A., *et al.* (1974) *Language Use and School Performance*, Academic Press, London

Delamont, S. (1976) *Interaction in the Classroom*, Methuen, London

Doyle, W. (1979) 'Student Management of Task Structures in the Classroom', paper presented at the Conference on Teacher and Pupil Strategies, St Hilda's College, Oxford

Furlong, V. (1976) 'Interaction Sets in the Classroom: Towards a Study of Pupil Knowledge', in M. Stubbs and S. Delamont, *Explorations in Classroom Observation*, Wiley, London

Gannaway, H. (1976) 'Making Sense of School', in M. Stubbs and S. Delamore, *Explorations in Classroom Observation*, Wiley, London

Garfinkel, H. (1967) *Studies in Ethnomethodology*, Prentice-Hall, Englewood Cliffs

Gergen, K.J. and Gordon, C. (eds.) (1968) *The Self in Interaction, Vol. I*, Wiley, New York

Goffman, E. (1959) *The Presentation of Self in Everyday Life*, Penguin, Harmondsworth

Hammersley, M. (1978) 'Strategy or Rule: Two Models of Action', synopsis of paper presented at SSRC Conference on Teacher and Pupil Strategies, St Hilda's College, Oxford

Hammersley, M. (1979) 'What is a Strategy? A Critique of Interactionist Strategy Analysis', unpublished manuscript

Hammersley, M. and Woods, P. (1976) *The Process of Schooling*, Routledge and Kegan Paul, London

Hargreaves, D. (1975) *Interpersonal Relations and Education* (revised ed.), Routledge and Kegan Paul, London

Hargreaves, D., Hester, S. and Mellor, F. (1975) *Deviance in Classrooms*, Routledge and Kegan Paul, London

Kounin, J.S. (1970) *Discipline and Group Management in Classrooms*, Holt, Rinehart and Winston, New York

Marland, M. (1975) *The Craft of the Classroom: a Survival Guide to Classroom Management in the Secondary School*, Heinemann Educational, London

Musgrove, F. and Taylor, P.H. (1969) *Society and The Teacher's Role*, Routledge and Kegan Paul, London

Nash, R. (1976) 'Pupil's Expectations of Their Teachers', in M. Stubbs and S. Delamont, *Explorations in Classroom Observations*, Wiley, New York

Payne, G. (1976) 'Making a Lesson Happen: an Ethnomethodological Analysis', in Hammersley and Woods (1976)

Snyder, B.R. (1971) *The Hidden Curriculum*, Alfred A. Knopf, New York

Stebbins, R. (1977) 'The Meaning of Academic Performance: How Teachers Define a Classroom Situation', in Woods and Hammersley (1977)

Stubbs, M. and Delamont, S. (eds.) (1976) *Explorations in Classroom Observation*, Wiley, New York

Torode, B. (1976) 'Teachers' Talk and Classroom Discipline', in M. Stubbs and S. Delamont, *Explorations in Classroom Observation*, Wiley, New York

Torode, B. (1977) 'Interrupting Intersubjectivity', in Hammersley and Woods (1977)

Wadd, K. (1972) 'Classroom Power', *Education for Teaching*, no. 89, autumn

Walker, R. and Adelman, C. (1976) 'Strawberries Strawberries', in M. Stubbs and S. Delamont, *Explorations in Classroom Observation*, Wiley, New York

Waller, W. (1932) *The Sociology of Teaching*, Wiley, New York

Werthman, C. (1963) 'Delinquents in School: a Test for the Legitimacy of Authority', *Berkeley Journal of Sociology 1878*, pp. 39-60

Willis, P. (1978) *Learning to Labour*, Tavistock, London

Woods, P. and Hammersley, M. (1977) *School Experience*, Croom Helm, London

Woods, P. (1979) *The Divided School*, Routledge and Kegan Paul, London

# 8 SYNTHESIS AND THE STUDY OF STRATEGIES: A PROJECT FOR THE SOCIOLOGICAL IMAGIN- ATION*

Andy Hargreaves

## Introduction: the Task of the Sociological Imagination

> What we experience in various and specific milieux . . . is often caused by structural changes. Accordingly, to understand the changes of many personal milieux we are required to look beyond them . . . To be aware of the idea of social structure and to use it with sensibility is to be capable of tracing such linkages among a great variety of milieux. To be able to do that is to possess the sociological imagination. (Mills, 1959, p. 17)

Some 20 years ago, C. Wright Mills defined the core feature of the socio-logical imagination as the ability and desire to connect the personal experiences of particular milieux to questions and conceptions of social structure. The implication of Mills's penetrating insight is that the task of the sociological imagination is to grasp the richness of personal and inter-personal experience (but not in a way which would amount to little more than a reiteration of the obvious), and to document the ways in which social structures impinge upon and partially shape the organisation of people's everyday lives (whilst trying to avoid mystifying the reader in the process).

Rather belatedly, for a host of reasons which cannot be entered into here,[1] sociologists of education are only now beginning to appreciate the significance and possibilities of the type of programme which Mills outlined so elegantly for the parent discipline, sociology. Many recent publications in the sociology of education contain a prefatory, almost obligatory section which surveys the achievements and shortcomings of the discipline in the past and then attempts to extract, from the wide variety of 'partial' explan-ations which have been produced so far, those elements which could be combined to provide the basis for a new, improved synthesis.[2] As Ivan Reid (1978) has pointed out, sociology of education in the 1970s has been characterised by a bewildering array of theoretical approaches. In

*I would like to offer my thanks to Peter Woods and Martyn Hammersley for com-menting upon previous drafts of this paper.

response to the confusion which such an assortment has alm
created, there has been a growing awareness of the necessity
alternatives and to create a synthesis of the broadest explan:
which would bond together classroom and society, social str
interpersonal interaction, and so on. In general, there is a sin.....y stateu
desire to end 'the war of the schools', as Bernbaum (1977) has expressed
it, and to appreciate that rather than there being several sociologies of
education, there is instead only one (Reid, 1978).[3]

However, while the necessity for synthesis is at last receiving a growing
amount of deserved and overdue attention within the discipline, the
attempts that have been made have been rather vague and have not contained any specific guidance as to how, precisely, the hopes for a synthesis
might be realised. Several writers have stressed that different approaches
are complementary (Banks, 1976), that they are simply alternative routes
for exploring the same territory (Reid, 1978), and that all researchers of
different theoretical persuasions should therefore stand above the conflict,
recognise these interests that they hold in common and work towards
their harmonious fulfilment (Karabel and Halsey, 1977). General appeals
of this kind, however, tend to gloss over the very real differences which
separate theoretical approaches, and which make the creation of any synthesis highly problematic. They also offer few concrete models which
might bring about this hoped for reconciliation.

In this chapter my aim is to offer an assessment of the various stances
which have been taken towards the problematic relationship that exists
between what have hitherto been competing approaches in the sociology
of education. I shall concentrate on what I take to be three significant
positions which have been adopted by writers seeking to establish some
kind of compatibility or integration between different theoretical approaches. These positions, I shall call gentle incorporation, necrolatry, and
splendid isolation. Having appraised each of these general stances, I shall
then consider three theoretical models each of which contains (though to
varying degrees of explicitness), a conception of the school-society relation. In other words, each contains a set of understandings as to how and
to what extent school and society, interaction and social structure are connected. The three models I shall call direct reproduction, relative autonomy
and the split-level model.

I want to propose the concept of 'strategy' as a way of connecting
social actions to structurally generated constraints. My aim is not to provide a comprehensive model of teacher or pupil strategies,[4] but to show
the urgent reasons why models of this kind need to be developed. Mills
was right to identify the central task of the sociological imagination as the

connection of personal troubles to public issues but subsequent efforts to achieve such a goal, at least in the realm of education, have fallen far short of adequacy.

## Part I Synthesis and Reconciliation: Some Prominent Stances

### 1. Gentle Incorporation

Here, from the standpoint of one chosen perspective, an assessment is made of preceding and competing approaches in the sociology of education with a view to demonstrating how the best elements from each position can be preserved and incorporated into the dominant model of the researcher's preference. The exact means by which this is to be achieved, though, is rarely specified.

An example is the work of Young and Whitty (1977). They emphasise the fundamental strength of the 'new' sociology of education in its recognition of the importance of culture and consciousness. They make out a convincing case for the inclusion of such features in any Marxist analysis of education. Otherwise, they suggest, any such analysis would be lacking in both rigour and subtlety. Yet, in their own writing, the lines of connection between structure and culture, or between society and the classroom remain blurred and obscure. There is little clarification, for example, of how the function of schooling as a reproducer of social class relations, is represented in the daily interchanges of classroom life. Clearly, there is considerable room here not only for empirical demonstration, but also for the close specification of a model which would give any such demonstration greater meaning.

By contrast, John Eggleston (1977) shows an affinity for a very different perspective than the Marxist standpoint adopted by Young and Whitty, but he too utilises the same strategy of gently incorporating some aspects of alternative approaches. Eggleston describes two perspectives which, he claims, have characterised investigations into the organisation of the school curriculum. These are the 'received' perspective (roughly equivalent to what has sometimes been called a 'normative' approach where any educational phenomenon such as the school curriculum is analysed in terms of the functions it seemingly performs for the school as an organisation and for the wider society); and the 'reflexive' perspective (roughly equivalent to the 'interpretive' approach, where the curriculum is seen as socially constructed, as the outcome of definitions which different groups and individua attempt to impose during negotiation with one another). Although Eggleston's attachment to the latter perspective remains strong, he attempts to transcend the two by establishing a 'restructuring' perspective which allows equal recognition of two facts: that individuals seek to impose their definitions upon the situations which they encounter, and that these situations are also characterised by an underlying structure of relationships which sets limits to the range of definitions that can be imposed. The restructuring perspective, it is argued, seeks to face squarely the realities of power and for support in this matter, Eggleston mentions (though very much in passing), the work of Karl Marx. Yet his preference for the reflexive perspective is patently indicated by his adoption of a pluralist view of power. Unlike the Marxist view where power is seen as tied to the structural positions which people occupy, Eggleston treats power as a resource which can be distributed more equitably amongst participants in the schooling process. Thus power, like knowledge, is negotiable. That Eggleston's primary objective is to combine these somewhat diluted notions of power and constraint with the reflexive perspective's emphasis upon how individuals try to impose their different definitions of the situation, is rendered transparent in three ways: in his failure to discuss the important contribution of Marxist perspectives in the sociology of education; in his pluralist conceptions of power and decision-making; and in the remarkable brevity of the section which he does devote to the 'restructuring' perspective. It would seem, then, that Eggleston's prime allegiance remains with the 'reflexive' perspective. The 'restructuring' perspective is thus not so much a clear alternative to this but more a minor incremental development of it.

In the conflict between different theoretical approaches, the most effective way to remove the threats posed by an opposing approach may be neither to obliterate it, nor even to isolate it, but rather, to incorporate its stronger features, translating them into the terms of one's own discourse. As Berger and Luckmann (1967) have noted

> The final goal of this procedure is to *incorporate* the deviant conceptions within one's own universe and thereby to liquidate them ultimately. The deviant conceptions must, therefore, be *translated* into concepts derived from one's own universe. (p. 133)

The way in which a number of Marxist researchers have incorporated some elements of the phenomenological tradition,[5] and the extension of Eggleston's 'reflexive' perspective, to subsume in altered form, some aspects of conflict and constraint are, in part, two very different instances of such a process. My argument here is not that all perspectives have equal weight and that they should therefore be combined in democratically equal proportions in the creation of any final synthesis. One perspective must serve as an anchorage point if a thoroughgoing relativism is to be avoided. However, when attempts are made to integrate the salient insights and concepts of other approaches into one's own, any translation of their meaning which occurs should be made absolutely clear, and the implications for concrete empirical work should be followed up.

## 2. *Necrolatry*

A second way of generating inclusive explanations involves appealing to the works of the traditional sociological 'masters'. Some writers choose to find the fuel for powerful future syntheses in the buried strata of the past. There is a return then, to founding fathers; to Marx, Durkheim and Weber or, in Karabel and Halsey's (1977) words, to 'the promise of the classical tradition' (p. 75). For them, Emile Durkheim 'provides an unequalled example of the way in which it is possible, and indeed necessary, to integrate microcosmic and macrocosmic levels of sociological analysis' (p. 74). Referring to one particular study of his, they continue:

> No sociologist of education has yet surpassed — in depth or in breadth — this investigation of the relationship between social structure and the process of educational transmission, written more than seventy years ago. This is a sobering commentary on the subsequent history of educational research. (p. 74)[6]

Although it would be reasonable to concur, to some extent, with Karabel and Halsey's appreciation of Durkheim's sophisticated understanding of structural connections and of the penetration of his historical investigations — qualities which are rarely matched by contemporary researchers — such a eulogy should not be allowed to obscure the fact that the relationships he establishes between school and society seem to be drawn a little too directly. In his work, there are no methodological correctives available in the form of detailed accounts and richly documented observations of curriculum and pedagogy. It would be unfair to blame Durkheim for this for there was no such methodological tradition available at the time he was writing. Nevertheless, the lesson that must be learned is that in going back to Durkheim or any other 'classic' source, we should not indulge ourselves in the scholarly ritual of reverence of academic ancestry for its own sake. Instead, we should continually strive to show how subsequent developments in sociological inquiry might enhance the relevance and penetration of any 'classical' analysis. There is no shame in updating.

By contrast, some writers (e.g. Banks, 1978), throw in their lot, not

with the work of Durkheim but with that of Max Weber. Weber was pre-
occupied with questions of power and stratification on the one hand, and
with questions of meaning and understanding on the other. The possibilities for applying some of the connections made between these issues to
the sociology of education are immense. However, given the attention
which Weber gave to the concept of *verstehen* (which referred to the complex processes of interpretative understanding) and to the concept of
*value relevance* (which enjoined sociologists to begin all their investigations by first studying the values held by their subjects and themselves), it
seems a pity that the full potential of his work has hardly been exploited
within the sociology of education. In so far as Weber's work has been
used in any systematic way, it has been applied only in studies of the
history of education.[7] As regards the wider implications of his work, all
that is available is a suggestive essay by Alan Dawe (1971) who argues
that a study of the organisation, structure and process of schooling should
commence with an analysis of the values of its members.[8]

Weber's studies of *verstehen* and *value-relevance* were never isolated
and were at all times integrated with his broader investigations of, say, the
relationship between *the Protestant Ethic and the Spirit of Capitalism*. For
him, the connection between interpersonal interaction and broader social
structures and historical processes was always remarkably explicit.

Although I myself would not adhere to a Weberian model of the social
structure (largely because of the excessive weight he gives to the importance of status groups as, in principle, separate from social class groupings
in society),[9] it is my belief that had British classroom research taken up
some of the suggestive integrating themes of Weberian action theory, then
the classroom might not have come to be depicted as such an isolated and
autonomous realm as it has often been. Any Weberian influence in classroom research has been second hand and has come largely via the work
of the phenomenologist Alfred Schutz who, in his critique of Weber
(Schutz, 1967), deepened the understanding of action and of problems
of interpretation but at the expense of neglecting Weber's equally important concerns of power, authority and stratification. Thus, while Schutz's
development of Weber has led to caution and sophistication in the interpretation of classroom processes, it has also directed attention away from
the influence of social and educational structures upon those processes. It
would seem, then, that there is a case for reconsidering the arguments and
theoretical framework of Weber alongside the developments of his work by
others.

A return to the venerated traditions of classical sociology is hardly
futile, then, so long as it is remembered that in themselves they cannot

provide theoretically sufficient and methodologically rigorous explanations of the relations between classroom processes and social structure. Truly, as C. Wright Mills recognised, the characteristic stamp of classical sociology is its very potential for connecting what he calls 'the personal troubles of milieux' to the 'public issues of social structure', but in this worthy enterprise, Mills displays the same leanings towards the macro-structural end of the spectrum as many of his eminent predecessors. This leads to assumptions about rather than detailed empirical inquiry into the experiential network of daily life which is presumed to be the product of such structures. The call for synthesis, for explanation of no less than the social totality, therefore, is not a new one and has been an integral part of much that is best in sociological investigation, even if the theoretical outcomes have usually been a little 'top heavy'. Where the controversy remains is in the choice of a dominant model (Marxist? Weberian? Durkheimian?) in terms of which this is to be achieved, and in the specification of the detailed mechanisms by which the different levels can be connected.[10] This latter requires the integration of 'classical' frameworks, where relevant, with more recent theoretical and methodological developments.

## 3. *Splendid Isolation*

Those who hold to this solution concede that it is necessary to connect the micro-processes of classroom and staffroom interaction to the social, economic and political relations within the wider society which shape and constrain the pattern of classroom events. But in so doing, they delegate this responsibility to other researchers. For them, the working out of a synthesis is someone else's job. It need not be their concern, given the specialised and complex division of labour that is available in academic research.[11] Thus, they do not *reject* alternative forms of theorising, but merely isolate themselves from it. This is a common practice in the sociology of education, even if it is rarely made explicit. More usually, there is an insinuation rather than a strong statement of disinterest. For example, some investigators make claims that they are interested in the *hows* rather than the *whys* of classroom life (D. Hargreaves, *et al.*, 1976; Pollard, 1979). A more overt stance has instead been taken by those interactionist and phenomenological sociologists from whom many educational researchers have subsequently received their inspiration. For instance, the phenomenologist Alfred Schutz, whose work has been held in high esteem by many classroom researchers, stated quite categorically that phenomenology and other modes of social scientific enquiry were complementary, although he stressed his own exclusive concern with the former. In his own words:

> the results of phenomenological research cannot and must not clash
> with the tested results of the mundane sciences, or even with the
> proved doctrines of so-called philosophies of the sciences . . . phen-
> omenology has its field of research in its own right and hopes to end
> where the others begin (Schutz, 1973, p. 115).

Another key figure for many classroom researchers, Erving Goffman
(1975), outlines a similar position which he puts with his usual panache
and feel for the controversial. He begins with a confession:

> I am not addressing the structure of social life but the structure of
> experience individuals have at any moment of their social lives. I per-
> sonally hold society to be first in every way and any individual's cur-
> rent involvements to be second: this report deals only with matters
> that are second. (p. 13)

In response to the anticipated criticism that focusing upon the nature of
personal experience alone has conservative implications, Goffman
expands a commonly used metaphor.

> The analysis developed does not catch at the differences between the
> advantaged and disadvantaged classes and can be said to direct
> attention away from such matters. I think that is true. I can only sug-
> gest that he who would combat false consciousness and awaken
> people to their true interests has much to do, because the sleep is
> very deep. And I do not intend here to provide a lullaby but merely
> to sneak in and watch the way the people snore. (p. 14)

Disarming statements of the kind which Schutz and Goffman make, offer
a proclamation of academic humility along with a recognition of the
worth and honest endeavour of other men's work, but they also mislead
the reader into accepting two rather dubious assumptions: that the
analysis of interaction and personal experience is a legitimately
autonomous area of investigation; and that the constitution of interpersonal interaction and the formal properties of commonsense knowledge are unaffected by wider social and political structures. This is not
a case which has been argued explicitly. But the assumptions *are* present
and can be seen in some of the detail of phenomenological and interactionist work. Two rather brief examples must suffice.

1. An important component of Schutz's phenomenology is his theory of commonsense knowledge and the formal properties it contains. One significant part of his argument is that commonsense knowledge is inherently contradictory. Thus, as one critic of Sharp and Green's (1975) work has pointed out, it is not particularly startling, but only natural that teachers' accounts are often confused and contradictory.[12] Standing in stark contrast to this viewpoint is the theoretical position of the Marxist Antonio Gramsci (1971). A central component of his analysis is that the contradictory character of commonsense thought is a product of what is often itself a contradictory relationship between two specific factors: (1) the way in which hierarchical relations of dominance and subordinacy in capitalist societies are ideologically expressed (through the media, etc.) on the one hand; and (2) people's everyday experience of those relations on the other (which is often discrepant with the range of accounts available in the dominant ideology). Thus, as two researchers into work experience in a chemical factory have noted, it is possible for workers to condemn strikes as communist-inspired in one breath (a view commonly purveyed through the media) whilst berating their own shop stewards for not being militant enough or prepared to go on strike, in the next (Nichols and Benyon, 1977). For Gramsci, such fragmentation in commonsense thought is not universal, but is a pathological feature of life within the social, economic and political relations of capitalist societies, and is also a reason why those relations are sustained. For him, such ways of thinking can be remedied through the politicisation of everyday consciousness which would be made possible by the production of a set of intellectuals organically connected to the interests of the working class. By contrast, for Schutz, there is no remedy.

I am not suggesting that *all* fragmented commonsense thinking is politically determined in this way, though I think there is a strong case for arguing that much of it is. However, the converse, that commonsense thinking is *naturally* contradictory seems an overstatement which has conservative implications. Whilst it might be true that some fragmentation is an inevitable feature of commonsense thought, there needs to be some consideration given to other cultures, both actual and possible where political awareness is/would be a consistent part of everyday thinking and where social theory and political practice are/would be an integral part of everyday life. Such considerations might lead not only to a redefinition of the formal properties of commonsense thinking on very different lines than those Schutz laid out but might also produce a substantial modification of how we define 'commonsense' in the first place.

2. A second example of the effect of macro-assumptions upon micro-

theory is that of the relationship between accounts and their social context (Scott and Lyman, 1968; Keddie, 1971; Esland, 1971). This view has been well summarised by David Hargreaves (1978).

> . . . phenomenologists . . . would *assume* as a central tenet of their perspective that . . . accounts given in different contexts (e.g. classroom versus staffrooms) or to different audiences (e.g. teachers, headteachers, parents, researchers) would naturally tend to vary by such situations and audiences (p. 14)

Now while it may be true that, empirically speaking, teacher accounts *do* vary, there is a need for greater caution when any claims are made about the *naturalness* of such variation. Although *some* variation in accounts might always be expected (especially in terms of the amount of detail offered) because of the division of responsibilities amongst school-related personnel, many substantive discrepancies in accounts may also arise because of the hierarchical nature of schooling and the control of information and knowledge within such a hierarchy. Many differences in accounts could probably be removed if control of and participation in schooling were organised on more thoroughly democratic principles.[13] When what teachers say to other teachers differs from what they say to parents, or headmasters, or researchers, for example, this is not a phenomenon which should be taken as 'natural' but one which might well be regarded as being specific to a particular kind of society at a particular time and as reflecting the distribution of power amongst those who are concerned with schools in this society. Once again, assumptions about what is 'natural' in the organisation and control of social institutions, appear to have intruded into assessments of what are presumed to be 'naturally' occurring features of everyday interaction.

My point should now be clear. The central strategy of the sociological imagination is 'synthesis'. The articulation of connections between the interpersonal relations of classroom life, and the structural properties of the wider society should be the defining characteristic of the research enterprise in the sociology of education. Such a task should not be regarded as the separate preserve of any one particular mode of sociological investigation but should instead be the focal concern of the sociological imagination itself. The making explicit of the manifold connections between various levels of analysis cannot be passed across to any other interested parties. It should *never* be someone else's job. This is because such connections are already unavoidably present but usually hidden, implicit and taken-for-granted in forms of theorising which appear to operate at one level only. For example, I have tried to show that some forms of interpretive theory imply a view of the social structure as organised on democratic, pluralistic principles. By this, unlike some commentators (Sharp and Green, 1975; Sarup, 1978), I do not mean that all groups are necessarily regarded as having equal weight in the negotiation and bargaining processes of political or classroom decision-making. Rather, the view that is usually held appears to be one where bargaining and conflict amongst a diverse range of groups characterises the organisation of society and its institutions—even if the power resources are distributed rather unevenly in that process.[14]

At the opposite pole, macro-theories which posit a strong relationship between society and schooling involve all kinds of assumptions which remain largely unsubstantiated by empirical evidence. There is little use, then, in operating only at one level of explanation, for such insular activity will always be contaminated by the unavoidable, if unwanted intrusions of various other levels (although here the intrusions will be of unclarified assumptions rather than carefully worked-out theory).[15]

The time is now ripe for all sociologists of education, either individually or in collective teams, to accept the central defining principle of their calling and to employ the full power and scope of the sociological imagination in understanding the complex processes of the educational system. If this principle is accepted, the real area of controversy that remains involves assessing competing views about the precise form that any synthesis would take. Most especially, any synthesis should address itself to questions regarding the functions, both intended and unintended, which schooling is seen to serve for a particular structure of society as a capitalist/advanced industrial one. These matters are ones which I shall now consider.

## Part II Schooling and Society: Some Competing Models

Within both Marxism and interactionism, some steps have already been taken into what can only be regarded as a potentially explosive area of investigation. From one side, theorists of class reproduction have become increasingly concerned with the extent to which schools actually do reproduce the structure of societal relations. Taking the different theories together, however, what remains unresolved between them is the degree of directness or indirectness of the reproductive process on the one hand, and the extent to which class reproduction is achieved 'efficiently' or not, on the other.

From the other side, interactionists have attempted to locate the origins of classroom constraints and to consider the mediating mechanisms by which they exert their effects. Here, any inadequacy in the understanding of the school-society relation has stemmed from a general reluctance to move beyond the school and its immediate environment when identifying the sources of these constraints. In short, the level of dependence of schooling upon society, together with the inadequacy of empirical proof regarding such dependence and its effects upon the interactive process, are coming to be taken as central problems in the sociology of education. I shall now consider what I take to be three general models, each of which offers a different explanation of the sort of connection which obtains between schooling and society, and hence of the determinations of classroom practice.

## 1. *Direct Reproduction Model*

In straightforward economic terms, there have been repeated attempts to implement reforms on the premise that the products of schooling are the raw materials of industrial prosperity. The necessity for schools to produce industrial workers with the requisite skills for an expanding and competitive capitalist economy has been stressed and acted upon ever since the 1870 Education Act. From there, through Fisher's 1918 Education Act, to the influential post-war reports of Crowther, Newsom and Robbins and right up to the startlingly explicit policy initiatives of James Callaghan and Shirley Williams (when 'recession', not 'expansion' became the overriding problem), the close linking of schooling to the levels and types of skill regarded as essential to the British capitalist economy at each particular stage of its development, has been a central theme in the official politics of education. Very similar links have also been made between the experience and curriculum of schooling on the one hand, and the future political stability of the nation on the other. Here the central theme has been one of education as a preparation for responsible political behaviour which would fall within the range of legitimate alternatives available in Western social democracies. Not only did Forster recognise and attempt to control this vital connection in his 1870 Act by extending mass education in anticipation of further extensions of the franchise, but the very same theme of political education as the antidote to 'extremism' has emerged much more recently, in discussions about the teaching of politics in schools (Tapper and Salter, 1978).

At this level of debate, although the connection between schooling and society is apprehended, it is not grasped with any great subtlety. Even where the link is conceptualised in negative terms, as for example in the Black Paper writers' view that progressive education produces 'a generation unable to maintain our standards of living when opposed by fierce rivalry from overseas competitors', it is nonetheless brutally direct (Cox and Boyson, 1976, p. 1). The failure of the economy is rooted in the failure of schooling.

Such straightforward and arguably crude connections have also been expressed in various kinds of educational theorising. For instance, functionalist explanations hinge upon the central point that schools select and socialise pupils for their adult roles in society. The school is viewed as a social system; a society in microcosm with its own network of roles and expectations, which allocates the pupil to and prepares him for his future place in society (Parsons, 1959). Consequently, it is argued, the school serves a useful function in serving the 'needs' of advanced industrial society. On the whole, this process is seen as a smooth and harmonious one and is regarded as being beneficial for both individual and society.

By contrast, whilst accepting that there is a general correspondence of schooling to society in that schools serve a preparatory function in maintaining societal stability, some Marxist explanations place a very different evaluation on that process. In such explanations, the interest lies not in how schooling reproduces society *in general*, but in how it reproduces a particular kind of society based upon hierarchical class relations, i.e. a capitalist society. I shall deal with two of the most prominent and influential examples of such Marxist work.

The first is an essay written by Louis Althusser (1971) which has been a source of inspiration for many other sociologists of education of a Marxist persuasion. Althusser argues that schooling, in capitalist society, is a salient means by which the existing relations between dominant and subordinate classes are perpetuated. In other words, in Althusser's terms, education *reproduces* the social relations of production (the relations of exploitation in economic, social and political life). As a consciousness-forming institution, an institution which is the prime repository of ruling-class ideology, schooling has a socially and politically soporific effect on the young, instilling in them an appropriate set of attitudes such that, as adults, they will have a quiescent response to a society based upon an exploitative set of class relations. To recapture Goffman's phrase, it would seem that for Althusser, the sleep is indeed very deep. Althusser states quite clearly that the process of schooling is 'ideologically' determined. He writes, that in addition to learning 'know how', for example:

> children at school also learn the 'rules' of good behaviour i.e. the attitude that should be observed by every agent in the division of labour, according to the job he is 'destined' for: rules of morality,

civic and professional conscience, which actually means rule of respect for the socio-technical division of labour and ultimately the
rules of the order established by class domination. They also learn
to 'speak proper French', to 'handle' the workers correctly . . .

In other words, there is a

reproduction of a submission to the ruling ideology for the workers,
and a reproduction of the ability to manipulate the ruling ideology
correctly for the agents of exploitation and repression. (p. 245)

Now there are many problems with Althusser's model, but two are of
particular relevance to this paper. Firstly, his account of the school-
society relation is a strongly deterministic one. It is true that, at points,
he makes concessions to the notion of 'relative autonomy', but these
are little more than parenthetic qualifications. Such considerations are
also concerned much more with the relative autonomy of the ideological superstructure as a whole from the underlying economic base,
than with that of schooling *per se* from the wider structure of social and
economic relations. For the most part, Althusser's explanation has a
markedly deterministic flavour about it. Teachers are cast in the passive
role of helpless agents of state repression (Erben and Gleeson, 1977), and
there is a clear implication that pupils also respond to the experience of
schooling in a uniformly submissive way. Their particular and varied
strategies from different brands of conformism to modes of rebellion
are given no space in Althusser's discussion. Yet, it is not at all clear why
teachers or indeed pupils act in the way they do, what the immediate,
concrete factors are which influence teacher and pupil behaviour, nor
how these are tied up with the class reproduction function of schooling.
In the case of teachers, there is no explanation of the contradictions and
dilemmas which they must try to resolve, of the particular ways in which
these contradictions are institutionally mediated, or of the historical
roots of the assumptions on which they base their responses to such
constraints. Teachers are treated as if they are simply cyphers; mere
bearers of 'the system'.

On the receiving end of this 'system' are the pupils. Their individual
and collective cultural responses to and reworkings of the concrete and
recurring situations they encounter are not acknowledged. This leads me
to the second criticism; that in Althusser's account, the process of class
reproduction in education is achieved almost effortlessly and without substantial resistance. Indeed it is the absence of any central concern for

'conflict' along with the convoluted language and high level of generality at which his theorising is pitched, that has invited comparison with functionalist forms of explanation.[16] Althusser ignores the fact that schools do not only generate passive acquiescence in their pupils, but also resistance and rebellion. Schools do not only reproduce class relations in general, but also the specifically conflictual aspects of those relations (Corrigan and Frith, 1977). Only a detailed ethnographically rich analysis, like that carried out by Willis (1977), will have the potential to reveal that classrooms are often saturated with conflict; that there is much less unquestioning acceptance of authority systems than Althusser suggests. Schools reproduce conflict as well as conformity even if these are only different ways of working out an otherwise unchanged set of class relations based upon dominance and subordination. Yet even here, whilst it is hardly the case that schools are the seedbed of the proletarian revolution they still produce insolence and indolence in the future workforce just as much as they generate consensus and conformity.

Understandings such as these have no place in Althusser's theoretical machine which steam-rollers along, flattening all reality in its path. There are no methodological checks in his highly structuralist account; no observations of the everyday routines of schooling. This does not prevent him, however, from making rather sweeping statements about the schooling process — the extract cited earlier is just one example of this. In short, Althusser's theoretical model, though remarkably insightful in places, is nonetheless deterministic, lacking in empirical verification and blind to the importance of conflict and change.

Even where attempts *have* been made by other researchers to provide some kind of empirical support for the Althusserian position, the data seems to have been chiselled away rather heavily at the edges to get it to fit the model. For example, in David's (1978) study of the part played by middle-class mothers in the William Tyndale dispute, the claim is made that the mothers 'felt threatened because their children did not seem to be acquiring either skills or know-how about the established order' (p. 190), yet none of the documented evidence that David provides shows that the mothers consciously apprehended the situation in quite these terms. The spurious imputation of 'intentions' in this way is insupportable. There is a need for much greater sensitivity than this when attempting to grasp the interrelations between case study data and individual consciousnesses on the one hand, and abstract theories and social structures on the other. It may well be that the inflexibility of the Althusserian model makes it and its adherents impervious to the insights which might otherwise be gained from carefully conducted case study work.

Criticisms of a similar order have been levelled at the widely dissem-
inated work of Bowles and Gintis (1976). These authors assert, almost
without equivocation, that there is a direct correspondence between
the social relations of production and schooling. While Bowles and Gintis
share with Althusser a fundamental interest in schools as consciousness-
forming institutions, unlike him, they see consciousness as being shaped
*directly* for the requirements of an expanding and changing capitalist
economy. They tend therefore to avoid developing other important concerns which Althusser took into account and indeed made the nub of
his thesis. These include the ideological role of schooling, the relationship of schooling to the state and the position and role of the state within the capitalist mode of production. Instead, Bowles and Gintis see
schools as reproducing, in microcosm, the social relations of the capitalist mode of production. In their own words, there is 'a structural correspondence between its social relations and those of production' (p.
131). Running through their work is a strong thread of certainty about
the tightness of this correspondence even if, from time to time, a few
cautionary disclaimers are inserted. Relations between the various participants in schooling 'replicate the hierarchical division of labour' (p. 131).
The organisation of the curriculum gives the student a preparatory
experience of alienated labour and of the fragmented character of work
in capitalist society. In general, 'by attuning young people to a set of
social relationships similar to those of the work place, schooling attempts
to gear the development of personal needs to its requirements' (p. 131).
Consequently, pupils are prepared not only for the experience of work
in general, but also for the specific form of work relations which apper-
tain to the occupational niche for which they have been selected and
are destined.

The analysis offered by Bowles and Gintis is a stunningly effective
and rather sharp corrective to the accounts of schooling which manifest-
ly set it up as an insulated and autonomous process and which suspend
judgement on the constraints exerted by the wider society.[17] It provides
a reassessment of what schooling achieves within society, but in doing
this, a great deal of subtlety and caution is sacrificed in the process.
Bowles and Gintis's model is hardly any less deterministic than
Althusser's and, as Banks (1978) suggests, quite clearly demands more
empirical verification than they are able to provide.[18] I will cite just one
example to illustrate my point. This refers to Bowles and Gintis's suggestive but as yet unproven assertion that as students '"master" one type of
behavioural regulation, they are either allowed to progress to the next
or are channelled into the corresponding level in the hierarchy of

production' (p. 132). Specifically, they argue that

> vocational and general tracks emphasize rule following and close
> supervision (as in the lowest levels of the hierarchy of the enter-
> prise).

Many investigators of British secondary modern schools who have exposed their incipient militarism in patterns of discipline and authority would
attest that this is true. But what is glossed over here is the extent to
which pupils conform or do not conform to an intendedly rule-following regime. Basil Bernstein (1977), for example, is in strong disagreement
with Bowles and Gintis when he suggests that

> The school in this respect is highly inefficient in creating a docile, def-
> erential and subservient work force. The school today has difficulty
> disciplining its pupils (p. 181).

His grounds for disagreement reside in his observation of a disparity
rather than a correspondence between the structure of the 'less able'
student's school experience and the structure of his future experience
as a manual worker. He notes that where, as in some 'progressive' ROSLA
programmes, an integrated code has been introduced, characterised by
less formal teacher-pupil relationships and some blurring of curriculum
boundaries, this creates an unconformity with the organisation of production in British capitalist society. Thus, at least for some of the lower
strata in British society, there will be the precise opposite of a correspondence between the social relations of schooling and production.

A second, possibly more significant point, is that even where rule following *is* emphasised in schools this may induce hostility rather than passive acceptance. As Bernstein (1977) has again recognised, the school
may 'indirectly and unwittingly' equip the future worker not so much
with 'right attitudes' but with a range of countervailing strategies extending from avoidance techniques through to forms of sabotage.

Paul Willis (1977) supplies what can be construed as empirically
grounded support for Bernstein's hypothesis in his study of twelve 'D'
stream 'lads' at Hammertown secondary school. These 'lads' responded
complexly to their educational and labouring environments, but the very
last label that could justifiably be pinned upon them would be 'passive'.
If anything, this pejorative would apply much more to the CSE 'ear'oles'
whom the 'lads' despised intensely. The 'lads' rarely displayed any leanings towards acceptance of the school's official order. More usually they

showed hostility and resentment in a succession of attempts to wrest control of the work process away from their pedagogical masters. There were correspondences, it is true, between school and work, but these were of a very different order than the ones suggested by Bowles and Gintis. The correspondences, in fact, occurred at the level of the informal; a world of 'mucking about' and 'having a laugh'; of practical jokes, sabotage, Paki-baiting and sexist ribaldry. This world had been carved roughly but creatively out of the tough environments which the 'lads' faced in both school and work. It was the attraction to and elaboration of this rugged 'informal' world which brought about an active opting for low-grade manual labour because of its correspondingly informal reward of 'being with your mates'. Strategic responses to institutional constraints and authoritarian relations therefore led to a stepping into and perpetuation of very similar relations on the shop floor, but through a process which was complex, mediated and uneven in its effects. To the extent that Willis's findings stand up to critical scrutiny, they should lead us to modify, though not reject, the correspondence principle advanced by Bowles and Gintis. It is sensitive observation and interpretation of classroom life that necessitates such a change.

A third relevant consideration when evaluating Bowles and Gintis's hypothesis about vocational tracks, is that if lower ranks are subjected to rule-following regimes, their response is by no means homogeneous. Peter Woods's (1979) account of secondary modern school pupils, for example, highlights a range of strategies from outright rebellion through to colonisation and indulgence in ritual and Hammersley and Turner (1980) identify similar variations in the responses of pupils who are conventionally lumped together as being simply 'conformist'. This diversity of response can again only be revealed by careful ethnographic study and must serve to modify considerably the notion of a direct, homogeneous correspondence between levels of schooling and levels of production.

It would be possible to offer further contrasts between ethnographic investigations and Bowles and Gintis's hypotheses. For example, readers may wish to examine Bowles and Gintis's claim that universities are characterised by 'a more open atmosphere' in the light of the case study work of Miller and Parlett (1976). Or they could compare Bowles and Gintis's claim that 'teachers and community colleges allow for more independent activity and less overall supervision', with the findings of the few studies available on (at least British) colleges of education (e.g. Bartholomew, 1976) which suggest that the notion of student autonomy, responsibility and so forth is one that exists at the level of ideology and within the theories which students appropriate, rather than at the level of their everyday practical experience. The everyday running of the college is quite frequently characterised by the saturation of students' time with face-to-face contact with tutors (thus reducing the time available for independent thinking), by the imposition of heavy workloads, by the close evaluation and grading of students' work, by careful monitoring of 'professional' conduct in schools, etc. Of course, a correspondence could still be claimed if Bellaby's (1977) assertion was accepted that universities create the generals of society who give the orders, and colleges train the lieutenants who learn to carry them out. But this thesis too demands substantiation through investigation of the structure and organisation of students' experience in college environments. In short, there may or may not be various kinds of correspondence obtaining between different levels of schooling and production. If there are, some consideration for the actual processes that go on inside educational institutions and indeed inside the work place would almost certainly lead to a substantial modification of the way in which these correspondences have been conceived—and of notions that have been held about the directness of their operation. Since Bowles and Gintis fail to grapple with individual consciousness first-hand, their account of the consciousness-forming process and the ways in which this serves the needs of capitalist relations of production often does not extend beyond the realm of the plausible. The insights of interactionism and case study work are thus begging for inclusion here.

## 2. *Relative Autonomy Model*

A sizeable cluster of Marxist writers have advanced a thesis which in many ways stands in direct opposition to the correspondence principle put forward by Bowles and Gintis. For these writers, schooling (like other parts of the superstructure) is relatively autonomous from the sphere of production. When and where correspondences do occur in significant proportions, this is not normal or usual but quite an exceptional and important occurrence. When two relatively autonomous spheres coalesce, challenging and complex explanations are called for. The central point of relative autonomy is not that it marks the severing of any connection whatsoever between schooling and production—this comprises a very different position which I shall examine shortly—but that any such connection is indirect, mediated and complex. The compelling task is to discover just why it is the case that, in Stuart Hall's (1977) words: 'In the superstructures, society reproduces the relations of production *outside* production *for* production.' (p. 37) Entry into this rather dense area delineated by the concept of 'relative autonomy' is perhaps best made through the penetrating, if sometimes almost impenetrable work of Basil Bernstein (1977).

Bernstein discusses two kinds of relation between education and production. These are *systemic* relationships and relationships of *classification*. Systemic relationships refer to the parallels, *whatever their cause*, between education and production. In so far as there is any correspondence between the distribution of pupils and the distribution of worker roles, between hierarchical relations in schooling and hierarchical relations required by the mode of production, and between skills and dispositions produced by the school and those required by the mode of production, this correspondence is always uneven and approximate. It is a tendency that is rarely fully actualised. Thus

> there are parallels (approximate correspondences) between the controls on the context of production and controls on the context of acquisition in education. These parallels in structures and contexts indicate the approximate or *relative correspondence* between education and production (p. 186).

Lest the point should be missed, Bernstein goes on to stress that

> only a small fraction of the output of education bears a *direct* relation to the mode of production in terms of the appropriateness of skill and disposition (p. 186).

Contrasting with the systemic relationships which indicate the degree of dependence of education upon production, Bernstein notes that the relative autonomy of education is signified instead by the extent to which it is actively and consciously integrated with production. Thus, in societies like Cuba and China where schooling and production are not totally isolated from one another, where they are not arranged in a neat sequence but where they interpenetrate and overlap, the two spheres are closely integrated; that is there is a low degree of relative autonomy between them. In capitalist societies, however, there is a strong classification between education and production. The two spheres are separate and only rarely interpenetrate in the living experience of those who inhabit them. Moreover, one might add that the looser role of the state as a co-ordinator of education and economic policy in capitalist societies, as opposed to, say, Soviet society, tends to enhance the separateness of the two realms. Strong classification, therefore, does not just indicate but actually *defines*, in Bernstein's terms, a marked degree of relative autonomy between education and production.

This creates a conundrum. On the one hand, there is an uneven tendency towards a correspondence between various aspects of education and various aspects of production. On the other, there is no definite economic determination of education by production, for the two spheres are, in capitalist societies, relatively autonomous:

> In this situation, the principles, contexts and possibilities of production are not directly constituted in the principles, contexts and possibilities of education. Education, that is, is not directly in rapport with a material base, although it is affected by such a base (pp. 189-90).

And yet, for all that, education still reproduces the social relations of production, though Bernstein is somewhat less emphatic about the tightness of this ultimate relation than is Althusser. Despite a relative autonomy between the structures and contexts of education and production, the reproductive work still gets done. How? Unfortunately, Bernstein does not really address this question.

An answer given by Bourdieu and Passeron (1977) is that it is precisely *because* of the relative autonomy of education from production that the reproduction of the social relations of production is secured. For them this *apparent* autonomy is significant ideologically, since it enables the reproduction of power relations (of the social relations of production) to be 'misrecognised'. This masking effect created by relative autonomy, transforms power relations into legitimate authority. Similarly, what Bourdieu and Passeron call 'the imposition of a cultural arbitrary' (i.e. of the culture of the dominant classes) upon pupils, becomes conventionally regarded as universally valid culture. The very relative autonomy of education from production thus brings about a pervasive and commonly accepted view of pedagogic action, work and authority as neutral and as unrelated to the interests of any particular class. Yet, the authors argue, underlying this apparent autonomy, the transmission of a 'cultural arbitrary' (i.e. of dominant culture) tends to produce in pupils a 'habitus' (what might be called a general pattern of conceiving, perceiving and believing) which is concordant with the dominant culture and its perpetuation. In their own rather difficult words, this habitus is the constellation of 'principle generating practices which reproduce the objective structures' (pp. 32-3). Relative autonomy, for Bourdieu, thus enables various ideological translations to occur; for murky realities to be transformed into glossy appearances. Through this process, dominant culture becomes simply culture in general, social gifts are translated into 'natural' gifts and cultural capital (the possession of linguistic and cultural characteristics that accord with those of the dominant class) becomes scholastic capital (seemingly neutral cognitive skills, abilities and qualifications). In short, a society based on class reproduction is instead conventionally regarded as being founded upon fair, meritocratic principles.

Paradoxically, then, since relative autonomy, in the normal run of events so successfully reproduces the social relations of production, its breakdown, signalled by the falling into line of the structures and processes of both education and production, i.e. by a correspondence between the two structures, anticipates much wider social, economic and political ruptures. Correspondence, that is, is the symptom of crisis (Finn, Grant and Johnson, 1977). Such crises are, to use a concept popularised by Althusser (1969), *overdetermined*. They are the product of 'multiple forces, rather than the isolated forces of modes or techniques of production [which are] ... structured in particular historical situations' (Williams, 1978, p. 88).[19] Under this view, then, correspondence points to the impending collapse rather than the harmonious continuation of the reproductive process, since it lays bare the connections between education and production which, in their specifically capitalistic form, had previously gone unnoticed. The Great Debate, the William Tyndale dispute and the general crisis in education have all been identified as instancing such a collapse (Finn, Grant and Johnson, 1977; Hall, 1977).

The point of view of 'relative autonomy' has much to commend it as an explanation of the relationship between schooling and society. It highlights the fact that the reproductive process is extremely complex and that it is achieved in indirect ways. It gives due weight to the question of events having *multiple* causes while recognising that this is very different from such events being *randomly* caused. There is something here for both the pessimist and the optimist. The pessimist can note Bourdieu's point that the very relative autonomy of schooling makes it all the more effective as an agency of reproduction because of the ostensibly neutral status which is conferred upon it. The optimist, meanwhile, can take heart in the view that because superstructural elements do not always directly reflect or actively service the economic base, it is always possible for radical groups to flourish, expand and exert their influence in the schooling system. Thus relative autonomy allows, in principle, for the possibility of radical social change (Whitty and Young, 1976). There is a potential, but no more than a potential openness here to historical and ethnographic investigation which might begin to uncover some of the concrete and historically variant determinations of patterns of schooling whilst locating these within the limits and constraints set by an enveloping class structure. Some purists would be dismissive of any such exercise and would not condone a 'theoretical practice' which, they felt, sank into mere eclecticism and historicism (Althusser, 1969), but theories always have a value beyond the intentions of their authors, and this should be exploited where further understanding might be gained as a result.

It is at this point where 'proof' is required and empirical verification is called for, that theories organised around the notion of relative autonomy become highly problematic. Most especially, as they stand, they have difficulty in establishing just *how* schooling and production have come to be relatively (as opposed to completely) autonomous; or in showing just *how*, despite or even because of this relative autonomy, schools come to serve the function of reproducing the social relations of production. Relative autonomy theories have been characterised by profound ambiguity, largely because explanations have been framed at the level of dense and abstract 'structural' theory. For this reason, there has been something of a mystique about the notion of relative autonomy and theories elaborated around it; a mystique which is extremely hard to penetrate.

There is considerable uncertainty, for example, as to who are the significant agents who maintain this system of clearly 'functional' autonomy, and as to how and why they are constrained or habituated to act in ways which tacitly and unintendedly lead to a perpetuation of the reproductive process.

At their most formal, the categories and concepts used in explanations resting upon the principle of 'relative autonomy', seem to take on a life of their own and even to cause one another. Althusser's general work is particularly open to this charge (Kolokowski, 1971). Basil Bernstein (1977), not uncharacteristically, also tends to commit this error from time to time. To give just one example:

> the systemic relationships between education and production constitute both the class and the material basis of education. In as much as this is the case, this relation indicates the dependency of education upon the mode of production (pp. 186-7).

This is pure tautology—a device which commentators have noticed before in Bernstein's work (Gibson, 1977).

Statements of this kind—and there are many of them—are simply true by definition. They cannot, in themselves, clarify just how far and under what concrete circumstances, schooling *is* dependent upon the mode of

production. Such abstract theorising where criteria of validity are generally internal to the model itself, often throws up statements and conclusions which fly in the face of experienced reality. For example,
Bourdieu and Passeron's (1977) thesis that the social relations of production are reproduced through the acquisition of a particular 'habitus' in
family and school appears to conform fairly closely to versions of a
rather simplistic 'dominant ideology' thesis which has quite rightly been
repudiated by several writers (e.g. Abercrombie and Turner, 1978; Tapper
and Salter, 1978). These critics argue that the transmission and smooth
assimilation of dominant ideology (in both content and form) has been
articulated far too neatly in much Marxist theorising. If anyone is taken
in by such ideology, they argue, it is only the members of the dominant
groups themselves. For the remaining majority, as Gramsci (1971) clearly
recognised, subjection to the dominant ideology or, in his terms, to the
dominant hegemony (a much more subtle and widely encompassing concept), produces not a homogeneity of world views, but a fragmentation
of commonsense thought. This is because the received range of ideas
that is available within the society is always combined with the half-
articulate consciousness derived from the experience of the everyday
world and one's place within it. Consequently, in the rather general and
formal manner in which it has often been couched, the relative autonomy
thesis, though somewhat subtler than the correspondence principle, nevertheless tends to gloss over and mystify many of the complexities of commonsense thinking and everyday experience.

Paul Willis (1977) has made an exciting attempt to ground the relative
autonomy thesis in a study of how working-class 'lads' are prepared for
the social relations of the shop floor. He notes that the relations which
they experience in the 'D' stream, relations which in many ways parallel those of the workplace, do not, by and large, occur within what he
calls a 'class paradigm', where their own behaviour or the teachers' reaction
to it, is a direct outcome of their class membership. 'Class' is not the
explicit context within which patterns of teacher-pupil interaction and
authority relations are framed. Instead, such patterns emerge, Willis
argues, within a separate 'educational paradigm' where most of the issues
are pertinent to the orderly running of the school and management of
the classroom, rather than to the more general questions of social class
control. These relations have class consequences, of course. They are a
crucial mechanism through which working-class kids actually come to
choose working-class jobs. This is a process that Willis has demonstrated
very ably. What he fails to elucidate however, are the reasons why the relations formed within an 'educational paradigm' serve reproductive

functions; why the parallels exist at all. It is at this point that Willis's account dissolves into a foggy rhetoric. We are told little more than that there is an 'articulation' of, or 'cross-valorisation' between the two structures. This is not very helpful.

Part of his failure to explain just why the 'educational paradigm' is structured in a parallel way to the 'class paradigm' may be rooted in the simple fact that his study is one of pupils rather than teachers. This is, perhaps, an illustration of why the study of pupil strategies, in isolation, is, in certain respects, insufficient if questions about class reproduction are to be tackled in a credible way. Thus, in Willis's account, there are no data available that would enable an assessment to be made of why teachers behave in the way they do, why they develop certain teaching strategies rather than others, what the constraints are which these strategies help resolve, and from where these constraints originate. That is, the most demanding question concerns how such parallels emerge and how they persist. Three of the simplest possible explanations seem implausible. 1) The parallels between the two structures (of education and production) are not the product of sheer ignorance, of teachers being the helpless carriers of dominant ideology — this was rejected in the discussions of Althusser and Bowles and Gintis. 2) Nor are the parallels the outcome of a conscious manipulation of bourgeois ideology on the part of teachers and other significant participants in the educational enterprise — this has been neatly refuted by Willis. 3) And the third possible reason for the existence of the parallels, that of mere chance, is not only wholly unsociological, but would also not be sufficient to account for the persistence of such parallels, even if it could explain their origin. Something more complex is needed, but which, in achieving subtlety, does not also degenerate into the misty verbiage of 'relative autonomy' theories as they have been presented so far.

I wish to suggest that if we want to know how it is that teachers can, within a relatively autonomous institution, engineer, enact and perpetuate a set of relations which are ultimately functional for reproducing the social relations of production, we need:

1. Studies of the dimensions of and variations in the commonsense thinking of teachers; of the assumptions which underlie not only their actions but also their accounts of such actions; of the historical and experiential origins of those assumptions.
2. Studies of the constraints which teachers experience; like class sizes, school buildings, shortage of materials, the incompatible goals of schooling (of discovery versus direction for example), and current

definitions of desirable educational practice held by influential personnel like headteachers and advisers. What would also be required here are studies of the extent to which the election of particular strategies and the construction of appropriate repertoires of strategies are based upon the assumptions mentioned in 1, and of the extent to which they bring about modifications of those assumptions.

3. Studies of the constraints which teachers have faced *in the past* and the strategies which they *then* developed to cope with these. Thus we may begin to discover how the accepted, legitimate pedagogic repertoires of the present are rooted in conflicts fought out in the past, along with the consciously developed but now taken-for-granted strategies which those conflicts produced.

4. Studies of the origins of the constraints experienced by teachers which they attempt, constructively, to resolve. These origins need to be located beyond the immediate, apparent and relatively obvious institutional level. For example, it is not enough simply to point to the problem of class sizes as one constraint with which teachers have to deal—more difficult questions also need to be asked about why, even at a time of high rates of unemployment amongst teachers, the opportunity has not been taken to reduce the teacher-pupil ratio.

5. Studies of the ways in which societal constraints are mediated in varying forms in different kinds of educational institutions. This will enable us to understand why the strategies which teachers develop in infant schools, for example, are different from those developed in middle schools which in turn are different from those developed in secondary schools and so on.

6. Studies of pupil responses (their own strategic solutions) to teacher strategies and of the interplay of teacher and pupil strategies; of their reciprocal effect upon one another. This will require some consideration of the extent to which teacher strategies emerge in response to an initial set of constraints, then undergo a process of 'drift' as they interlock with pupil strategies. Some understanding is needed here of the detailed workings of this strategic, coping cycle and of the degree to which it can move away from or even over-ride the constraints that are first encountered.[20]

7. Studies of the origins of pupil responses; of the sources of their strategic repertoires. Such investigations would tread various pathways—some of them promising avenues and others empty culs-de-sac. But some mileage might be gained by studying how conversational and interact-

ional strategies are acquired during early childhood socialisation and how pupil perspectives and strategic orientations emerge in the peer group both in and out of school. In short, what is required is a study of the cultural, familial and institutional origins of pupil perspectives and strategies.

8. Perhaps most crucially of all, studies of the cultural aspects of teacher and pupil groupings which throw up, contain and perpetuate the strategic repertoires that these groups employ in negotiation with one another. The occupational, professional and general cultural dimensions of the teachers' shared world need to be studied here to see how they interlace and make up that complex constellation of characteristics which is usually rather crudely expressed as the possession of 'middle-class values'. On the other hand, the class origins of pupil cultures in the family and thus, indirectly in the world of work in which their parents are involved; in street corner life; and in the institutional meeting place of the school also require investigation. Only by looking at both sides of the equation simultaneously, will we come to forge the necessary connections between what appear to be specifically institutional questions about the interplay of teacher and pupil strategies, and those wider, more inaccessible questions to do with the organisation and reproduction of social class relations. This is where the institutional and class levels of analysis can be joined, where the educational and class paradigms can be connected by more than sheer rhetoric. It is also a means by which the association between class problems and classroom problems might be grasped in a way that does not just amount to dissolving one into the other.

9. Quite simply, as a way of clarifying many of the previous points, careful and painstaking studies of infant schools, middle schools, comprehensive schools, public schools, universities, colleges of education, etc, which are informed by, at the same time as they contribute to the development of a much broader thesis which seeks to explain the relationship between schooling and capitalism. Together, such studies, by giving access to the teacher's and pupil's perspective and situation might enable us to answer the fundamental question: why do teachers and pupils behave the way they do? Focusing on this area of teacher and pupil strategies and their origins might then make it possible to build that desperately needed bridge which would connect the organisation of schooling to the reproduction of capitalist social relations.

All these considerations taken together demand that we assemble a careful and delicately worked out Marxist theory incorporating a concern for historical detail, which can be combined with theories rooted in the phenomenological and interactionist traditions and with the sophisticated methodologies appropriate to them. We may then begin to shed some light on some hitherto unsolved mysteries: exactly *why* do relatively autonomous institutions reproduce the social relations of production; just *how* is this reproduction accomplished through the day-to-day interactions between school personnel; and *why* is it that teachers are, wittingly or unwittingly, the active agents of this process. For an adequate resolution of these problems, our conceptual armoury should consist not only of 'mode of production', 'class reproduction', 'correspondence' and 'relative autonomy', but should be expanded to include such concepts as 'meaning', 'interpretation', 'coping' and 'strategy'.

## 3. *The Split-Level Model*

A third formulation of the relation between school and society is not part of the Marxist framework, and in many respects, stands in direct opposition to it. This formulation is most common in interactionist studies of education, though its presence is tacit and unacknowledged in most of them. But an explicit, though somewhat brief and speculative, outline has been provided by Woods (1977) in what is a much broader discussion of teachers' survival strategies. The core of Woods's argument is that there is often a total separation in schools between two kinds of control: *social* control and *situational* control. *Social* control refers to 'training for induction into capitalist society'—it is therefore an integral feature of the process of schooling as one of class reproduction. *Situational* control is quite different—this arises out of the teacher's need to accommodate to a set of immediate constraints like the teacher-pupil ratio or the raising of the school-leaving age which are a part of the situation in which he finds himself. Woods asserts that these two types of control are 'quite separate'. In his view, patterns of teacher-pupil interaction, curriculum construction and teacher survival are therefore determined at two distinct, autonomously constituted levels. This autonomy is not *relative* autonomy, for in the latter case, while each level has its own determinations and effects, these patterns of determination are still located within the bounds of an enclosing structural context. By contrast, for Woods, the autonomy is *complete* and the different levels (social and situational) are totally split from one another. Elsewhere in a discussion of pupil strategies, Woods (1978) presents a similar view when he claims that the institutional dimension cuts across the class one, rather than, say, corresponding with or mediating it.

Woods's account, then, stresses the importance of the problems of teacher survival; of accommodation to mounting institutional constraints. The patterns of control that result are therefore viewed as situational in origin. In consequence, much of what goes on in schools is regarded as having no connection with those questions which Marxists would hold to be central; questions of class division, of social class reproduction, and of the contribution that schooling makes to this. As a result, Woods's account can be read as presenting an *alternative* to that which has been offered by Marxists; as an explanation which hinges on the sources and consequences of survival strategies. How valid is this split-level model, and how far are questions of teachers' and indeed pupils' strategic accommodation separate from those of class reproduction?

The central problems appear to revolve around the conceptions of the *situation* which have been embraced by interactionists. Woods's stressing of the importance of the *situation* as a constraining influence upon teacher behaviour, reflects a more widespread concern on the part of many interactionists (a concern which, interestingly, few critics are prepared to concede) with the extent to which social behaviour in general is shaped by the situations in which people find themselves (e.g. Denscombe in this volume and 1979). In contrast to many other adherents of the 'interpretive approach' (mainly phenomenologists) who focus almost exclusively on how individuals are conscious of and even define situations themselves in personally and situationally unique terms (see Ball in this volume), interactionists reserve the right to provide accounts of actions which view them as a response to situational constraints, even when the people studied are not themselves aware of being constrained in this way. There is a possibility here that connections might be made between situational and structural factors for, as Hammersley (1980) notes

> Making a clear distinction between analytic and member conceptions
> of the situation lays the basis for the investigation of how the situations
> facing actors are structurally produced, and thus provides a link to the
> macro level.

This most promising avenue is one which few interactionists have explored. The work of Becker (1952) stands out as one of the rare exceptions here. Although Becker's account is somewhat over-simple, he did at least glimpse the relations between the social class structure; the situational problems which pupils from different social classes created for their teachers in terms of teaching, discipline and the maintenance of standards of cultural

propriety; and the teachers' differing typifications and treatments of
pupils from each class grouping which arose as a result. Becker thus displayed an elementary grasp of the sorts of connections that obtain between the school *situation* on the one hand and social structure on the
other. Unfortunately the potential in Becker's work has not been taken
up by most other interactionists. On the whole, they have chosen to keep
*the situation* separate from any notion of a wider social structure which
might ultimately produce it.[21]

On the other hand, one of Woods's central points is that situational
control has been confused with social control by some Marxist writers,
with the result that 'the products of the situation have been subsumed,
erroneously, under the latter, and survival strategies have not been proper-
ly identified' (p. 291). To some extent, it is possible to sympathise with
Woods's complaint about some Marxist accounts of the determinations
of classroom practice. Sharp and Green (1975) are the most readily
identifiable culprits here. They explain 'busyness' in the infant school
as an outcome of the problems that teachers experience in connection
with the high teacher-pupil ratio, but they seem to regard this *situational* constraint (of the teacher-pupil ratio) as some kind of mysterious
emanation from the capitalist mode of production. Thus, as presented,
their explanation exposes them to the charge that they have unjust-
ifiably subsumed situational features under the rubric of social-
structural concerns. Woods's response is to argue for the separateness
of the situation and social structure and to draw a set of conclusions
for policy which are opposed to the Marxist view that 'change in the situation would make little material difference' (p. 290). If teachers were
liberated from a host of situational constraints, he argues, then education
could be put before survival and the schooling process would be human-
ised as a result.

The split-level model and the emphasis it gives to the impact of situational factors on classroom relations thus gives rise to quite markedly different policy implications from those advanced by Marxists who argue
that any meaningful change in education would not be possible without,
at some stage, fundamental changes being wrought in the capitalist mode
of production. Is the priority which Woods attaches to *the situation*
justified?[22]

While situational factors have often been mistakenly subsumed under
or identified with structural factors, this does not automatically mean that
no connections can be forged between them. Factors which are ostensibly
*situational* in nature such as the teacher-pupil ratio, the teaching week, the
raising of the school leaving age, school buildings, the dilemmas of progres-

sive education and so on, may well have their origin in the changing social, economic and political conditions of capitalist society. Just because the complex interrelation of the two levels has rarely been demonstrated so far, does not mean to say that no such connections exist. In this sense, the Great Education Debate of the mid 1970s and the economic crisis which accompanied, indeed heralded it, may have done more to prod the sociological imagination into life than any other events in recent years. Its emphases on, among other things, the necessity for evaluation and testing, the importance of maintaining educational standards at all levels and the closer linking of education with industry, all to service and expand a flagging capitalist economy, publicly expressed, in a way which no sociologist could ever have done, the connections between schooling on the one hand, and politics and the economy on the other. The crisis unveiled the correspondence between the two spheres.[23]

What is astonishing, some two and a half years later, however, is the extent to which the fears about centralised control of the curriculum and about the exertion of direct political control over schooling at all levels have just not materialised. Instead, there has been a gentle, if rapid, filtering of the new rhetoric (and its accompanying practices) of 'assessment', 'evaluation', 'standards', and so on into the everyday working assumptions of the advisory service, the DES, colleges of education and so forth. A new context is being shaped, a new set of situations is being framed, in which present and future teachers are finding and will find themselves. The language and practice of 'accountability' is so quickly becoming a part of college 'curriculum' courses and of educational practice in general, that its political and economic origins will soon be lost sight of. It will become just one more set of elements to be considered as part of *the situation* and to be taken into account by the teacher when formulating his survival strategies. The social, political and economic origins of the other situational features mentioned earlier need to be studied in a similar way. As a result, we may discover that situation and social structure cannot be readily divorced from one another except in a purely analytic sense. We may then get an insight into how teacher and pupil strategies are a response to situational problems which are structurally produced, and thus gain some purchase on just how the everyday practices of schooling and the organisation of capitalist society are connected. The split-level model will, I fear, direct us away from rather than towards these tantalisingly complex, but extremely important issues.

## Conclusion

I have argued for the centrality of the study of teacher and pupil strategies to the sociology of education. Mills's call for the connection of various milieux to understandings of the workings of social structure involved no less than the full scope of the sociological imagination itself. In the sociology of education, that imagination might best be employed in the study of teacher and pupil strategies, of the situational constraints in response to which they are fashioned, and of the relation (present or past) of such constraints to wider structural concerns. While the language of strategy analysis has so far been confined to interactionist research, this need no longer be the case. All too frequently, *the situation* has been regarded as the outer limit of constraint upon teacher and pupil behaviour.[24] Concerns which have normally been thought to be the proper province of interactionist research should now be linked with and included in theories about the operations of social structure. Studying strategies with this end in view, an end might be brought to the 'splendid isolation' of many interactionist and other interpretive researches; an isolation which in any case has always been less than complete because of the unwanted (though usually unrecognised) intrusions of 'foreign' influences. This kind of programme might also provide the acid test for establishing the validity of various abstract theories about the relationship of schooling to society.

The plea I am making is a contentious one. I am not asking for this or that particular researcher to engage in a study of strategies with a view to generating or contributing to the production of a synthesis in the sociology of education. I am saying, for theoretical and moral reasons, that such considerations are the responsibility of everyone who works in that field. This is no easy task. It may only be achievable through the development of carefully co-ordinated teamwork. The gargantuan size of the task should not deter us, however for upon its achievement rests not only the fulfilment of the sociological imagination in the sphere of education, but also the framing of realistic proposals for reform which would be based on a sounder knowledge of the connection between schooling and society and thus of the determinants of classroom practice.

## Notes

1. A useful historical overview of the emergence and decline of different approaches within the sociology of education has been provided by Barton and Walker (1978).
2. Lest this should read as a pejorative description, I should add that I include some of my own work within this category.
3. There are notable omissions in these two overviews of approaches within the

sociology of education. Marxism is not discussed at all in Bernbaum's work. In Reid's book only a very small amount of attention is paid to it and here it is juxta-posed with other kinds of conflict theory. These omissions seem remarkable (though less so in Bernbaum's text, which was written earlier), given the growing importance of a whole range of Marxist approaches to the study of education in recent years.

4. I have attempted to outline the rudiments of such a model elsewhere – A. Hargreaves (1978 and 1979).

5. Such tendencies can also be seen in the work of Sharp and Green (1975) whose treatment of the concept 'consociates' is at variance with its use in phenomen-ological research (D. Hargreaves, 1978) and in the work of Willis (1977) whose con-ceptions of 'meaning' and 'culture' do not square with the usage of these terms in phenomenology and symbolic interactionism.

6. The study referred to is Durkheim's *L'evolution Pedagogique en France*.

7. These are studies about the control of schooling by different status groups within society. See, for example, Scotford-Archer and Vaughan (1971) and Collins (1971).

8. One very recent exception is the work of King (1978), though the Weberian model which he adopts only emerges sporadically and is not particularly well devel-oped.

9. For a critique of this view, see Westergaard and Resler (1975).

10. Marx, of course, has been as much an object of necrolatry as Durkheim and Weber. I am deferring my discussion of him and the more contemporary guises in which he appears until Part II.

11. To a certain extent, this appears to be the position taken by Hammersley (1980).

12. See D. Hargreaves (1977 and 1978).

13. This is clearly the implication of Hunter's (1979) argument.

14. By contrast, the central component of the Marxist position is that power and control may be exerted even in the absence of overt conflict – and that the pro-cess of hegemony as a constellation of assumptions about the workings of society and its institutions, a constellation which is *partly* a product of ideological accounts of such workings, plays an important, stabilising role. This process, one which Lukes (1974) has called 'the supreme and most insidious exercise of power', receives no attention within interactionist approaches.

15. Thus, unlike Hammersley (1980), I am arguing that approaches articulated at one level only, tend to provide not just *incomplete* accounts of the schooling pro-cess, but also *distorted* ones.

16. This has led Althusser to be tarred with the unflattering epithet of 'the French Parsons' by Alvin Gouldner (1976).

17. Most of the articles in this volume are representative of such a position, where the classroom and school are treated in isolation from wider structural concern While there is much good case study work here which illuminates the complexity and diversity of school life, the unique and personal aspects of schooling (Ball, 1980) and the bewildering assortment of contextual variations that can be found in pupil behavi (Bird, 1980), all these factors have perhaps been overstressed at the expense of the structural context which might, if only in part, produce such variations.

18. They do, of course, provide some statistical evidence in support of their argument, but as Mackinnon (1977) points out, this is often rather shaky.

19. Williams uses the concept of *overdetermination* in a more subtle and complex way than Althusser whom he takes to task for not applying it to his theory of ideolog and for converting what is always a historically contingent process into a structural principle.

20. I have tried to outline this coping cycle in more detail in A. Hargreaves (1978)

21. This is true of Denscombe (1979).

22. It should be borne in mind that Woods's own definition of the *situation* is itself somewhat ambiguous. He defines it as widely as 'the meeting point of institutional momentum and societal developments where it impinges on any individual teacher' (p. 290). Here, it is difficult to see how any changes in the *situation* could be effected *without* simultaneous changes occurring within the society as a whole.

23. A similar argument has been made by Whitty (1978).

24. This criticism applies to Denscombe's article in this volume.

# References

Abercrombie, N. and Turner, B.S. (1978) 'The Dominant Ideology Thesis', *British Journal of Sociology*, vol. 29, no. 2

Althusser, L. (1969) *For Marx*, Allen Lane, Harmondsworth

Althusser, L. (1971) 'Ideology and Ideological State Apparatuses', in *Lenin, Philosophy and Other Essays*, New Left Books, London

Ball, S. (1980) 'Initial Encounters in the Classroom and the Process of Establishment' (in this volume)

Banks, O. (1976) *The Sociology of Education* (third ed.), Batsford, London

Banks, O. (1978) 'School and Society', in L. Barton and R. Meighan (eds.), *Sociological Interpretations of Schooling and Classrooms: a Re-appraisal*, Nafferton, Driffield

Bartholomew, J. (1976) 'Schooling Teachers: the Myth of the Liberal College', in Whitty and Young (1976)

Barton, L. and Walker, S. (1978) 'Sociology of Education at the Crossroads', *Educational Review*, vol. 30, no. 3

Becker, H. (1952) 'Social Class Variations in the Teacher-Pupil Relationship', *Journal of Educational Sociology*, vol. 25, no. 4

Bellaby, P. (1977) *The Sociology of Comprehensive Schooling*, Methuen, London

Berger, P.L. and Luckman, T. (1967) *The Social Construction of Reality*, Penguin, Harmondsworth

Bernbaum, G. (1977) *Knowledge and Ideology in the Sociology of Education*, Macmillan, London

Bernstein, B. (1977) 'Aspects of the Relations Between Education and Production', in *Class, Codes and Control, Vol. 3* (second ed.), Routledge and Kegan Paul, London

Bird, C. (1980) 'Deviant Labelling in School: the Pupils' Perspective' (in this volume)

Bourdieu, P. and Passeron, J.C. (1977) *Reproduction in Education, Society and Culture*, Sage, London

Bowles, S. and Gintis, H. (1976) *Schooling in Capitalist America*, Routledge and Kegan Paul, London

Collins, R. (1971) 'Functional and Conflict Theories of Educational Stratification', *American Sociological Review*, vol. 36

Corrigan, P. and Frith, S. (1977) 'The Politics of Education', in Young and Whitty (1977)

Cox, C.B. and Boyson, R. (1976) *Black Paper 1975*, Dent, London

David, M.E. (1978) 'The Family-Education Couple: Towards an Analysis of the William Tyndale Dispute', in G. Littlejohn, *et al.* (eds.), *Power and the State*, Croom Helm, London

Dawe, A. (1971) 'The Relevance of Values', in A. Sahay (ed.), *Max Weber and Mod-*

*ern Sociology*, Routledge and Kegan Paul, London

Denscombe, M. (1979) 'Keeping 'em Quiet: the Significance of Noise for the Practical Activity of Teaching', in P. Woods (ed.), *Teacher Strategies*, Croom Helm, London

Denscombe, M. (1980) 'Pupil Strategies and the Open Classroom' (in this volume).

Eggleston, J. (1977) *The Sociology of the School Curriculum*, Routledge and Kegan Paul, London

Erben, M. and Gleeson, D. (1977) 'Education as Reproduction: a Critical Examination of Some Aspects of the Work of Louis Althusser', in Young and Whitty (1977)

Esland, G. (1971) 'Teaching and Learning as the Organisation of Knowledge', in M.F.D. Young (ed.), *Knowledge and Control*, Collier-Macmillan, London

Finn, D., Grant, N. and Johnson, R. (1977) 'Social Democracy, Education and the Crisis', in Centre for Contemporary Cultural Studies, *On Ideology*, Working Papers no. 10

Gibson, R. (1977) 'Bernstein's Classification and Framing: a Critique', *Higher Education Review*, vol. 9, Spring

Goffman, E. (1975) *Frame Analysis*, Penguin, Harmondsworth

Gouldner, A. (1976) *The Dialectic of Ideology and Technology*, Macmillan, London

Gramsci, A. (1971) *Selections from the Prison Notebooks*, Lawrence and Wishart, London

Hall, S. (1977) 'Review of the Course', Open University Course E202, *Schooling and Society*, Unit 32, Milton Keynes

Hammersley, M. (1980) 'On Interactionist Empiricism' (in this volume).

Hammersley, M. and Turner, G. (1980) 'Conformist Pupils?' (in this volume).

Hargreaves, A. (1978) 'The Significance of Classroom Coping Strategies', in L. Barton and R. Meighan, *Sociological Interpretations of Schooling and Classrooms: a Re-appraisal*, Nafferton, Driffield

Hargreaves, A. (1979) 'Strategies, Decisions and Control: Interaction in a Middle School Classroom', in J. Eggleston, *Teacher Decision-Making in the Classroom*, Routledge and Kegan Paul, London

Hargreaves, D.H. (1977) 'A Phenomenological Approach to Classroom Decision-Making', *Cambridge Journal of Education*, vol. 7, no. 1

Hargreaves, D.H. (1978) 'Whatever Happened to Symbolic Interactionism?', in L. Barton and R. Meighan, *Sociological Interpretations of Schooling and Classrooms: a Re-appraisal*, Nafferton, Driffield

Hargreaves, D.H., Hester, S.K. and Mellor, F.J. (1976) *Deviance in Classrooms*, Routledge and Kegan Paul, London

Hunter, C. (1979) 'The Politics of Participation – With Specific Reference to Teacher-Pupil Relationships', in P. Woods (ed.), *Teacher Strategies*, Croom Helm, London

Karabel, J. and Halsey, A.H. (1977) *Power and Ideology in Education*, Oxford University Press, New York

Keddie, N. (1971) 'Classroom Knowledge', in M.F.D. Young (ed.), *Knowledge and Control*, Collier Macmillan, London

King, R. (1978) *All Things Bright and Beautiful*, Wiley, Chichester

Kolokowski, L. (1971) 'Althusser's Marx', *Socialist Register*, vol. 8

Lukes, S. (1974) *Power: a Radical View*, Macmillan, London

Mackinnon, D. (1977) 'Revision I', Open University Course, E202, *Schooling and Society*, Unit 13, Milton Keynes

Miller, C.M.L. and Parlett, M. (1976) 'Cue Consciousness', in M. Hammersley and P. Woods, *The Process of Schooling*, Routledge and Kegan Paul, London

Mills, C.W. (1959) *The Sociological Imagination*, Penguin, Harmondsworth

Nichols, T. and Benyon, H. (1977) *Living with Capitalism*, Routledge and Kegan

Paul, London

Parsons, T. (1959) 'The School Class as a Social System', *Harvard Educational Review*, vol. XXIX, Fall

Pollard, A. (1979) 'Teacher Interests and Changing Situations of Survival Threat in Primary School Classrooms', in P. Woods (ed.), *Teacher Strategies*, Croom Helm, London

Reid, I. (1978) *Sociological Perspectives on School and Education*, Open Books, London

Sarup, M. (1978) *Marxism and Education*, Routledge and Kegan Paul, London

Schutz, A. (1967) *The Phenomenology of the Social World*, Heinemann, London

Schutz, A. (1973) *Collected Papers I*, Martinus Nijhoff, The Hague

Scotford-Archer, M. and Vaughan, M. (1971) 'Domination and Assertion in Educational Systems', in E.I. Hopper (ed.), *Readings in the Theory of Educational Systems*, Heinemann, London

Scott, M.B. and Lyman, M.S. (1968) 'Accounts', *American Sociological Review*, December

Sharp, R. and Green, A. (1975) *Education and Social Control*, Routledge and Kegan Paul, London

Tapper, T. and Salter, B. (1978) *Education and the Political Order*, Macmillan, London

Westergaard, J. and Rester, H. (1975) *Class in a Capitalist Society*, Heinemann, London

Whitty, G. and Young, M. (1976) *Explorations in the Politics of School Knowledge*, Nafferton, Driffield

Whitty, G. (1978) 'School Examinations and the Politics of School Knowledge', in L. Barton and R. Meighan, *Sociological Interpretations of Schooling and Classrooms: a Re-appraisal*, Nafferton, Driffield

Williams, R. (1978) *Marxism and Literature*, Oxford University Press, Oxford

Willis, P. (1977) *Learning to Labour*, Saxon House, Farnborough

Woods, P. (1977) 'Teaching for Survival', in P. Woods and M. Hammersley, *School Experience*, Croom Helm, London

Woods, P. (1978) 'Relating to Schoolwork: Some Pupil Perceptions', *Educational Review*, vol. 30, no. 2

Woods, P. (1979) *The Divided School*, Routledge and Kegan Paul, London

Young, M. and Whitty, G. (1977) *Society, State and Schooling*, Falmer, Brighton

# 9 ON INTERACTIONIST EMPIRICISM*

## Martyn Hammersley

The substantial consensus which characterised the sociology of
education in the 1950s and 1960s has been replaced by a baffling array
of different approaches. There are not only normative functionalism,
conflict theory, interpretive and Marxist versions, but even distinct
varieties of each of these (Woods and Hammersley, 1977; Karabel
and Halsey, 1977; Hammersley, 1978). In the face of this fragmentation, some writers have called for a synthesis, claiming that the
various approaches are in fact complementary (Banks, 1978; Bernbaum,
1978). There is some truth in this. Many of the differences go no deeper
than terminology; others have more to do with political emphasis than
serious intellectual disagreement.[1] However, there *are* some fundamental
differences between available approaches; and indeed the synthesising
manifestos indicate this by the way in which they underplay those
approaches with which their authors have limited sympathy (Delamont,
1978). Given this, any attempt to rebuild the fragments into a replica
of the earlier consensus seems doomed to failure. In my view the way
forward lies neither in radical sectarianism nor naive eclecticism. Much
more likely to be productive is research which operates within a particular approach, while at the same time recognising its deficiencies and the
aid other traditions may offer in overcoming these. This may well result
in some kind of *rapprochement*, but if it does it will have a solid found-
ation, being neither an eclectic synthesis nor an incorporation masque-
rading as synthesis. I shall argue in this chapter that, despite its faults,
interactionism offers a promising basis for such *rapprochement*; and I
shall indicate some of the directions in which it must be developed if it
is to fulfil this promise.

Interactionism is not a monolithic tradition, nor is it clearly marked
off from other forms of sociology. Despite much talk about competing
paradigms, the discipline is not composed of a set of mutually exclusive,
internally coherent approaches, but rather of a number of loosely defined,
overlapping, and in important respects internally inconsistent, frameworks.
What I shall be recommending here, then, is one version of interactionism,
and indeed one which draws in a number of places on competing approache

*My thanks to Andy Hargreaves and Jeff Evans for their comments on earlier drafts
of this paper. They will still disagree with some of what I have to say.

198

## Interactionist Empiricism: the Marxist Critique

Interactionism was one of the central elements of 'the new sociology of education', that inchoate opposition movement which emerged in the late 1960s. As might be expected, once it was no longer in opposition the 'new sociology' began to splinter and interactionism has come under increasing attack from neo-Marxist and neo-Durkheimian directions. The core of this critique is that interactionism is empiricist (Sharp and Green, 1975; Whitty, 1974; A. Hargreaves, 1978). By this is meant, in part, the tendency of interactionists to neglect macro-level theory. However, these critics are not pointing to a gap that needs to be filled, but rather to what they claim is an inherent defect of the approach. The argument is often presented along the lines that interactionist work focuses on appearances and neglects the underlying forms which produce those appearances. And this formulation is sometimes laced with the claim that these appearances are ideological, and that any study which restricts itself to them is itself ideological.

In many versions of this argument, therefore, interactionism is not simply charged with an accidental neglect. Rather, it is claimed, interactionism is *unable* to theorise the larger social system, and in particular to recognise the way in which events in a setting are produced by features of that larger system. This inability derives, it is said, from a presupposition that actors are free to define and construct the world in any way they wish. Allied to this is a failure to go beyond recounting the views of participants to ask how these views are generated and what consequences they, and the actions deriving from them, have.

A number of things must be said about this critique. Firstly, the appearance/reality formulation is a device for rhetorically assigning priority to one set of phenomena rather than another. It must, therefore, be treated very warily. Secondly, in many ways what we have here is the construction and demolition of a straw man (Hargreaves, D.H., 1978). Furthermore, what force the critique has applies more to interactionist *rhetoric* than practice. Thus, for example, it is not true that interactionist work treats the actor as completely autonomous. The situations actors face are assigned a considerable role in shaping their perspectives and thus their actions. Even where the critique does apply to interactionist practice, no argument is provided which demonstrates that interactionism is *necessarily* empiricist. Finally, to claim that micro phenomena can only be understood correctly in terms of the right macro scheme is to beg the question of how we produce and test the latter; and also to confuse the completeness of an explanation with its validity.

The Marxist critique is therefore in important respects misconceived. Nevertheless, while it is incorrect to claim that interactionism is *inherently* empiricist, I think it must be conceded that, as currently practiced, interactionist ethnography does display distinct empiricist tendencies.[2]

1. Much of the work in the interactionist tradition tends to be ahistorical and to lack a comparative dimension. Almost all our work is on British and American settings, and we ignore the implications of this neglect of other socio-cultural contexts. Indeed, we make little use of existing historical and anthropological material.[3]

2. Most interactionist work disregards the ways in which different social phenomena are systematically related to one another, and the role of institutionalisation and unintended consequences. We *do* tend to assume a simplistic pluralist macro theory as a backdrop to our studies. While the notion of societies as self-maintaining systems may be rightly discredited, some notion of the systematic interrelation of the institutions of a society is essential. On the other hand, occasionally, in glossing the wider macro context, we find interactionists resorting to functionalist arguments without paying much attention to the well-known problems of this theoretical scheme (Woods, 1977b; Marsh, Rosser and Harré, 1978). Similarly, most recent interactionist work, unlike earlier versions of interpretive sociology, fails to locate itself within theories of societal development; it has become detached from these just as it has become detached from more specific historical and comparative concerns. Despite the fact that Weber is often cited among the pantheon of interpretive forefathers, little use is made by interactionists of his substantive work: he is revered largely for his discussion of the concept of action and for his methodological writings.[4]

Thus, while in some respects the recent criticisms of interactionism are mistaken, there are some very important ways in which much interactionist work in the sociology of education and elsewhere does suffer from empiricism. I want now to look at some of the solutions which have been adopted for dealing with this problem.

## Combating Empiricism[5]

Two major strategies seem to have been adopted for dealing with interactionist empiricism. The first prescribes the abandonment of the interactionist framework for one or other macro-structural approach. Thus we have the current rush to critical theory (Young, 1975 and 1977), political economy (Open University, 1977), reproduction theories (Bourdieu and Passeron, 1977), discourse analysis,[6] etc. However, this 'solution' doesn't

solve the problems it is a response to, except in the magical way of swap-
ping them for different problems; among them precisely those interactionism criticised in functionalism ten years or so ago. Sometimes what
are involved are simply differences in formulation. An example is the issue
of determinism where this strategy entails replacing the bald assertion
that humans are active in creating the social world by the claim that
human actions are the product of social forces. Both these statements are,
of course, true. Some of the problems are more serious however:[7]

(a) These approaches trade on the notion of function without having
made much progress in the analysis of this concept; indeed they often
use it in a cruder way than some functionalists.[8]
(b) They presuppose a crude conception of the relationship between
structurally induced situation and social action. Thus, for example,
Bowles and Gintis take over Parsons's speculations about the impact
of forms of social organisation on personality; Althusser simply
assumes that ideological state apparatuses successfully inculcate
ideology. As a result of this they fail to recognise the existence and
importance of multiple adaptations and locally generated cultures.
(c) Their methodological status is either largely speculative or is basically
suspect, relying naively on forms of data which are highly question-
able.[9] This last point indicates an advantage of ethnographic empiricism. Whatever the deficiencies of interactionist work on schooling,
we do now have a range of studies of schools and classrooms which
are reasonably well-grounded empirically and which provide at least
some basis for the development and testing of theory.

But there is more. Many of these macro theories, as they stand at present,
themselves lack a comparative dimension. They also frequently have a
very limited historical dimension, being concerned primarily with aspects
of the development of modern capitalism in its Western forms, and often
with inadequate recognition even of the variations within that field. This
makes it difficult for them to distinguish between what is specific to the
particular type of society they are analysing and what, on currently available evidence, seems to characterise all societies.[10] This first solution,
then, on current evidence has little to commend it.

The other way of dealing with the problem of micro-empiricism which
has been adopted is the pursuit of macro theory through an ethnographic
case study. What often results is the incorporation of interactionist
analysis, in an appropriately 'sawn off' form, into one or other of the
currently fashionable Marxist or Durkheimian approaches.[11] This is

certainly to be preferred to the first strategy, but it still involves problems
The central one is overambition: in a single study the attempt is made not
only to reconcile different sociological approaches but also to document a
substantial chunk of the social world. It expands the focus of the research
and, as a result, a single case study is no longer a sufficient data base. One
cannot infer the structure and operation of the education system of a
society from a case study of a single school or a few classrooms or pupils
in it.[12] Yet this is what Sharp and Green and Willis tend to do.[13]
The attempt to extend the focus of the research in this way may also, if
only for reasons of time, reduce the depth and quality of the case-study
work.[14]

In summary, then, the strategies which have been adopted to deal with
interactionist empiricism do not provide effective solutions to the problem
The solution it seems to me requires the rejection of something which is
common both to recent interactionist work and to Marxist ethnography.
Each displays a very limited amount of specialisation in the research task.
For the first, research consists almost entirely in the production of ethnographic case studies; for the second, this is also the primary task except
that it is assumed to be essential at the same time, and in the same depth, to
analyse the socio-historical context in which the case is located. Instead of
a single standard task I suggest that what is required is an explicit division
of labour. There are two aspects to this. On the one hand, it involves a
differentiation of task; and on the other, increased attention to the co-
ordination of research.[15]

## A Division of Labour: the Differentiation of Research Product

At present we have no systematic basis for deciding what kinds of work
need to be done and what the priorities are. What follows is a tentative
first attempt to conceptualise the field. We can begin from the common
distinctions between macro and micro levels and formal and substantive
theory. I use the term 'macro' to refer to studies which theorise patterns
of interrelation between many different types of setting which are directly
related to one another by causal networks. This may involve tracing linkages across the structure of a national society or even of the world
system.[16] Basically, then, macro/micro refers to the scope of a study: how
many different types of linked settings does the research examine.

I am using formal/substantive in the Glaser and Strauss sense.[17]
Once again here the two forms of theory operate at different levels of
abstraction. But this time the more abstract formal theory does not conceptualise a large area of continuous terrain, it theorises patterns in particular types of society or setting on the basis of analogy with other pat-

terns in often very remotely related societies and settings. Substantive theory, on the other hand, operates at a lower level of abstraction, ranging from theories about the internal workings of a particular society or institutional sector down to accounts of particular settings.

Using these two dimensions, we can recognise four complementary kinds of research and research product:[18]

| | Formal | Substantive |
|---|---|---|
| **Macro** | For example:<br><br>Marx on types of society and the dynamic of historical development<br><br>Durkheim on The Division of Labour<br><br>Parsons on The Social System | For example:<br><br>Marx and Weber on capitalism<br><br>Durkheim on the history of education in France<br><br>Bernstein on the shift from closed to open forms of schooling |
| **Micro** | For example:<br><br>Mead on mind, self, act and society<br><br>Goffman on the presentation of self, interaction ritual and framing<br><br>Glaser and Strauss on Status Passage<br><br>Sacks on the organisation of conversation | For example:<br><br>Hargreaves and Lacey on differentiation and polarisation of values among pupils<br><br>Werthman on 'delinquents in schools'<br><br>Dumont and Wax on Cherokee pupils in the classroom<br><br>Woods on Showing them Up and Having a Laugh |

As I indicated in my discussion of attempts to combine ethnographic case-study with macro analysis, I believe there are good reasons to suggest that any piece of research should be explicitly directed predominantly towards one and only one of these four goals. Without a clear distinction between these different goals and the single-minded attempt to pursue one of them, it seems to me that the value of the research product is likely to be seriously reduced. On the other hand, in doing this, a study must draw as much as possible, and as explicitly as possible, on work of the other three kinds.

These four types of research product are, in my view, complementary and of equal value. Yet interactionists have focused almost entirely on micro-formal and micro-substantive work. There seem to be several reasons for this neglect of macro theory. One is the tendency to anti-determinism. In many of the arguments symbolic interactionists put forward to justify the approach it seems that processes of interpretation and social interaction are to be treated not simply as mediators of wider socio-cultural factors, but, in fact, as fully insulating interaction from such factors. Take, for example the following characteristic statement:

> rather than viewing behaviour as a simple 'release' from a pre-existing psychological structure (such as drives, personalities, emotions or attitudes) or as a consequence of an external coercion by social 'facts' (cultures, structures, organizations, roles, power), the interactionist focuses upon emergence and negotiation – the processes by which social action (in groups, organizations or societies) is constantly being constructed, modified, selected, checked, suspended, terminated and recommenced in everyday life. (Plummer, 1975, p. 13)[19]

Such an assumption denies the relevance of the society in which a setting is located for the patterns of activity which occur there and thus rules out any kind of macro analysis: the field is restricted to substantive and formal micro theory.[20]

Another reason for the emphasis on case studies and the consequent neglect of macro analysis is the claim that only social action in localised settings can be systematically and rigorously studied

> Some theories are too extensive or too vague. The parts of them that can be operationalized into testable hypotheses might be too few or too trivial in the context of the theory as a whole to have any value. Though all manner of 'evidence' might be found to support a theory, there might be other equally plausible explanations, some of them diametrically opposed. Also, such theories commonly leave much contradictory evidence unexplained. The truth is that they are not 'scientific' theories, though they are often put through the scientific operational formula. As Jack Douglas has said: 'we must stop treating macroanalyses *as if* they were scientific arguments, that is, arguments based on carefully done, systematic observations of concrete phenomena'. [Douglas, 1971, p. 11]

That is why, scientifically, middle-range theory is on much firmer ground. It falls between the 'minor working hypotheses' of everyday life and the all-inclusive 'grand' theories. Addressing itself to limited and clearly defined problems, it more easily acquires the generality, economy and clarity that theory requires. Thus it is more amenable to scientific testing. (P. Woods, 1977a, p. 10)

While it is certainly easier to establish the internal validity of small-scale case studies, and substantive and formal theory based on them, we should not dismiss macro theory as unscientific and restrict our investigations only to those areas where reasonably high levels of internal validity are available. For one thing this would distort the nature of the explanations for social phenomena we can develop, since any case study presupposes some conception of the larger whole in which the case is located. It would also prevent the improvement of the levels of validity available in those areas. Thus, the importance of macro work which, currently at least, necessarily relies on cruder forms of data, must be recognised by interactionists; and they must start to do such work themselves.

Indeed, interactionism has a number of important advantages as a basis for macro analysis. Firstly, contrary to most forms of structural functionalism and Marxism, it does not *presuppose* the existence of a tightly integrated social system. As a result, and because of its associated methodological orientation, it does not employ the assumption that the very existence of a particular institution must mean that it plays a role in the reproduction of the system. Instead, the field is wide open for the *investigation* of the pre-conditions and consequences of a particular form of institutional organisation.[21]

Secondly, interactionism does not assume that a particular institutional order, whether the 'mode of production' or the 'normative order', is somehow basic. As a result it avoids those scholastic discussions about 'determination in the last instance' which arise for proponents of the other approaches once they begin to recognise the complexity of the social world.

Finally, interactionism does not assume that class is the *basic* element of social structure. Thus, for example, it does not encourage the automatic tracing of all beliefs and actions back to class groupings.[22]

By minimising prior assumptions about the nature of macro structure, interactionism allows for the development and testing of forms of macro theory which avoid the self-confirming tendencies characteristic both of structural-functionalism and of Marxism.[23] Pluralism, so often the butt of critics, is not built into interactionism in the way that functionalism is built into these other approaches. It is quite possible for consensus to be discovered by interactionists. It may be that a high degree of social integration underlies the pluralism suggested by interactionist work at the micro level. Alternatively, it may be that pluralism is functional for structural integration.[24] The difference between interactionism and the other approaches is that the interactionist cannot get away with assuming or simply asserting the existence of social or structural integration. He has to demonstrate it.

Interactionists must begin to work at the macro level, then. Furthermore, in line with the earlier criticism, this research must be comparative and historical in nature. Of course, this is an area where it will be particularly necessary to draw on work in other traditions as a resource.

I argued earlier that, while misconceived, the Marxist critique of interactionism as empiricist had some force. There is also a sense in which this critique does not go far enough. Interactionism has not only suffered from what might be called macro-empiricism, a neglect of the macro level, it has also succumbed to micro-empiricism, an under emphasis on theory at the micro level, in particular a failure to develop its most fundamental concepts.

The concept of 'strategy' offers a good example of this theoretical underdevelopment. This concept is central to interactionist theory and research, yet not only is its reference unclear, but crucial issues surrounding it remain unexplored. Most interactionist studies of strategies take the form of a specification of some problematic situation followed by an account of the strategies actors use to cope with this.[25] What is missing is any account of the nature of strategies in relation to other forms of social action, of how situations come to be seen as problematic, of how particular strategies are selected and of how the strategies of one group relate to those of others in the same setting.[26]

There is a need then for theoretical work at the micro level too, in particular research directed towards the development of the strategy model and of the other concepts central to interactionism: perspective, identity and negotiation.[27]

### A Division of Labour: the Co-ordination of Research

A division of labour requires co-ordination as well as differentiation. Research of the four kinds outlined earlier must be co-ordinated by work in each area drawing on and being drawn on by that in the others. But co-ordination is also necessary *within* each type.

There is a tendency built into ethnography to minimise the importance of the selection of a research problem and setting. It is embodied, for example, in the injunction attributed to Everett Hughes that, given a setting, one should look for the problem for which that setting is the most appropriate research site; rather than choosing a setting according to its

suitability for a pre-defined problem. There is sense in this recommend-
ation, of course, both as a way of minimising the dangers of bias arising
from theoretical presuppositions, and as a strategy for coping with the
problem that one can only get a very crude idea of the nature of a
setting before investigating it. However, the adoption of this stance makes
the co-ordination of research very difficult. Obviously we have to trade-
off two sets of conflicting considerations, and perhaps we need a range
of studies which make different trade-off decisions. If so, what we currently lack are studies which put the problem of co-ordination first, for
example by adopting a critical case approach: identifying a location
where evidence supporting or refuting a theory is most likely to be found.
The usual example of this strategy cited is the Affluent Worker study.[28]
The investigation of middle schools may provide an example nearer
home:

> the middle school . . . holds a central position not only chronologic-
> ally in the hierarchy of educational institutions but also sociologically
> as a focal point for studying the dilemmas which teachers face and
> the constraints with which they must cope in the schooling system
> of British society.[29]

The claims of critical cases must not be exaggerated of course: they never
illuminate everything nor do they answer questions definitively, and they
do involve a heightened danger of theoretical bias. Nevertheless they are
an important research strategy currently underused.

Another way in which research might be usefully co-ordinated is through
parallel studies. Thus, for example, at the micro level, if one compares
teaching by Open University central academics with the work of a teacher
in a secondary school classroom, certain illuminating parallels and contrasts
emerge. Both are concerned to pitch their teaching at an appropriate level
for their audience and both are aware that they may have to motivate
their audiences in various ways. On the other hand, where the secondary
school teacher has to decide how to do these things on the spot, in the
immediacy of the classroom, the Open University 'lecturer' has much
time to consider and make these decisions. However, unlike the secondary
school teacher, the feedback he gets about the response of his audience is
little, poor and late. Furthermore, he is aware that his teaching is open to
public scrutiny, not least by his academic colleagues; and he has much
better feedback about their responses than about those of students. The
different contingencies which the two categories of teacher face go some
way to explaining the forms of teaching which have emerged in the two

situations.[30] Equally, parallel studies of secondary school pupils and Open University students may point up important features of *their* situations. The linking of studies in this way gives each some comparative analytic leverage, but it may also provide the basis for the development of more formal theory.

Another kind of co-ordination is team research on a particular locality. In this way one may be able to investigate, for example, the relationship between pupil adaptations and both the organisation of the school and that of the community and family life in which the pupils participate. Alternatively, in a single study it may be possible to examine the links between the pastoral organisation of school, the police and the social welfare apparatus and the effects of these on the career patterns of 'deviant' pupils. A team approach makes possible the investigation of a number of different settings and the linkages between them.[31] Team-work also facilitates the triangulation of data.[32]

Even in the case of single naturalistic studies by individual researchers there is room for increased co-ordination. There is a tendency for attention to focus on teachers and pupils in state secondary schools so that even within the micro-substantive quadrant there are vast tracts under-investigated or uninvestigated: higher/further education, primary and nursery education, private and special schools; headmaster's offices, staff-rooms, pastoral organisation, playgrounds, local educational authority offices, and of course the DES. Furthermore, settings outside the education system where selection and socialisation processes occur have been almost entirely neglected by sociologists of education.[33]

In addition, the current, almost exclusive, focus of ethnographers interested in schooling on contemporary settings must be complemented by micro analysis of historical settings. The link-up with social and local history is important here. In addition, we need to take full account of the historical dimensions of existing work in the field. The work of Hargreaves (1967) and Lacey (1970), for example, was done in the early sixties, almost 20 years ago. There have no doubt been important changes in the process of schooling since then, and we must take account of these when relating our work to these earlier studies. Conversely, we might be able to use their work to investigate these changes. Similarly, research must be done in other societies besides Britain and America, and work already done by anthropologists and historians used for comparative analysis.[34]

Perhaps even more importantly, even in areas like teacher typification of pupils where there is now quite a body of work, much still remains to be done in developing and testing out the available accounts. Thus, for

example, there is still uncertainty about the consequentiality of typifications, and about how typifications displayed in various different contexts (the report form, staffroom discussion, research interviews, etc.)
relate to what teachers do in the classroom. In addition we only have hints
about the kinds of theories which underlie and are used to legitimate
typifications.[25] Even more remains to be done in the area of pupil
typifications.

A crucial basis for the co-ordination of research is the detailed public
evaluation of existing work. One of the consequences of interactionist
empiricism has been that little effort has gone into the evaluation of
studies: their findings seem to be treated either as true and unproblem-
atic or rejected out of hand and ignored. The purpose of such evaluation
is to assess how valid a study's findings are and, more importantly, to
discuss the *ways* in which they are misleading. This allows us to determine how the findings can be legitimately interpreted and what kinds
of further research are necessary. Evaluation also provides a basis for
views about how future research in the field might be better designed
and executed, capitalising on hindsight.[36]

## Conclusion

In summary, then, interactionist work within the sociology of education
has been empiricist, but this is not an inherent feature of the approach.
While this empiricism has had at least one major advantage – it has saved
interactionism from the speculative excesses characteristic of a number
of other sociological approaches – it has seriously limited the value of the
work produced by interactionists. The strategies generally adopted for
dealing with the problem of empiricism have been counterproductive.
What is required is an explicit division of labour and a shift of some of
the emphasis currently placed on studies of particular settings to theoretical work, both macro and micro, and to the evaluation of previous
work. Also, more co-ordination of micro-substantive case studies is required so that they are usable for macro and micro, formal and substantive theorising. By restructuring our work in this way I think we can do
research which is neither speculative nor empiricist.

## Notes

1. The replacement of 'selection' and 'socialisation' by 'class reproduction' and
'cultural reproduction' is simply terminological. The alternating stress on constraint
or autonomy is a product of varying political emphasis.

2. By empiricism I do not mean the philosophical doctrine that sense impressions are the sole basis of knowledge; but rather the only remotely related sociological sense of an over-concentration on concrete empirical studies and a neglect of theory construction and of the theoretical context of any study.

3. For a useful collection of anthropological material on educational settings see Spindler (1974).

4. There may, of course, be a good reason for this: that in his substantive and especially his later work, Weber was close to being a structuralist. See Turner (1977). Bauman (1978) argues that even in his methodological writings Weber was not an interpretive sociologist in the current sense of that term.

5. There is one way of dealing with the failings of interactionism which I shan't discuss here: the retreat into ethnomethodology. This is best described as an attempt to 'dissolve' rather than solve the problems faced by interactionism, and indeed by other forms of sociology. In my view it is an attempt which totally fails; albeit in a productive way, since it has given rise to some excellent empirical work.

6. The key sources for this approach are authors like Barthes and Foucault.

7. I am not suggesting that these problems are *necessarily* involved in the approaches mentioned, simply that as currently developed these approaches display such problems. I would add that any attempt to solve them is likely to result in a *rapprochement* with interactionism.

8. This applies to the work of Althusser (1971), Bourdieu and Passeron (1977) and Bowles and Gintis (1977). For sophisticated treatments of this concept see Isajiw (1968) and Munch (1976).

9. Althusser (1971) provides an example of a purely speculative approach. This is the product of an epistemology which instead of merely recognising the theory-laden nature of all data, and despite its attempts to distinguish between science and ideology, plunges into relativism by claiming that theory fully determines data. Bowles and Gintis (1977) exemplify the reliance on highly problematic evidence (I am refer-ring both to the quantitative and the historical material). Furthermore, *Schooling in Capitalist America* presents their analysis without the qualifications which they them-selves made in the articles on which it is based (Mackinnon, 1977).

10. Incidentally, I cannot understand the appeal of Marx and the neglect of Weber except as a response to their respective political positions. Thus, for example, Weber's theory of class is far more coherent, developed and useful than that of Marx. Indeed, Marx, in his concrete analyses, such as the Eighteenth Brumaire, uses a model of class which, in important ways, is quite close to that of Weber.

11. D. Hargreaves (1978) argues the case in relation to Sharp and Green (1975). In Willis (1977) the problem erupts in his treatment of 'rationality' and 'ideology' where he relies on Lukacs's 'solution' to the problem of knowledge. For a discussion of Willis see Hammersley and Turner (1979).

12. And, of course, the correct unit of analysis is not the national society but the world system: Worsley (1967); Frank (1967); Wallerstein (1974).

13. Sharp and Green do say that their work is exploratory but the way in which they formulate their findings in the book does not take the tentative, qualified form one might expect from this; nor is their work generally treated by others as explor-atory. Willis carried out 'comparative case studies' in other schools, but he makes little reference to them in the study.

14. D. Hargreaves (1978) argues that this is the case with Sharp and Green (1975).

15. What is recommended here is a division of labour between research projects, *not* between particular researchers.

16. This dimension must not be confused with the notion of centrality (Shils, 1961) or power: a study of the DES or of the managerial elite of a large corporation would be relatively micro study.

17. Glaser and Strauss (1968). The idea of formal theory derives from Simmel.

See Wolff (1950).

18. This schema arose out of discussions with David Hargreaves. However, he may not agree with the way I have formulated it or the use to which I have put it.

19. This formulation is very similar to that of Blumer (1969).

20. Rock (1979) argues that this position is central to interactionism. As Rock also suggests, interactionism is very loosely structured and incorporates a number of distinct tendencies. Only some of these rule out macro analysis and I see no reason to assign them priority. As counter evidence, I would cite the fact that the work of Everett Hughes and his students was firmly located in a macro theory; albeit one often only vaguely expressed. See Becker (1951) and Simpson (1972).

21. Even where structural-functionalism and Marxism have recognised functional autonomy (Althusser, Bourdieu, Bernstein) they still assume, without explanation or documentation, that this functional autonomy functions to maintain the system. (A. Hargreaves makes this clear in the chapter included in this volume.) It may, but this must be demonstrated not assumed.

22. Willis (1977) is characteristic of the historicist tradition within Marxism in this respect. Some other Marxists have recently come to recognise that many social differences and conflicts do not arise from class divisions. See Hirst (1976); Laclau (1977) recognises some autonomy – but adopts the expedient of claiming that class determines 'in the last instance'!

23. This particular aspect of Popper's (1966) critique of Marxism seems to me to have much force.

24. The terms social and structural integration are derived from Lockwood (1964).

25. See for example the studies referenced in Lofland (1976). Lofland recommends this format for the writing up of ethnographic research.

26. For a detailed discussion of these problems see Hammersley (1979). This criticism applies to some of my own work, for example, Hammersley (1976).

27. Though see Ball (1972) on identity and Strauss (1978) for an attempt to develop the concept of negotiation.

28. Goldthorpe, *et al.* (1968-9). It is also, of course, a central element in analytic induction. See Lindesmith (1947) and Cressey (1953).

29. A. Hargreaves (1978). Andy Hargreaves has indicated that the idea of middle schools as a critical case for investigating the constraints and dilemmas facing teachers only emerged over the course of his research (personal communication).

30. I am drawing here on the work of Judith Riley on OU academics and my own work on secondary schoolteachers.

31. Willis's (1977) work points to the importance of this but in the absence of a team his documentation of the organisation of the school and of the culture of the shop floor is inevitably limited.

32. For a discussion of some of the advantages of team research see Douglas (1976). Of course, while the larger the team the more can be done, the organisational problems are likely to be simultaneously increased.

33. For example military and police academies, theological seminaries, religious and political sects and movements, not to mention the family.

34. For an example of some of the ways in which anthropological work might prove useful see McDermott (1976), for instance footnote 14, pp. 273-4.

35. One such theory is embodied in the notion of contagion: see Cicourel, *et al.* (1975) and Hargreaves, Hester and Mellor (1976). Contagion theory has of course been worked up into more respectable sociological form by Sutherland (1956).

36. Unfortunately, much research at the moment provides rather little documentation of the research process so that evaluation is difficult. See D. Hargreaves (1978) and Hammersley and Turner (1979) for attempts to evaluate particular studies. D. Hargreaves (1977) is an evaluation of some aspects of a whole field of research.

# References

Althusser, L. (1971) 'Ideology and Ideological State Apparatuses', in B. Cosin, *Education, Structure and Society*, Penguin, Harmondsworth

Ball, D. (1972) 'Self and Identity in the Context of Deviance: The Case of Criminal Abortion', in R.A. Scott and J.D. Douglas, *Theoretical Perspectives on Deviance*, Basic Books, New York

Banks, O. (1978) 'School and Society', in Barton and Meighan (1978)

Barton, L. and Meighan, R. (1978) *Sociological Interpretations of Schooling and Classrooms: A Reappraisal*, Nafferton, Driffield

Bauman, Z. (1978) *Hermeneutics and Social Science*, Hutchinson, London

Becker, H.S. (1951) 'Role and Career Problems of the Chicago Public School Teacher' unpublished Ph.D thesis, University of Chicago

Bernbaum, G. (1978) 'Schooling in Decline', in Barton and Meighan (1978)

Blumer, H. (1969) *Symbolic Interactionism*, Prentice-Hall, Englewood Cliffs

Bourdieu, P. and Passeron, J.P. (1977) *Reproduction in Education, Society and Culture*, Sage, London

Bowles, S. and Gintis, H. (1977) *Schooling in Capitalist America*, Routledge and Kegan Paul, London

Cicourel, A.V. *et al.* (1975) *Language Use and School Performance*, Academic Press, London

Cressey, D. (1953) *Other People's Money*, Free Press, Chicago

Delamont, S. (1978) 'Sociology and the Classroom', in Barton and Meighan (1978)

Douglas, J.D. (1971) *Understanding Everyday Life*, Routledge and Kegan Paul, London

Douglas, J.D. (1976) *Investigative Social Research*, Sage, London

Frank, A.G. (1967) *Capitalism and Underdevelopment*, New York

Glaser, B., and Strauss, A. (1968) *The Discovery of Grounded Theory*, Weidenfeld and Nicolson, London

Goldthorpe, J., *et al.* (1968-9) *The Affluent Worker*, 3 vols, Cambridge University Press, Cambridge

Hammersley, M. (1976) 'The Mobilisation of Pupil Attention', in M. Hammersley and P. Woods, *The Process of Schooling*, Routledge and Kegan Paul, London

Hammersley, M. (1978) 'Swings and Roundabouts in the Sociology of Education', *Ethnography*, no. 2

Hammersley, M. (1979) 'What is a Strategy', unpublished manuscript

Hammersley, M. and Turner, G. (1979) '"Labour" and "Rules"', *Ethnography*, no. 3

Hargreaves, A. (1978) 'The Significance of Classroom Coping Strategies', in Barton and Meighan (1978)

Hargreaves, D.H. (1967) *Social Relations in a Secondary School*, Routledge and Kegan Paul, London

Hargreaves, D.H. (1977) 'The Process of Typification in Classroom Interaction', *Br. J. Educ. Psychol.*, 47, pp. 274-84

Hargreaves, D.H. (1978) 'Whatever Happened to Symbolic Interactionism', in Barton and Meighan (1978)

Hargreaves, D.H., Hester, S. and Mellor, F. (1976) *Deviance in Classrooms*, Routledge and Kegan Paul, London

Hirst, P.Q. (1976) 'Althusser and the Theory of Ideology', *Economy and Society*, vol 5, part 4, November

Isajiw, W.W. (1968) *Causation and Functionalism in Sociology*, Routledge and Kegan Paul, London

Karabel, J. and Halsey, A.H. (1977) *Power and Ideology in Education*, Oxford University Press, Oxford

Lacey, C. (1970) *Hightown Grammar*, Manchester University Press, Manchester

Laclau, E. (1977) *Politics and Ideology in Marxist Theory*, NLB

Lindesmith, A. (1947) *Opiate Addiction*, Principia Press

Lockwood, D. (1964) 'Social Integration and System Integration', in G.K. Zollschan and W. Hirsch, *Explorations in Social Change*, Routledge and Kegan Paul, London

Lofland, J. (1976) *Doing Social Life*, Wiley, New York

McDermott, R.P. (1976) 'Kids Make Sense: An Ethnographic Account of the Interactional Management of Success and Failure in One First Grade Classroom', unpublished Ph.D. thesis, Stanford

Mackinnon, D. (1977) Open University Course, E202, Schooling and Society, Unit 13, Milton Keynes

Marsh, P., Rosser, E. and Harré, R. (1978) *The Rules of Disorder*, Routledge and Kegan Paul, London

Munch, P. (1976) 'The Concept of "Function" and Functional Analysis in Sociology', Phil. Soc. Sci. 6, 1976, pp. 193-213

Open University (1977) E202 Schooling and Society, Milton Keynes

Plummer, K. (1975) *Sexual Stigma*, Routledge and Kegan Paul, London

Popper, K. (1966) *The Open Society and its Enemies*, 5th revised ed., 2 vols., Princeton University Press

Rock, P. (1979) *The Making of Symbolic Interactionism*, Macmillan, London

Sharp, R. and Green, A. (1975) *Education and Social Control*, Routledge and Kegan Paul, London

Shils, E. (1961) 'Centre and Periphery', in *The Logic of Personal Knowledge, Essays Presented to Michael Polanyi on his Seventieth Birthday*, Free Press of Glencoe, pp. 117-30. Reprinted in E. Shils (1975) *Centre and Periphery*, University of Chicago Press

Simpson, I.H. (1972) 'Continuities in the Sociology of Everett C. Hughes', *Sociological Quarterly*, vol. 13, Fall, pp. 547-65

Spindler, G. (1974) *Education and Cultural Process*, Holt, Rinehart and Winston, New York

Strauss, A. (1978) *Negotiations*, Jossey-Bass

Sutherland, E. (1956) *The Sutherland Papers*, edited by A. Cohen, A. Lindesmith, and K. Schuessler, Indiana University Press, Bloomington

Turner, B.S. (1977) 'The Structuralist Critique of Weber's Sociology', *Sociology*, vol. 28, no. 1, March

Wallerstein, I. (1974) *The Modern World System: Capitalist Agriculture and the Origins of the European World-Economy in the Sixteenth Century*, Academic Press, London

Whitty, G. (1974) 'Sociology and the Problem of Radical Education Change: Towards a Reconceptualisation of the "new" Sociology of Education', in M. Flude and J. Ahier, *Educability, Schools and Ideology*, Croom Helm, London

Willis, P. (1977) *Learning to Labour*, Saxon House, Farnborough

Woods, P. (1977a) 'The Ethnography of the School', Units 7-8, Open University course E202 Schooling and Society, Milton Keynes

Woods, P. (1977b) 'Teaching for Survival', in P. Woods and M. Hammersley, *School Experience*, Croom Helm, London

Woods, P. and Hammersley, M. (1977) *School Experience*, Croom Helm, London

Wolff, K. (1950) *The Sociology of Georg Simmel*, Free Press, Chicago

Worsley, P. (1967) *The Third World*, 2nd ed., Weidenfeld, London

Young, M.F.D. (1975) 'Science as Alienated Labour', paper presented to the BSA Sociology of Science Study Group, February

Young, M.F.D. (1977) 'School Science – Innovations or Alienation', in P. Woods and M. Hammersley, *School Experience*, Croom Helm, London

# CONTRIBUTORS

Stephen Ball, Lecturer in Education, University of Sussex.

Cathy Bird, Educational Studies Unit, Brunel University.

Martyn Denscombe, Senior Lecturer in Sociology, Leicester Polytechnic

Peter French, Research Associate, School of Education, University of Bristol.

Martyn Hammersley, Lecturer in Educational Studies, The Open University.

Andy Hargreaves, Lecturer in Educational Studies, The Open University.

Margaret MacLure, Research Associate, School of Education, University of Bristol.

Robert J. Meyenn, Research Fellow, Department of Educational Enquiry, University of Aston in Birmingham.

Glenn Turner, Research Student, Faculty of Educational Studies, The Open University.

Peter Woods, Senior Lecturer in Educational Studies, The Open University.

# SUBJECT INDEX

# AUTHOR INDEX